Collins

DISAPPEARING WORLD

ISBN: 978-0-00-726118-5

ISBN: 978-0-06-143444-0 (in the United States)
FIRST U.S. EDITION Published 2008

Text © Alonzo C. Addison 2007
Photographs © as per credits on p. 272
Design © HarperCollins Publishers 2007
Maps © Collins Bartholomew Ltd 2007

Printed in Italy

10 09 08 07
7 6 5 4 3 2 1

DISAPPEARING

101 of the Earth's Most
Extraordinary and
Endangered Places

WORLD

Alonzo C. Addison

An Imprint of HarperCollinsPublishers

CONTENTS

FOREWORD

In 1959, following the decision to build the Aswan High Dam on the Nile, the people of the world came together to save Egypt's great temples at Abu Simbel and Philae from the rising waters. The United Nations Educational, Scientific and Cultural Organization (UNESCO) launched an international safeguarding campaign, capturing the hearts and minds of children and adults across the globe. Some fifty countries assisted, accelerating archaeological research and moving the temples to higher ground. A few years later, in 1965, at a White House conference in Washington, D.C., the concept of combining natural and cultural site protection was proposed in a "World Heritage Trust". In 1972, exactly 100 years after the world's first National Park was created at Yellowstone in the United States of America, these ideas culminated in a unique international legal instrument to protect and conserve cultural and natural sites of "outstanding universal value" to humankind. Officially known as the *Convention Concerning the Protection of the World Cultural and Natural Heritage* and ratified by 184 member states of UNESCO as of October 2006, the World Heritage Convention today helps protect and conserve 851 properties in 141 countries.

With the celebration in 2002 of the thirtieth anniversary of the World Heritage Convention, the World Heritage Committee engaged in a critical reflection on the results it has achieved, as well as on the road ahead. Among their conclusions, the members stressed the need to increase public awareness, involvement, and support for World Heritage as the Convention entered its fourth decade. It is thus with pleasure that I welcome this new book celebrating World Heritage while highlighting the range of risks sites face. Presenting a unique perspective on how our world is changing, the dramatic images and stories in this book present some of the challenges faced by the world's most treasured places. In these pages 101 sites from the World Heritage List, including all thirty on the List of World Heritage in Danger as of July 2007, are presented.

Although the selection of the sites and perspectives on their status on the following pages are neither those of UNESCO or of the World Heritage Committee, it is my hope that this richly illustrated volume will help awaken a greater awareness and concern for the protection of our shared World Heritage.

The public's assistance is needed if our heritage is to live on. The opportunities to help are numerous – from visiting responsibly to avoiding products made from threatened or endangered species, or doing our part to prevent pollution or climate harming emissions, we can all aid in the conservation and protection of these universally valued places. Through our collective efforts we can keep all of these sites from disappearing.

FRANCESCO BANDARIN
Director, UNESCO World Heritage Centre

INTRODUCTION

In these pages the dramatic stories behind some of the most extraordinary and endangered World Heritage Sites are detailed. Drawing from the UNESCO World Heritage List, we explore the top natural and cultural wonders of the world and the challenges they face in the twenty-first century.

In the following chapters, 101 sites are grouped in ten categories of key risks, from conflict to theft, development, unsustainable tourism, pollution, natural disasters, management and financial constraints, changing uses, invasive species, and climate change. More often than not, however, a site is under pressure from several of these factors. Three levels of threat are identified: from those in clear **danger**, as defined by UNESCO, to those deemed **at risk** or in **guarded** condition based on recent field reports from international experts and Non-Governmental Organizations and conservancies.

The variety of challenges faced by these sites range from the immediate, such as in Garamba National Park in the Democratic Republic of the Congo (DRC) where the last two northern white rhinoceroses in the wild fight for survival, to the longer term, such as at the Rice Terraces of the Philippine Cordilleras where ancient fields are slowly falling away as younger generations move to the cities. In some cases, such as at Mount Nimba in West Africa, man's actions are the threat, while in others, such as the Monuments of Thatta in Pakistan, it is our lack of action that is the challenge. Some, such as Machu Picchu are being loved to death, while others such as

Bamiyan have been torn apart by conflict and intolerance. In many cases the solutions are complex or beyond the reach of any one government, as along the Great Barrier Reef or on Mount Kilimanjaro, where global climate change is eroding the ecosystem. In others, well-managed sites may be included for the potential of disaster beyond their immediate control, as in the case of spills off the Dorset and East Devon Coast, or the risk of a major volcanic eruption to the Historic Centre of Naples.

While this list is representative of the challenges our shared World Heritage is faced with today, it is but a small sampling of the sites under threat in a rapidly changing world. The choice of included properties is solely ours—although many were considered and are worthy of the recognition such a grouping brings, the sites included are those we believe currently at greatest risk and most in need of our collective focus and care.

Although the challenges are highlighted here, the bigger story is of the many who have worked for so long to conserve the World's Heritage. Many of our great places would not even have survived to make it into these pages if it were not for the untiring efforts of thousands of selfless individuals around the world. From the rangers in the DRC who risk their lives every day for little or no pay, to the architects, archaeologists, and restorers who have spent years in harsh conditions at sites from the temples of Angkor to the ruins of Borobudur, this book is dedicated to all who strive to preserve and protect our World Heritage.

World Heritage Site location map

Constraints

Changing Uses

Invaders

KEY:

IN DANGER

AT RISK

GUARDED

Disasters

Climate Change

CONFLICT

The world is, sadly, never without conflict in one continent or another – and some areas have endured generations of war and unrest. UNESCO World Heritage Sites in these zones are affected by the subsequent instability in the area, whether through civil war, religious conflict, internal coups, or marauding gangs of poachers, and the subsequent difficulties in their management and conservation stemming from the conflict in the region.

Conflict is no respecter of location, whether it is a rain forest, tropical forest, wetland, national park, site of architectural or archaeological importance, or holy city. Once warfare starts, the evidence of centuries of culture, religious belief, archaeology, or thriving ecosystems can be destroyed in hours, never to be recovered or replaced.

War has, unfortunately, been with us for a long time. The first written mention of war dates back to 2700 BC, although there were undoubtedly earlier conflicts. During the UNESCO campaign to safeguard the temples at Abu Simbel, archaeological evidence pointing to a battle 13,000 years ago was unearthed.

In this chapter, we see how places as unique and diverse as Samarra in Iraq, Virunga National Park in the Democratic Republic of the Congo (DRC), Kosovo's Medieval Monuments in Serbia, and the Old City of Jerusalem and its walls are all vulnerable, and attempts to save them are ongoing.

Rebel forces and guerrillas exploit natural resources – they need funds for their cause and so, for example, they slaughter elephants for their ivory, which they sell on the black market. Thousands of elephants have been culled in this way. The rebels need transport and roads, and so trees are felled and vegetation ripped up, which leads to deforestation and destruction of natural habitats. Nesting birds are driven from the trees and species put at risk. Without the cover of the forests and trees, the animals are driven out into the open, where they are killed for food, or trade. Reptiles, amphibians and fish are hunted, while rivers and waterways are polluted and illegally mined.

Local people, the innocent victims, are forced by the conflict to leave their homes and become refugees, but through their need to survive, they also become unwitting destroyers, contributing to the escalating damage brought about by the unrest. They are often driven into protected areas, where their need for fuel can lead to illegal tree felling, while the subsequent fires sometimes result in further destruction. The need for food leads them to graze their cattle on fragile ecosystems, poach protected species, or indulge in large-scale fishing, with subsequent diminution of fish stocks.

Religious conflict, intolerance and pogroms can have a devastating effect on historic monuments and statues, with the loss of churches, mosques, minarets and monasteries. Icons, frescoes, wall paintings, furniture and other irreplaceable items that have existed for centuries can be destroyed in minutes, as can any centuries-old statue deemed idolatrous by new régimes.

Whatever the conflict, the presence of opposing forces, rebels, or large-scale gangs of poachers frequently means there is no adequate protection of listed sites, habitats and species, be they animal, vegetable or mineral. Rangers, wardens, management and peacekeepers are driven away, leading to looting and destruction. In forests and parks the lack of supervision often leads to illegal traffic in wildlife and subsequent dwindling numbers of protected species, while at historic sites or in religious buildings, historic items are looted, paintings stolen, and mosaics ripped up.

In 2000, UNESCO and the United Nations Foundation set up a pilot project of conservation of natural heritage in war time. The first project was to conserve World Heritage Sites in the Democratic Republic of the Congo, and was launched for four years. The goal was to ensure the conservation of World Heritage Sites in the DRC, both during periods of civil unrest and in the long term, by mobilizing financial, logistical, technical and diplomatic support at regional and international levels, to strengthen the conservation of the sites. This project functioned as a learning process to inform efforts and develop mechanisms to conserve similar sites in conflict regions around the world. Here, as elsewhere, local government plus international support and community education is vital.

Archaeological Remains of the Bamiyan Valley
Afghanistan

IN DANGER

KEY THREATS Conflict | Theft | Development | Tourism | Pollution | Disasters | Constraints | Changing Uses | Invaders | Climate

At the crossroad of civilizations between East and West, Bamiyan was for more than 1000 years a major focus of Buddhist culture and an important stop on one of the "silk routes" between China, central Asia, India and the Roman Empire. Officially known as the Cultural Landscape and Archaeological Remains of the Bamiyan Valley, this site represents the artistic and religious developments which, from the first to the thirteenth centuries AD, characterized ancient Bakhtria, integrating various cultural influences into the Gandhara school of Buddhist art. The Bamiyan Buddhas, the tallest in the world, were among Asia's greatest treasures, surviving numerous conflicts until their destruction by the Taliban in March 2001.

World Heritage Site inscribed 2003
Inscription on the List of World Heritage in Danger: 2003
http://whc.unesco.org/en/list/208

OPPOSITE PAGE: The view in 1963 of the Large Buddha with a traditional mud-brick fortified house in the foreground.

ABOVE RIGHT: An armed boy guards the vast cave complex at Bamiyan.

The Taliban destroyed the many Buddhas and other statues throughout Afghanistan because they believed them to be idolatrous and un-Islamic.

The Bamiyan valley was a thriving area for religion, philosophy and art and was the site of several Buddhist and Hindu monasteries.

The hands and faces were probably carved wooden insets and perhaps covered with copper. Before the destruction, rows of peg holes were visible in the vicinity of the upper halves of the faces and lower arms.

The Large Buddha may have represented Vairocana, the "Light Shining throughout the Universe Buddha" and been painted red, while the smaller statue is thought to have been the Buddha Sakyamuni (not a woman as thought by locals in recent times) and was painted blue.

Some 240 km (150 miles) west of Kabul at an altitude of 2500 m (8200 feet) in the Hindu Kush, Bamiyan was partly inhabited and urbanized from the third century BC. It was in the first century AD under the Kushana emperors that it became a major Gandhara Buddhist site, and was at its peak from the fourth century AD to the eighth.

The two colossal standing Buddhas were hewn out of the sheer valley walls, while the rich surface details were formed from mud, straw and horsehair, secured by wooden pegs inserted in the stone and coated with a fine stucco. They were reportedly richly painted and decorated with gold and jewels. The 55-m (180-foot) high Large Buddha was probably cut from the sixth century AD, while the smaller 38-m (125-foot) statue came 50 years earlier. The valley was a pilgrimage site and the statues may have served as a beacon for travellers. Although the figures were almost completely destroyed, staircases and passages carved in the rock around the niches have survived. More than 700 caves and monasteries remain today of a reported 12,000, although weather, neglect, the destruction and use as shelters have all taken their toll. They were once richly decorated with art, statues and frescoes from the fifth to the eighth century, with influences from Hellenistic, Roman and Sassanid traditions.

Fortifications from early Islamic rule in the ninth century to the time of Bamiyan's sacking by Ghengis Khan in 1221 have survived. Today this rich cultural landscape is struggling with the challenges of modernization, development, the ravages of the Taliban and two decades of civil war.

third–sixth centuries AD — major Buddhist site, Buddhas built

ninth–twelfth centuries — Muslim fortress town

1650–1750 — Aurangzeb (1618–1707), the last Mughal emperor, ordered his troops to shoot off the legs of the Large Buddha. Nadir Shah, the succeeding Persian emperor, is said to have directed artillery at the statues in a second failed attempt to destroy them.

1978–present — civil war and ongoing conflict; power vacuum leads to looting, theft and destruction at many sites and museums

1920–1970s — archaeological studies undertaken

500 AD **1000 AD** **1500 AD** **2000 AD**

1221 — Genghis Khan sacks town and monasteries – Bamiyan is abandoned for long periods and never regains its past glory

1981 — Afghanistan submits World Heritage nomination, but the site lacks legal structures and protection and nomination is deferred

630 — Chinese traveller Hsüan-tsang describes a hub of commerce and Buddhist religion with more than 1000 monks, and two statues finished with plaster and decorated with gold and fine jewels

April 1997 — after less than a year in power, the Taliban government declares that it will destroy the Buddhas; UN Secretary General appeals; Taliban declares it will not destroy Buddhas

Dec 1998, 1999, 2000 — UN General Assembly adopts successive resolutions of concern over the destruction of cultural artefacts in Afghanistan and requests all parties to protect their common heritage

AD 400 — first written record

16 Feb 2001 — the press report an order to destroy the Bamiyan Buddhas as idolatrous and un-Islamic; UNESCO issues urgent appeal for the preservation of Afghanistan's heritage

1 March 2001 — Taliban Information and Culture Minister tells AFP, 'The work started about five hours ago but I do not know how much has been destroyed. It will be destroyed by every means. All the statues are being destroyed.'

10 March 2001 — ambassadors from all fifty-four states of the Organization of the Islamic Conference (including Pakistan, Saudi Arabia and the United Arab Emirates – the only nations to recognize the Taliban regime) join calls to spare the monuments. A religious delegation including the Mufti of Egypt is flown to Afghanistan to try to convince the Taliban not to destroy the country's culture.

11 March 2001 — Taliban forces destroy the Buddhas of Bamiyan with dynamite and artillery. Locals claim to have seen Pakistani and Saudi engineers on site helping with the destruction while others claim that Al Qaeda was involved.

July 2003 — inscribed on both the World Heritage List and the List of World Heritage in Danger; UNESCO begins major international campaign to develop management plan, document the site and shore up and stabilize the remains.

A Colossal Tragedy

Bamiyan is officially "in Danger", having been placed on the List of World Heritage in Danger simultaneously with its World Heritage inscription in 2003. It has suffered from systematic theft, neglect, lack of maintenance and the tragic deliberate destruction by the Taliban in 2001.

The site is in a fragile state of conservation, which is not surprising considering that it has suffered from long term abandonment, successive military actions and the intentional destruction by the Taliban. Although the "imminent collapse" feared in 2003 has been averted by a major UNESCO campaign to reinforce and shore up the Buddha niches, enormous amounts of work remain to be done across the vast site.

BELOW LEFT: Interior of a hillside cave once richly decorated and used by Buddhist monks.

BELOW RIGHT: More than 700 caves are cut into the sheer cliff face.

OPPOSITE PAGE (LEFT): A traveller on horseback is dwarfed by the feet of the Large Buddha in 1963.

OPPOSITE PAGE (RIGHT): Preserving the Large Buddha's fragments post-destruction.

"The destruction of the giant Buddhas before the eyes of the international community on 11 March 2001 was a tragedy on the colossal scale of the statues themselves. The Afghan people and the international community at large regretted it. This destruction ... testifies to an important tragic event in the history of human civilization and an act of deliberate eradication of the tangible heritage [and] cultural identity of people in the twenty-first century AD."
— THE GOVERNMENT OF THE TRANSITIONAL ISLAMIC STATE OF AFGHANISTAN, WORLD HERITAGE NOMINATION, MAY 2003

Samarra Archaeological City
Iraq

A once powerful capital, Samarra ruled over the Abbasid Empire from Tunisia to Central Asia for fifty-six years in the ninth century. Built in AD 836 by Caliph Al-Mu'tasim, it replaced Baghdad as the focus of the Abbasid world and grew to be the largest Islamic city of its day, spanning roughly 57 sq km (22 sq miles). Located in central Iraq along the Tigris river 125 km (75 miles) north of Baghdad, the site was largely abandoned in 892 and more than 80 per cent of the ancient city remains unexcavated. Known for its unique 52-m (170-foot) high spiral ramped minaret, the 42,000 sq m (450,000 sq ft) Great Mosque was the largest in the world when it was built in 849.

Built of fired-brick and gypsum mortar, the Great Mosque spans 264 by 159 m (980 by 520 ft) with walls 2.5 m (8 ft) thick by 10 m (33 ft) high supported by forty-four regularly spaced semi-circular towers. It was the largest mosque in the Islamic world when it was built between 849 and 852. The unusual Spiral Minaret (Al-Malwiya) may predate the mosque by fifteen years. It is 32 m (105 ft) square at the base, shifting to a spiral of five layers rising 54 m (180 ft) high.

The Al-Askari shrine, although not part of the World Heritage Site, is one of the holy sites of Shia Islam. It is home to the tombs of Ali Al Hadi, the tenth imam, who died in 868, and his son Hassan al-Askari, the eleventh imam, who died in 874.

® World Heritage Site inscribed 2007
Inscription on the List of World Heritage in Danger: 2007
http://whc.unesco.org/en/list/276

OPPOSITE PAGE: The famous minaret of the Mosque of al-Mutawakkil is 52 m (170 ft) high, with a square base, and a spiral exterior staircase, up which the caliph is said to have ridden on a white Egyptian donkey. There are traces of a wooden pavilion at the top to protect the muezzin.

ABOVE RIGHT: The golden dome of the Al-Askari Mosque after the bombing of 2006. Although it was more recently built and not part of the inscribed site, the shrine's suffering illustrates the danger conflict has brought to Samarra.

Among the other monumental remains are: the 1.25-sq-km (0.5-sq-mile) Caliph's Palace, one of the largest imperial buildings to have survived from late antiquity; the Abu Dulaf Mosque north of the city, a smaller version of the Great Mosque with a second, smaller spiral minaret; Husn al-Qadisiyya, an unfinished round city largely unexcavated and abandoned several decades before Samarra was built; the Al-Huwaysilat Palace; the Balkuwara (Al-Manqur) Palace; Al-Ma'shuq Palace; Bayt al-Zakharif house; Al-Musharrahat Palace; Al-Istablat houses and palace compound; Al-Ja'fari Palace; the artificial mound of Tel Al-Alij and a (presumed) mausoleum, Qubbat al-Sulaybiyya.

In the Midst of War and Sectarian Strife

Given the current political situation in Iraq, Samarra's heritage is at extreme risk. Multinational forces have at times occupied the archaeological site and a small bomb caused minor damage in April 2005. Although not part of the World Heritage Site, nearby in the modern city, the danger from sectarian strife has been painfully illustrated by terrorist attacks. On 22 February 2006 an insurgent bomb destroyed the golden dome of the Al-Askari shrine, one of Shia Islam's holiest sites. A second attack on 13 June 2007 destroyed the shrine's two 36-m (118-foot) gilded minarets. UNESCO and the UN have announced over US$5 million in international support to help rebuild the shrine once stability returns. With the chaos of war and limited management and protection, Samarra is in danger from terrorism, uncontrolled agricultural encroachment, illegal excavation and illegal dumping of rubbish.

Manovo-Gounda St Floris National Park
Central African Republic

With a wealth of flora and fauna, this is the largest protected savanna in west and central Africa, covering 17,400 sq km (6700 sq miles) in the northern Central African Republic near the border with Chad. The vast savannas are home to a wide variety of species, from endangered elephants to cheetahs, leopards, wild dogs, red-fronted gazelles and buffalo, while various types of wildfowl are to be found in the annually flooded low-lying northern plains. Threaded by five major rivers the park ranges from swamps to grassland and bushy wooded savanna to gallery forest. Once well-protected, many of the fifty-seven mammals here are now in great danger.

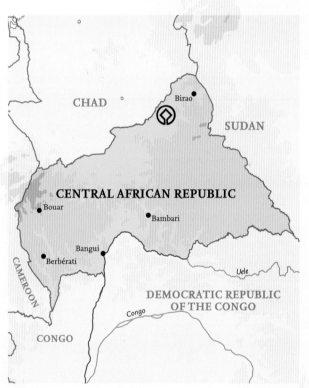

⊚ World Heritage Site inscribed 1988
Inscription on the List of World Heritage in Danger: 1997
http://whc.unesco.org/en/list/475

OPPOSITE PAGE: Since the early 1980s, the number of elephants has plummeted as uncontrolled poaching has reached emergency levels. Staff numbers are very low for the size of park, and the resources available are inadequate.

ABOVE RIGHT: Once abundant, the hippopotamus is now in serious danger here as caravans of professional poachers move through the park.

Refugees and villagers are also a problem for the animals: chased from their lands, they graze cattle in the reserve, clear the forest for new farms, and mine streams in the hope of finding diamonds. When they are unable to plant crops safely, the wildlife becomes a last source of food.

There were still 500–700 hippopotamuses here in 1998. Today numbers cannot be obtained.

Some 418 species of birds are also present including threatened shoebill, pallid harrier, lesser kestrel and black-winged pratincole.

Extinction of Species

Ravaged by years of war and poaching, this park is literally on the verge of extinction. Since raids by horsemen from Darfur in the early 1980s, the situation for elephants, crocodiles, hippopotamuses, leopards, antelope, buffalo and giraffe has continued to deteriorate.

A major highway bisects the reserve, allowing easy access for armed camel trains of hundreds of professional poachers from Chad and Sudan. In the late 1990s, they killed four rangers and systematically slaughtered the elephants. The black rhinoceros, critically endangered at the time of the park's inscription on the World Heritage List in 1988, is long since extinct here. Elephants, once numbering in the tens of thousands, have seen a 95 per cent reduction in numbers, to just 500 by 2005.

Renewed fighting in the region and an overspill of the conflict in Darfur have brought all enforcement to a standstill. It is impossible to obtain numbers for the once plentiful hippopotamus. Caravans of Sudanese poachers are active across the entire region, openly hunting down the last remaining elephants. Although one rebel group in the Central African Republic signed a peace agreement in April 2007, the situation is still so unstable that international monitoring teams have been unable to enter the park.

With the elephants on the verge of disappearing and other species such as Buffon's kob, Defassa waterbuck and topi and hartebeest nearing extinction, it seems likely that without immediate emergency measures this sanctuary's value, like its wildlife, will be lost forever.

Kahuzi-Biega National Park
Democratic Republic of the Congo

IN DANGER

KEY THREATS Conflict | Theft | Development | Tourism | Pollution | Disasters | Constraints | Changing Uses | Invaders | Climate

Dominated by two spectacular extinct volcanic cones, Kahuzi and Biega, this vast area of primary tropical forest is home to nearly 90 per cent of the world's endangered eastern lowland gorillas. In the Albertine Rift area near Lake Kivu and the Rwandan border, the World Heritage Site covers 6000 sq km (2300 sq miles) of diverse habitats, from marshes and swamps to rainforest and bamboo and montane forests. The park's 194 recorded species of mammal include the endangered African forest elephant and eastern chimpanzee, ten species of monkey, forest buffalo, hippopotamus, bongo and seven species of duiker. Other species once known to be here include 224 birds, 48 reptiles and 31 amphibians.

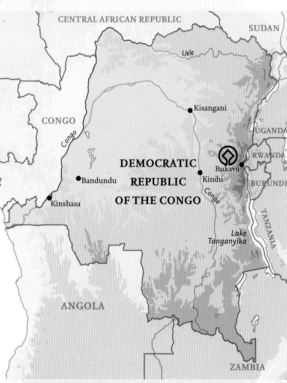

Made up of two sections linked by a narrow corridor, the park is being cut in half by encroaching farmland in one of Africa's most densely populated areas, with 300 people/sq km (780/sq mile).

The Democratic Republic of the Congo has the world's largest reserves of coltan or columbite-tantalite, a dark ore used to make electronic capacitors and specialist coatings for everything from satellites to children's games.

◎ World Heritage Site inscribed: 1980
Inscription on the List of World Heritage in Danger: 1997
http://whc.unesco.org/en/list/137

ABOVE RIGHT: The eastern lowland gorilla subspecies (*Gorilla beringei graueri*) is the largest living primate. In the wild, the male can reach weights of more than 225 kg (500 lb) and measure 1.83 m (6 ft) in height. They are predominantly herbivorous with a diet consisting of leaves (they have often been seen to take only a few leaves from a plant rather than strip entire branches, in order to allow it to regrow) as well as occasional fruits, seeds, bamboo shoots and insects.

Gorilla Warfare

Once known as the "Sanctuary of the Gorillas", Kahuzi-Biega cannot make this claim any more. In an area ravaged by years of civil war and ensuing chaos, the gorillas are disappearing. The cluster of roughly 250 that had made their home in the high mountains (between 2100 and 2400 m [6900–7900 feet]) of the park in the mid-1990s had been reduced to only 96 by 2001. In the expansive western lowlands of the park it is estimated that 90 per cent, or 7200, of the former group of 8000, have been destroyed. Poachers, invasive species – including the highland liana which threatens the gorilla's food supply – and habitat loss make the picture bleak.

Since 1994, when thousands of Rwandan refugees (the border is only 30 km [19 miles] away) overran the park and drove off the rangers, Kahuzi-Biega has been in crisis, a situation only made worse by the 1998 civil war. In 2000 a tenfold rise in the price of coltan (the mineral ore columbite-tantalite) sparked a "gold rush", as more than 15,000 miners flooded the forests to dig and pan for it. With them came massive bushmeat hunting, illegal airstrips and ivory poaching, which eliminated the elephants. Although condemned by the UN Security Council, the rebels' exploitation of resources continued and the following year, with 95 per cent of the park in the hands of armed gangs, it became too dangerous to visit. International assistance from the UN, UNESCO and Non-Governmental Organizations and talk of peace are slowly helping in efforts to take back the park, but Mai-Mai and Hutu rebels still pose a threat to the rangers: for example, in April 2006 a patrol post was overrun and numerous hostages taken.

Comoé National Park
Côte d'Ivoire

One of the largest protected areas in West Africa, Comoé National Park encompasses 11,492 sq km (4437 sq miles) of savanna, forests and grassland. Roughly 500 km (310 miles) upriver from Abidjan in the northeast of Côte d'Ivoire, the park is characterized by its great plant diversity. Because of the presence of the Comoé River, which runs for 120 km (75 miles) through the park, it contains plants which are normally only found much farther south, such as shrub savannas and patches of thick rainforest. The park is home to at least 150 species of mammals, including fourteen primates.

IN DANGER

KEY THREATS Conflict | Theft | Development | Tourism | Pollution | Disasters | Constraints | Changing Uses | Invaders | Climate

Atlantic Ocean

World Heritage Site inscribed 1983
Inscription on the List of World Heritage in Danger: 2003
http://whc.unesco.org/en/list/227

ABOVE RIGHT: Comoé lies in rebel territory and wildlife protection staff currently have no access to it. Among the sufferers in the Côte d'Ivoire's civil war have been the elephants who are poached for their ivory. It is impossible to find out exactly how many survive, but these rows of tusks provide a disturbing image.

The Côte d'Ivoire's civil war has had a dramatic toll on the elephants whose ivory it was named after. No-one knows the current elephant population in Comoé, but with the numbers at the only other major reserve in the country (Tai) having fallen from 3000 in 1980 to fewer than 100 today, the worst is feared.

West Africa's largest game reserve, the park has the Côte d'Ivoire's greatest concentration of wildlife, including lions, baboons, crocodiles, elephants, 21 species of pig, hippopotamus, black and white colobus, waterbuck, kob and roan antelope among others.

More than 400 species of birds have been recorded, including vultures, cranes, turtledoves and parrots.

The park is home to at least three World Conservation Union (IUCN) Red List endangered species: the Diana monkey (Cercopithecus diana), the chimpanzee (Pan troglodytes) and the African elephant (Loxodonta africana). It also has several officially vulnerable species including the lion (Panthera leo) and dwarf African crocodile (Osteolaemus tetraspis).

Unsafe to Enter

Following coups in 1999 and 2001, the Côte d'Ivoire was embroiled in civil war from September 2002 and Comoé has suffered dramatically. The director of the park could not gain access, field stations were looted and rangers and Non-Governmental Organizations were forced to abandon their efforts. In the absence of management and patrols, poaching accelerated from pre-war levels. The large mammal community, including the majority of primates, is heavily threatened. Elephant, roan antelope and waterbuck are particularly at risk, despite vigorous anti-poaching campaigns.

Damage to habitat is also a threat: encroaching populations, overgrazing by cattle, timber harvesting and uncontrolled burning for land clearance and by poachers continue, although some progress has been made in increasing awareness among the adjoining populations. However, resources are limited and conservation needs, such as the establishment of wildlife corridors to adjoining reserves in Burkina and Ghana, will struggle to attract funding.

Virunga National Park
Democratic Republic of the Congo

Africa's oldest national park, and one of the most diverse ecosystems in the world, Virunga is located in the eastern reaches of the Democratic Republic of the Congo (DRC), on the border with Rwanda and Uganda. Covering an area of 7900 sq km (3050 sq miles), it comprises a wide variety of habitats, from swamps and lush wetlands to montane, bamboo and lowland forests, steppes and the glaciers and snowfields of Rwenzori at 5000 m (16,400 ft), as well as lava plains and savannas on the slopes of active volcanoes. One of the most important conservation areas in Africa, Virunga holds 2077 identified plant species and has more bird and mammal species (706 and 196 respectively) than any other African park.

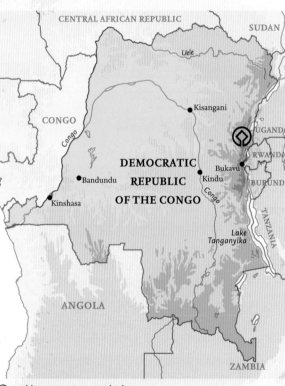

® World Heritage Site inscribed 1979
Inscription on the List of World Heritage in Danger: 1994
http://whc.unesco.org/en/list/63

Dian Fossey, renowned champion of the gorilla and author of Gorillas in the Mist, *started her career here. Murdered in 1985, she was one of "Leakey's Angels."*

Called "silverbacks" after the patch of greyish hair they develop on their backs at maturity, male mountain gorillas are easy to recognize in the wild. They typically weigh 204–227 kg (450–500 lb), and reach heights of 1.5–1.8 m (5–6 ft)

The heavily forested slopes of extinct volcanoes of the Virunga Range are home to more than half of the world's mountain gorillas. Only some 700 survive, including roughly 100 in Virunga National Park.

The DRC is Africa's third largest country, roughly the size of Western Europe, and site of more than half of Africa's rainforest.

With three neighbouring national parks (Bwindi and Mgahinga in Uganda and Volcano in Rwanda), Virunga is the last home for the world's few remaining critically endangered mountain gorillas.

In addition to the mountain gorilla, threatened species include elephant, hippopotamus and Rwenzori duiker. The park is home to a vast diversity of creatures, from rare golden monkeys to chimpanzees, golden cats to lions and the Rwenzori otter shrew to 78 amphibians and 109 reptiles including the horned and Jackson's chameleons. Birds, from crowned eagles to Rwenzori touraco, also inhabit Virunga.

Rangers – the Heroes of Virunga

In the early 1990s, in the wake of the genocide in neighbouring Rwanda, more than 1 million refugees fled to the park, leading to massive poaching and deforestation – 600 metric tonnes of fuel wood were being burned daily. The productive fisheries of Lake Edward have enabled the human population, already one of the densest in the DRC, to multiply several-fold, increasing the strain on the forest. The eruption of Mt Nyiragongo over the town of Goma in 2002 sent a reported 200,000 people into the forest.

Ravaged by war and its consequences since the early 1990s, Virunga is arguably the world's most dangerous park. Overrun by armed factions (Interahamwe, Mai-Mai, NALU, ADF, ex-FAZ, ex-FAR and ex-FAC), as well as invading farmers, fishermen, pastoralists and refugees (including some remaining Rwandan Hutu), its plant and animal species have suffered massive losses. Fewer

OPPOSITE PAGE: The mountain gorilla (Gorilla beringei beringei) was identified in 1902 and is a subspecies of the eastern gorilla. Hunting, destruction of its forest habitat and capture for the illegal pet trade have led to a dramatic decline, threatening the species with extinction.

ABOVE RIGHT: In the early 1970s there were 30,000 hippos in Virunga, but poaching by rebel groups has led to a massive decline in numbers. By October 2006 only 629 remained, a 98 per cent decline.

than 100 mountain gorillas cling on here, reduced from an already critical 320 in 1989. Elephants and hippopotamuses are targeted for their ivory, which is regularly collected from militia camps and sent via adjoining countries to the international black market.

Since 1996 an estimated 120 rangers have been killed in the line of duty. Despite insubstantial and irregular wages, 480 continue to risk their lives every day to protect the gorillas. Six tourists were taken hostage in 1998 – two never returned and tourism has been on hold ever since.

Sadly, the situation is only worsening. Despite a ceasefire and moves toward reunification, in early 2007 Mai-Mai rebels, perhaps emboldened by a shift of UN peacekeepers to monitor elections, increased their

BELOW LEFT: A park guard looks over the 15 sq km (6 sq miles) of forest and rare mountain gorilla habitat slashed and burned in May and June 2004 by thousands of Rwandan refugees who poured across the border. Illegal timber extraction to make valuable charcoal destroys vital habitat and is a serious and continuing problem.

BELOW RIGHT: The elephant population in Virunga is hunted for its ivory and numbers are rapidly decreasing.

OPPOSITE PAGE: Poaching of wildlife continues while park staff lack the resources to fully patrol the 650-km (404-mile) long boundary. The area of the park where the gorillas live is only 425 sq km (164 sq miles). A ceasefire in early 2007 has allowed rangers to resume operations.

attacks and have been slaughtering hippopotamuses at an unprecedented rate. A group of 200 rebels recently attacked three patrol posts, killing yet another ranger and seriously injuring four. In January 2007 charcoal extractors killed two silverback gorillas, reportedly eating one. In July the violence reached new depths as four gorillas were murdered execution-style, in a clear message to the world. The Ugandan army has deployed troops along the River Ishasha on the border in an effort to save the park's largest remaining group (134) of hippopotamuses. The rangers say that in this violent period of national reunification their work is even more dangerous and unpredictable than during the recent civil war (which involved nine African nations and directly affected the lives of 50 million Congolese).

Medieval Monuments in Kosovo
Serbia

Representing the exceptional synthesis of Byzantine and Western ecclesiastical culture that developed in the Balkans between the thirteenth and seventeenth centuries, this group of four monuments in Kosovo illustrates the fresco style and distinctive architecture of the Palaiologian Renaissance. The site consists of the Dečani Monastery (inscribed in 2004), plus the Patriarchate of Peć Monastic Church, Church of the Virgin of Ljeviša at Priština, and Gračanica Monastic Church in Prizren (all added in 2006). Sharing donors, builders and master painters as well as architectural principles, their Byzantine-Romanesque fusion emanates from the height of the Serbian Nemanjic dynasty in the fourteenth century.

⊚ World Heritage Site inscribed 2004, 2006

Inscription on the List of World Heritage in Danger: 2006

http://whc.unesco.org/en/list/724

Remnants of a large walled monastic complex, the four domed churches of the Patriarchate of Peć feature extensive wall paintings. The thirteenth-century frescoes of the Church of Holy Apostles are in a unique, monumental style, while early fourteenth-century frescoes in the church of the Holy Virgin represent the appearance of the Palaiologian Renaissance style.

At the exquisite fourteenth-century church at Gračanica, long cycles of paintings on the walls, domes and in the narthex are preserved almost in their entirety.

The c. 1306 Church of the Virgin of Ljeviša reflects the political and religious upheavals of the region: converted to a mosque in the mid-eighteenth century, it reverted to a church following liberation from the Turks in 1912. During restoration in the 1950s, murals plastered over during the Turkish period were found and restored (although less than 30 per cent were salvageable).

ABOVE RIGHT: The Dečani Monastery, at the foot of the Prokletije mountains in western Kosovo, represents the last important phase of Byzantine-Romanesque architecture in the region and is the largest of all medieval Balkan churches. Built in the mid-fourteenth century as the church and mausoleum of the Serbian King, the original iconostasis, marble floor and interior furniture are all preserved. Its treasury is the richest in Serbia, including about sixty exceptional icons from the fourteenth to seventeenth centuries.

This group of churches illustrates the evolution of the Palaiologian Renaissance architectural form from the first appearance of the cross-in-square plan with five domes at Ljeviša to its unique manifestation at Peć with three separate churches united by a narthex, to its culmination in the structure at Gračanica.

Kristallnacht in Kosovo

The victims of centuries of conflict, these threatened edifices have suffered repeated damage over the years. From the Serbian-Turkish wars (1876–78), to World War I, and the more recent regional conflict, they have been attacked, looted, burned, rebuilt and abandoned. Since the end of the latest war in 1999, some 120 churches and mosques across Kosovo have been destroyed or severely damaged, despite the presence of UN and NATO-peacekeepers. On March 17–18, 2004, in a vast pogrom reminiscent of Kristallnacht, mobs burned dozens of religious buildings. In Prizren, the Church of the Virgin of Ljeviša, which had evaded an earlier bombing, was left damaged but standing, the only one of six to survive. Today armoured peacekeepers guard the sad site, ringed with barbed wire and piles of trash.

Yet violence continues. Three years later, on March 30, 2007, an attack on Dečani with an anti-tank rocket reiterated the ongoing risk. The World Heritage Committee placed the collective monuments on the "in Danger" list in 2006 in an effort to bring support for urgently needed emergency conservation work and protect them in this strife-torn region. Until there is a lasting peace, these monuments remain in grave danger.

Los Katíos National Park
Colombia

Extending over 720 sq km (278 sq miles) in northwestern Colombia, Los Katíos National Park comprises low hills, forests and humid plains. Forming the southern end of the Central American land bridge, the site has been a filter for the interchange of species between North and South America since the Tertiary Era. As a result, an exceptional biological diversity is found in the park, which is home to many threatened animal species, as well as many endemic plants.

AT RISK

KEY THREATS Conflict | Theft | Development | Tourism | Pollution | Disasters | Constraints | Changing Uses | Invaders | Climate

⊚ **World Heritage Site inscribed 1994**
http://whc.unesco.org/en/list/711

ABOVE RIGHT: The forests of Los Katíos, for a long time off-limits due to limited access and guerrilla activity, are increasingly threatened as they are burned to clear land for new farms.

The Atrato is the fastest flowing river in the world, emptying 4.9 million litres (1,077,850 gallons) of water into the Caribbean every second.

Only 1 per cent of the park area has ever been developed, making it one of the best preserved in the region.

On the border with Panama, Los Katíos forms a transfrontier World Heritage Site with Darién National Park. Running along the Atrato River, it is split between swamp forest and rainforest. Roughly 20–25 per cent of the 669 known plants are endemic. The park is home to more than 250 bird species (including several endemic hummingbirds) and some 500 vertebrates (excluding fish). Threatened animals include the manatee, American crocodile, bush dog, giant anteater, Central American tapir, sloth, armadillo and numerous primates. The park also protects outstanding scenery, particularly the Tendal and Tilupo waterfalls and the Ciénagas de Tumaradó swamp.

Biodiversity at Risk

Guerrilla activity in the region has caused severe management constraints and illegal timber harvesting has become rife. Situated at the border of two continents, the park is also at risk from development (it is on the route of the long-planned Pan American Highway) and illegal traffic in wildlife (of crocodile, jaguar and otter skins and of live monkeys, parrots and other birds) between continents.

Old City of Jerusalem and its Walls

IN DANGER

KEY THREATS Conflict | Theft | Development | Tourism | Pollution | Disasters | Constraints | Changing Uses | Invaders | Climate

As a holy city for Judaism, Christianity and Islam, Jerusalem has been of great symbolic importance for thousands of years. Among its 220 historic monuments, the Dome of the Rock stands out: built in the seventh century, it is decorated with beautiful geometric and floral motifs. It is recognized by all three religions as the site of Abraham's sacrifice. The Wailing Wall marks the quarters of the different religious communities, while the Resurrection rotunda in the Church of the Holy Sepulchre houses Christ's tomb.

The safeguarding of the monumental, religious and cultural heritage of the Holy City of Jerusalem has been one of UNESCO's main concerns since 1967 as it has guided and financed the restoration and conservation of a number of monuments and religious and cultural properties.

The area within the walls contains four distinct quarters: the Muslim in the east with the Dome of the Rock, the Jewish in the southeast with old synagogues and the sacred wall of the temple destroyed by the Romans, the Armenian in the west and the Christian in the northwest with the Church of the Holy Sepulchre.

On medieval European maps Jerusalem was placed at the centre of the world.

⊚ World Heritage Site inscribed 1981
Inscribed on the List of World Heritage in Danger: 1982
http://whc.unesco.org/en/list/148

OPPOSITE PAGE: Many of Jerusalem's ancient monuments are deteriorating through lack of conservation.

ABOVE RIGHT: The ancient honey-coloured stones of the city wall show the wear of centuries of conflict. Like many things here, maintenance, conservation and encroaching development are controversial.

A City Divided

Jerusalem is an exceptional city in that there is no general political agreement as to its status; certain states declare that they abided by the situation defined in the 1947 United Nations partition plan which considered Jerusalem as a corpus separatum located in neither Israel nor Jordan. Its placement on the List of World Heritage in Danger in 1982, the year after it became a World Heritage Site, was a recognition by the World Heritage Committee of the danger to religious properties, threats of destruction following uncontrolled urban development and the general deterioration in the state of conservation of the city's monuments because of the disastrous impact of tourism and a lack of maintenance. Almost 2000 years after the Romans destroyed the Great Temple, the religious monuments here continue to be flashpoints. At the intersection of history, faith and politics in a region torn by generations of conflict, the heritage of Jerusalem remains in danger.

Baalbek
Lebanon

GUARDED

KEY THREATS Conflict | Theft | Development | Tourism | Pollution | Disasters | Constraints | Changing Uses | Invaders | Climate

One of the largest and most celebrated sanctuaries of the Roman empire, Baalbek is renowned for its exquisitely detailed and colossal architecture. Its six surviving Corinthian columns were the tallest in the ancient world. First occupied more than 5000 years ago, the extensive site is located in central Lebanon on fertile plains northeast of Beirut. A minor agricultural centre during Phoenician times, Baalbek, or "Lord of the Bekaa valley", included the sun god Baal among its three deities. It was renamed Heliopolis by the Greeks, and its triad of gods were appropriated as Jupiter, Bacchus and Venus after the arrival of the Romans in the first century BC.

Ⓦ World Heritage Site inscribed 1984
http://whc.unesco.org/en/list/294

Under the World Heritage Convention (1972), signatories commit not to "damage directly or indirectly the cultural and natural heritage situated on the territory of other States Parties to this Convention."

Under The Hague Convention for the Protection of Cultural Property in the Event of Armed Conflict (1954) and its two protocols, signatories "undertake to respect cultural property … within the territory of other High Contracting Parties by refraining from any use of the property and its immediate surroundings or of the appliances in use for its protection for purposes which are likely to expose it to destruction or damage in the event of armed conflict; and by refraining from any act of hostility, directed against such property."

OPPOSITE PAGE: A fighter jet leaves a vapour trail in the sky behind the remaining six towering 22-m (72-ft) cut stone columns of the Temple of Jupiter, the tallest in the Roman world.

ABOVE RIGHT: The magnificent Temple of Bacchus has a front row of unfluted Corinthian columns, which mask a further row of fluted columns. Internally, a good deal of the original structure and decoration is preserved.

One of the finest examples of Imperial Roman architecture at its apogee, Baalbek's temple acropolis attracted thousands of pilgrims before its closure and destruction after the empire's shift to Christianity.

Progressively built over three centuries with colossal structures, Baalbek features the Temple of Jupiter (c. AD 60), the Temple of Bacchus (c. 120–125), the grand court (c. 150), the Temple of Venus (third century), the Propylaea (under Caracalla [188–217]) and hexagonal court (under Philip the Arab [244–249]). The Temple of Jupiter measures 88 × 48 m (290 × 158 feet) and once had fifty-four columns. The foundation wall of the unfinished temple podium contains three enormous stones, the famed "trilithon" weighing 800 tonnes each. An even larger block, the 1000-tonne "Stone of the Pregnant Woman", still sits in its quarry south of the site entrance. At 21.5 × 4.8 × 4.2 m (70.5 × 15.7 × 13.8 feet), it is the largest hewn stone in the world.

Shaken by Conflict

In July 2006, renewed conflict between Israel and militants in southern Lebanon placed five World Heritage Sites at risk as intensive bombing and shock waves threatened ancient structures. An oil spill affected the site of Byblos, while bombs fell only 300 m (1000 feet) from Baalbek's ruins. Although structures in the Old City were destroyed, the World Heritage Site escaped with only minor damage. One block of stone fell at the site and cracks on the lintels of the temples of Jupiter and Bacchus probably widened because of the vibrations. Baalbek remains in guarded condition.

THEFT

Theft, the taking without permission of something belonging to another, is a threat to many UNESCO World Heritage Sites. From looting of objects to poaching of species, and theft born of ignorance, the scale and variety of the removal of non-renewable species, resources and valuable objects is distressing in the extreme. The abundant and varied plant and wildlife, including internationally threatened species, and monuments and antiquities will be lost forever if action isn't taken.

In poorer countries, where economic depression results in low subsistence levels, local people inevitably turn to any free source of food. Poaching ensues – not just for food, but also for trade, often on commercial scales. With few alternatives in impoverished areas, bushmeat is sadly an increasingly popular source of provision and income. And the conflict endemic in many poor regions has resulted in easy accessibility to ever more powerful weapons, compounding the problem.

A ready international market results in the culling of game, mammals and cetaceans for their eggs, shells, horns or flesh. Species at risk include turtles, elephants, and rhinos. Illegal fishing leads to diminishing food supplies for larger fish and their subsequent reduction in numbers. A further consequence is the loss of young birds, which are used in some countries as bait for blue crab fishing. In some cases, animals are hunted simply for the fun of it, as in the former Oryx Sanctuary in Oman – where virtual loss of the species has resulted in the first removal of a site from the World Heritage List.

Theft through ignorance has led to valuable sources of food for wildlife being lost. Increasing populations in areas such as national parks are threatening the local ecosystem. Agriculture is the main source of income, but many people are attracted by the wildlife and other opportunities these places afford. The newcomers bring with them sheep, goats and cattle, which literally steal the grazing from indigenous species, while pasture land is converted into cropland.

Other means of producing income result in illegal mining and logging – a tempting prospect when one can earn several times the daily average wage. Driven by international demand often continents away, endangered woods, such as mahogany in the Río Plátano Biosphere or hardwoods in the Sumatran rainforest and on the slopes of Kilimanjaro, are being cut from the forests, leaving gaping holes. The illegal loggers further decimate the surrounding areas – roads are hacked out for vehicle access and the subsequent deforestation causes soil erosion and sedimentation of streams.

Elsewhere, the ongoing interest and desire for antiquities means that wherever there is a site of archaeological significance, looting becomes a problem – the ready market of collectors across the world is not all comprised of honest citizens. The second-century BC city of Hatra in Iraq and seventh-century BC Cyrene in Libya are just two important sites that have lost valuable objects.

Ignorance, too, often results in the destruction of centuries-old structures – the Great Wall of China being a prime example. It seems that familiarity breeds contempt, and the looting of bricks and soil, and unsupervised quarrying, has eaten away at many segments of this ancient monument. The cultural value of sites such as this is undermined both by local people and visitors, who extract archaeological objects for souvenirs or to sell to tourists and collectors.

Large-scale projects for improving conservation of the sites are currently under way. For example, in the Democratic Republic of the Congo, UNESCO launched an emergency programme to save all sites in danger and international donors have contributed millions in financial aid to the fund; while in other parts of the world local regional initiatives bring together experts and funding to establish conservation priorities.

IN DANGER

KEY THREATS Conflict | Theft | Development | Tourism | Pollution | Disasters | Constraints | Changing Uses | Invaders | Climate

Garamba National Park
Democratic Republic of the Congo

Established in 1938, Garamba is one of Africa's oldest national parks. Once the last home in the wild of one group of the northern white rhinoceros population, Garamba may already have earned the grim title of the site of its extinction. Covering 4920 sq km (1900 sq miles) in the northeast of the country near the border with Sudan, the park's savannas, grasslands and woodlands, interspersed with swampy depressions and gallery forests along river banks are home to a number of other threatened mammals. The chimpanzee, elephant and hippopotamus are all at risk, as is the world's last known population of Congo giraffe. The park is still home to a number of species including buffalo, hartebeest, kob, warthog, leopard, lion and antelope.

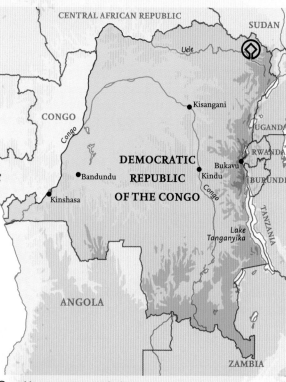

◎ World Heritage Site inscribed 1980
Inscription on the List of World Heritage in Danger: 1984–1992, 1996
http://whc.unesco.org/en/list/136

OPPOSITE PAGE: This image of a dead rhinoceros in Garamba National Park illustrates vividly the callous nature of the international horn trade.

ABOVE RIGHT: Although half their numbers were slaughtered, during the war-torn years of the 1990s, buffalo live on in the park.

Despite their size (up to 4.2 m [13.8 ft] in length) and weight (up to 3600 kg [7940 lb] for males) rhinoceroses are surprisingly agile and can run up to 40 km/h (25 mph) for short periods.

The world's second largest land mammal, the white rhinoceros of Africa is not white but slate grey. Its name may come from the Boer "wijdt" for its wide lips, or from the pale mud it likes to wallow in.

Two subspecies exist in separate parts of Africa. Once close to extinction, the southern population is now relatively secure, unlike the critically endangered northern population.

Ten northern white rhinoceroses survive in captivity and a breeding programme is underway.

Prior to recent wars and massive poaching, Garamba had the highest density of elephants in all of Africa. It was also the site of the first successful program to domesticate the African elephant.

The Deadly Horn Trade

For 50 million years the white rhinoceros survived the perils of life in the African savanna, but in one century, man has driven the species to the brink of extinction. Although banned by almost all nations, the international horn trade continues, driven by demand for use in Asian medicine and for dagger handles in the Middle East. Policing has forced the trade further underground.

Before 1900, the northern white rhino ranged from the Congo to Chad, the Central African Republic, Sudan and Uganda. In 1960 there were 2250, but by 1970 poaching had cut the number to 700 and in 1980 to just 100. By 1984, only thirteen survived. Emergency action and protection led to a small recovery to thirty-two animals by 1993. But war returned and more than 80,000 Sudanese refugees and armed militias entered the park. Over half of the elephants, hippopotamuses and buffalo were slaughtered, rangers were attacked and facilities looted. By 1999 the situation was critical as UNESCO, Non-Governmental Organizations and international donors helped the guards to reassert control. In June 2003, as progress was being made, armed gangs returned and by April 2004 janjaweed militia from Sudan's Darfur had increased the killing, operating donkey trains of poached animals. A plan to move a few animals to a reserve in Kenya was drawn up, but politics and conflict got in the way. The Democratic Republic of the Congo's (DRC) vice president said that only two rhinos remained by the middle of 2006. Today the number is unknown. The DRC has since held elections and conflict seems to be winding down, but the UN remains on alert, with its largest peacekeeping force in this troubled nation.

Okapi Wildlife Reserve
Democratic Republic of the Congo

A vast expanse of emerald forest, rivers and waterfalls, the Okapi Wildlife Reserve spans 13,730 sq km (5300 sq miles), or an area almost half the size of Belgium, in the northeastern Democratic Republic of the Congo. Guarding about one-fifth of the Ituri Forest near the border with the Sudan and Uganda in the vast Congo river basin, the reserve takes its name from the shy, diminutive forest "giraffe" which calls it home. More than a decade ago the reserve held 5000 of the estimated 30,000 okapi surviving in the wild.

The Congo basin, of which the reserve and forest are a part, is the largest drainage basin in Africa.

Four forest types, an immense flora and 376 bird species grace this dramatic scenery. Its fifty-two mammal species range from elephant to chevrotain, aardvark and genet, and include thirteen primates and eleven duiker antelopes. In addition, some 10,000 nomadic Mbuti and Efe hunters live in the Ituri Forest.

The okapi shares its face with the giraffe but has the body of an antelope and a striped hind portion not unlike a zebra. Small by comparison to their long-necked cousins, they stand 1.5–2 m (5–6.5 ft) high at the shoulder and can reach up 1.9–2 m (6.2–8.1 ft).

The blue tongue of an okapi is so long it can wash its own eyelids and clean its ears with it!

◈ World Heritage Site inscribed: 1996
Inscription on the List of World Heritage in Danger: 1997
http://whc.unesco.org/en/list/718

OPPOSITE PAGE: The Mbuti pygmies' way of life, hunting in this wilderness, is documented by Colin Turnbull in his classic book, The Forest People.

ABOVE RIGHT: Shy creatures, the okapi – the closest living relatives of giraffes – have survived by avoiding contact with others.

Guns versus Game

The site has suffered from years of poaching, illegal mining and encroachment. Ivory hunters, armed rebels, refugees, miners and farmers have hacked away at this once luxuriant reserve. With the 1964–1966 rebellion, conflict arrived. The early Okapi Station was abandoned and animals were killed, in a prelude to what would happen in successive waves with the 1994 refugee crisis, the 1997 civil war and violence ever since. Poaching of elephants for ivory and other species for bushmeat has become worse as the human population around the park has grown, armed factions have moved in and miners have come for gold and coltan (columbite-tantalite ore). The fighting brought cheap weapons, enabling the poachers to move up from snares to AK-47s and bigger arms. In 1995 an estimated 5700 elephants were in the park – a greater density than in Maiko or Kahuzi-Biega National Parks. Today their number is not known but destruction has been extensive – the elephants are most threatened, but primates, okapi and other edible species have also suffered.

More positively, international assistance and dedicated staff have made progress – Operation Tango in 2000–2001 cleared the park of miners and poachers for a time. Recent elections and signs of a long-term peace are hopeful, but armed bands continue to roam.

Niokolo-Koba National Park
Senegal

IN DANGER

KEY THREATS Conflict | Theft | Development | Tourism | Pollution | Disasters | Constraints | Changing Uses | Invaders | Climate

Located in a lush area along the banks of the Gambia river in southern Senegal, the gallery forests and savanna woodland of Niokolo-Koba National Park support a diversity of wildlife including many rare species and taxonomically distinct types. Key large mammals include Derby's elands (largest of the antelopes), roan antelope, hartebeest, kob and buffalo. The site is one of the largest protected areas in West Africa, covering some 9130 sq km (3525 sq miles) near the border with Guinea, and is home to 84 mammal, 350 bird, 36 reptile, 20 amphibian and 60 fish species. Among these are crocodiles, chimpanzees, baboons, lions, leopards, hippopotamuses and the last remaining elephants in Senegal.

⊗ World Heritage Site inscribed 1981
Inscribed on the List of World Heritage in Danger: 2007
http://whc.unesco.org/en/list/153

OPPOSITE PAGE: The Niokolo-Koba National Park is home to several species of monkeys including the Vervet monkey. Vervets have a mixed diet, although their favourite food is fruit.

ABOVE RIGHT: The Gambia river and its tributaries, the Koulountou and the Niokolo-Koba rivers flow through the park. The rivers are home to a wide variety of reptiles, amphibians and fish.

Many of the key species in the Niokolo-Koba National Park have almost been eradicated.

In 1990–1991 there were 8000 buffalo in the park. In 2006 this had reduced to 457 – a reduction of 94 per cent.

In 1990–1991 there were 5000 hartebeest in the park. In 2006 this had reduced to 149 – a reduction of 97 per cent.

In 1990–1991 there were 24,000 kob in the park. In 2006 there were only 92 – a reduction of 99 per cent.

In 1990–1991 there were 33,000 waterbuck in the park. In 2006 there were only 10 – a reduction of 99 per cent.

Guns versus Game

Despite the best efforts of the Department of National Parks and recent support from the international donor community, the Niokolo-Koba has suffered a dramatic and continuing decline since it was inscribed on the World Heritage List. With most of the large mammals lost to poaching, the park was placed on the List of World Heritage in Danger in 2007.

Slaughter for the commercial bushmeat trade has been of unprecedented proportions, bringing elephants here to the verge of extinction and decimating species like kob and waterbuck. Native ungulates are now outnumbered three to one by cattle, goats and sheep.

With the high value of bushmeat providing a strong incentive for continued killing, particularly in this poor rural area with few alternative livelihood options, the ongoing danger is extreme.

The park is also threatened by the proposed construction of a dam upstream which would halt the vital seasonal flooding that sustains much of the flora and by a major trans-national highway. The giraffe has been extinct here for a half century – the World Heritage Committee warned in 2007 that if any more species are extinguished, the site's "outstanding universal value" will be lost and that it should be removed from the official list of World Heritage Sites.

IN DANGER

KEY THREATS Conflict | Theft | Development | Tourism | Pollution | Disasters | Constraints | Changing Uses | Invaders | Climate

Aïr and Ténéré Natural Reserves
Niger

From the orange sea of sculpted dunes of the Saharan Ténéré desert in the east to the majestic formations of the volcanic Aïr massif in the west, this vast reserve across the north of Niger is one of the world's most beautiful and remote spots. The largest protected area in Africa, it covers some 77,000 sq km (30, 000 sq miles), with a core sanctuary of one-sixth of the total area for the addax (desert antelope). Aïr's nine, roughly circular massifs rising above a rocky plateau contain a small Sahelian (semi-arid southern Saharan) pocket with a unique climate, and flora and fauna. Both Aïr and Ténéré reserves boast an outstanding variety of landscapes, plant species and wild animals.

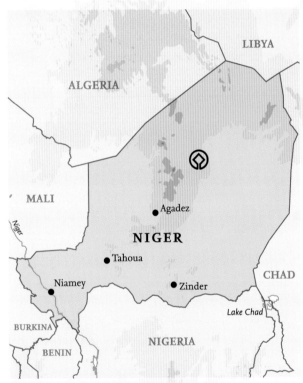

The Addax is a critically endangered desert antelope that lives in isolated regions of the Sahara. Its distinctive double twisted horns can reach 120 cm (4 ft) in length on the males.

The endangered slender horned gazelle was once the most common of its species, ranging from Algeria and Mauritania to the Nile river in Egypt and Sudan. Using a nasal-blood cooling process and capable of obtaining all its water from its food, if necessary, it is the most desert-adapted of all the gazelles.

◎ World Heritage Site inscribed 1991
Inscription on the List of World Heritage in Danger: 1992
http://whc.unesco.org/en/list/573

ABOVE RIGHT: The sparse vegetation and arid soils of the Aïr and Ténéré reserves are at risk from over-extraction for animal fodder and erosion.

Several threatened species live in the Aïr massif, including the addax and ostrich. At one time the addax population had fallen to just fifteen animals, but is believed to now be recovering. The dama gazelle is down to just a few hundred survivors, the ostrich is near extinction locally, the slender horned gazelle is so rare it has been seen only once and the endangered scimitar-horned oryx is presumed to be extinct in Niger, not having been seen for more than twenty years.

A Robbed Desert

In danger almost since its inscription in 1991, this vast reserve has been plagued by military conflict, poaching, kidnappings, looting of equipment, commercial extraction of resources and an ongoing lack of management. Although it is the world's second largest producer of uranium, Niger remains one of the poorest countries. Because of limited capacity to patrol and monitor the site, let alone manage it, illicit activities are able to continue unabated. Illegal timber and hay extraction continues and poaching is threatening several of the endangered species while the vehicles the thieves use are eroding soil and destroying vegetation. Clashes between security forces and Tuareg pastoralists have renewed in the region, with three people being killed in an attack on a garrison in the reserve in February 2007.

Hatra
Iraq

A large fortified city under the influence of the Parthian Empire, Hatra flourished as a trading centre for 400 years from the second century BC. Southwest of Mosul in a semi-arid desert between the Tigris and Euphrates, Hatra was once, like Palmyra, a major caravan stop. Capital of the first Arab kingdom, it withstood invasions by the Romans in AD 116 and 198 thanks to extensive fortifications. An outer clay wall was followed by a deep, 300–500-m (980–1640-foot) wide trench and a 2-m (6.5-foot) high stone inner wall. Four gates and some 163 defensive towers completed the fortifications. Hatra finally fell in AD 241 to the Sassanids and was razed and abandoned.

AT RISK

KEY THREATS Conflict | Theft | Development | Tourism | Pollution | Disasters | Constraints | Changing Uses | Invaders | Climate

⊚ World Heritage Site inscribed 1985
http://whc.unesco.org/en/list/277

ABOVE RIGHT: A member of the Iraqi Civil Defense Corps patrols the ancient remains of the city.

In a region torn by religious and civil strife, Hatra was an early example of tolerance, famed in ancient times for its pantheon of gods from multiple cultures. It had temples to the gods Nergal (Sumerian and Akkadian), Hermes (Greek), Atargatis (Syro-Aramaean), Allat and Shamiyyah (Arabian) and Shamash (Mesopotamian).

The ancient remains of the city, especially the temples where Hellenistic and Roman architecture blend with Eastern decorative features, attest to the greatness of its civilization.

Unguarded in a War-torn Land

Hatra, which remains mostly unexcavated, is in a precarious situation as the breakdown of order in the country has resulted in limited protection for archaeological sites. Isolated and once largely forgotten, the expansive site is now subject to looting. Although military guards were present in 2003 and portions of Hatra (including the small museum) had been fenced off to protect them from raiders, the current situation seems bleak as the authorities do not have the resources required to protect the site or to implement an appropriate management and conservation policy.

AT RISK

KEY THREATS Conflict | Theft | Development | Tourism | Pollution | Disasters | Constraints | Changing Uses | Invaders | Climate

Río Plátano Biosphere Reserve
Honduras

Located on the watershed of the Río Plátano, behind the Mosquito coast of Honduras, this 5000-sq-km (1900-sq-mile) reserve is part of one of the largest and last undisturbed tropical rainforests in Central America. Blanketed by mature wet forests, the humid landscape has an abundant and varied plant and wildlife. Thirty-nine species of mammals and 377 birds have been recorded here. In its mountainous reaches, which slope down to the Caribbean coast, fewer than 1000 indigenous people continue their traditional way of life.

⊚ World Heritage Site inscribed 1982
http://whc.unesco.org/en/list/196

OPPOSITE PAGE: Mahogany and other hardwoods from the reserve's great forests are gradually disappearing as they are looted for the international furniture trade or destroyed by slash and burn colonists.

ABOVE RIGHT: Best reached from the coast, the Río Plátano is the primary transportation artery in this vast roadless reserve. Too shallow in many places for a motor vehicle, locals use small dugout canoes called pipantes to navigate the river.

By 1995 the scarlet macaw (a national emblem), jaguar, tapir, and crocodile had reportedly been driven from the reserve.

Ladino smallholders are often financed by commercial cattle-ranchers in order to take advantage of the lack of property records. After two years, the farmers sell the land rights to cattle-ranchers and move further into the forest.

Among the lesser-known animals here are white-faced, mantled howler, and spider monkeys, three-toed sloths, pacas, kinkajous, coatimundis, tayras, Central American otters, pumas, jaguarondis, collared and white-lipped peccaries, and red brocket deer.

Rare or endangered mammals here include jaguar, giant anteater, ocelot, margay, Central American tapir and Caribbean manatee. Notable birds include king vulture, harpy eagle, great curassow, crested guan and scarlet, green and military macaws. Almost 200 reptile and amphibian species include at least 7 poisonous snakes, American crocodile, brown caiman, green iguana and leatherback, loggerhead and green turtles.

Massive Timber Extraction

Encroachment for logging and farming has placed this vast rainforest reserve at risk. The southern and western zones are subject to massive extraction of precious hardwood including mahogany (caoba), liquidamber and palm. More than 10 per cent of the forest cover has been lost and the destruction continues. Uncontrolled commercial hunting of wild animals is reducing the fauna. On the coast, marine turtles are under threat because of the stealing of eggs and the poaching of hawksbill turtles for their shells. Encroachment in the west by cattle ranchers, and ladino slash-and-burn colonists, is further reducing the forest's canopy. In addition, although a massive hydroelectric project (Patuca II) was abandoned, new dam proposals could emerge. The introduction of exotic species (such as tilapia fish) is threatening to undermine the complex ecosystem here. Although major international support has come recently, with limited capacity to manage such a vast site, the risk to this rainforest remains.

Islands and Protected Areas of the Gulf of California
Mexico

AT RISK | KEY THREATS Conflict | Theft | Development | Tourism | Pollution | Disasters | Constraints | Changing Uses | Invaders | Climate

Separating Baja California from the Mexican mainland, this vast protected area comprises 244 islands, islets and coasts in the Gulf of California. The rugged islands, with high cliffs and sandy beaches, are set off by the reflection from the turquoise waters. The site is home to 695 vascular plant species, more than in any other marine and island property on the World Heritage List. Equally exceptional is the number of fish species: 891, of which 91 are endemic. The site contains 39 per cent of the world's marine mammal species and a third of the world's marine cetacean species. It is the only home to one of the world's rarest sea mammals, the critically endangered vaquita, or harbour porpoise, and totoaba.

Driven by a need for fresh produce and drinking water, the United States now uses as much as 90 per cent of the water that flows through the Colorado River. As a result, very little of the water now reaches the Colorado River delta.

An underwater paradise, the diversity and abundance of marine life and transparent waters make this site a haven for divers.

The Sonoran desert ecosystems present here are the richest in the world, with the greatest biodiversity.

The world's two largest cacti, the cardón and saguaro, which can reach heights of 15 m (50 ft) can be found in the desert.

World Heritage Site inscribed 2005
http://whc.unesco.org/en/list/1182

OPPOSITE PAGE: Roughly a quarter of the gulf's 900 islands were protected when it was inscribed on the World Heritage List in 2005.

ABOVE RIGHT: Overfishing is just one of the reasons marine life in the Gulf of California is at risk. This critically endangered vaquita was caught in a gill net that was meant to catch sharks and other fish.

Stretching from the Colorado River delta at the north to the Pacific Ocean at the south, the waters of the Sea of Cortez (as it is known locally) are home to 80 per cent of Pacific Ocean mammals. They include blue, fin, California grey and pilot whales, California sea lions, fur and elephant seals and dolphins. Also present are loggerhead, leatherback, hawksbill, green and olive ridley sea turtles, giant manta rays and hammerhead and whale sharks. The rocky coasts and rugged islands are home to hundreds of resident and migrant bird species, including Heerman's gulls, elegant terns, blue-footed boobies, least and black storm petrels and yellow-footed gulls.

Overfishing and the Vanishing Vaquita

The turquoise waters here once teemed with fish and supplied 60 per cent of Mexico's annual catch, but overfishing, illegal takes and deregulation of the Mexican fishing industry have caused steep declines in key harvests including sardine, shrimp and shark. The vaquita porpoise is in extreme danger: fewer than 300 now remain and between 40 and 80 die each year after being caught in gill or trawl nets. As there are so few big fish, fishermen have to go after smaller and less desirable fish and the entire ecosystem, from predator fish to marine mammals and seabirds, suffers. The gulf and islands are also at risk from pollution, invasive species, such as cats and buffel grass, unregulated tourism and development. Years of drought and the damming of the Colorado River has reduced the inflow of water at the north of the Gulf to a trickle, altering the salinity of the ecosystem and threatening habitat for animals such as the vaquita.

The Great Wall
China

AT RISK

KEY THREATS Conflict | Theft | Development | Tourism | Pollution | Disasters | Constraints | Changing Uses | Invaders | Climate

Begun in the fifth century BC, what has come to be known as the Great Wall is actually a series of many walls built, repaired and extended by successive Chinese dynasties. Winding like a giant dragon across a great expanse of desert, grassland, mountains and plateaux in northern China, it ranks as the world's longest man-made structure and the largest military construction. It ranges from the well-known crenellated stone sections near Beijing to endless stretches of mud-brick and tamped earth in other regions. A symbol of ancient China, its historic and strategic importance is matched only by its architectural value.

⊚ World Heritage Site inscribed 1987
http://whc.unesco.org/en/list/438

OPPOSITE PAGE: Most of the Great Wall remains vacant, decaying and inaccessible as is evident in this early twentieth-century photograph. But despite its worn state, it is still a formidable fortification .

ABOVE RIGHT: Several million tourists a year crowd onto a few restored sections, The wear and tear, and swarms of stalls, are taking their toll.

It is estimated that less than 30 per cent of the original wall survives in good condition – which is remarkable, nonetheless, given the age and extent of the monument.

The claim that the Great Wall is visible from the Moon or space is in doubt. With a maximum width of 9 m (30 ft), the wall would be impossible to discern from the Moon as it would be far thinner than a human hair. Shuttle astronauts have said that it is not visible with the unaided eye from low-level orbits (500 km/300 miles).

Known as Wanli Cháng Chéng, literally the long wall of 10,000 li (a unit of measure), it traverses the provinces of Liaoning, Hebei, Beijing, Tianjin, Shanxi, Inner Mongolia, Ningxia, Shaanxi and Gansu.

Protection laws were enacted, from 1 December 2006, making it illegal to remove bricks or stones, drive vehicles along the wall or build houses up against it. Enforcement of the laws will be challenging as no-one has properly delineated the full length of the wall or defined what is, and is not, protected.

Around 475 BC three of the states that became China started building fortifications to protect their borders. With China's unification in 221 BC under Emperor Qin Shin Huang, these sections were joined together to form a defensive system against invasions from the north. In the succeeding Han, Sui, Northern and Jin dynasties construction continued. Little of the earliest wall survives, but sections of the Han wall are visible today.

After the defeat of the Mongols in 1449 by the Ming dynasty (1368–1644), wall building was renewed, and stone and brick were used to extend stretches, especially near the capital. The main portion runs in a rough arc across the bottom edge of Inner Mongolia for about 6500 km (4000 miles) from Shanhaiguan pass near the gulf of Bo Hai to Jiayuguan pass (Gansu province).

A Monumental Challenge

Protecting the Great Wall is a monumental challenge in itself. After Mongolia was annexed during the Qing dynasty's rule, the wall's usefulness decreased and maintenance of large portions of it was discontinued. Today it suffers from neglect in many areas, the elements in others, and the wear and tear caused by visitors at the rebuilt sections near major tourist centres. But perhaps the biggest threat is the slow and seemingly innocuous destruction and brick-by-brick looting. Portions that had survived for 2000 years have vanished in recent decades and there are reports of quarrying in many locations. Rich soil is taken to improve fields and bricks are removed for local construction work. In some areas, sections have been blasted through to make way for paths, roads or buildings.

Archaeological Site of Cyrene
Libya (Libyan Arab Jamahiriya)

AT RISK

KEY THREATS Conflict | Theft | Development | Tourism | Pollution | Disasters | Constraints | Changing Uses | Invaders | Climate

A colony of the Greeks of Thera (Santorini), Cyrene was the leading city of the Libyan pentapolis and one of the principal urban centres of the Hellenic world. Chronicled by Herodotus and Synesius and with its praises sung by Pindar and Callimachus, a thousand years of history are recorded here. Founded in 631 BC, it was the capital of the ancient kingdom of Cyrenaica. Romanized in 74 BC and rebuilt by Hadrian in AD 120, it remained a great centre until the earthquake of AD 365. Active until the time of the Arab invasions in AD 643, it is today one of the most impressive complexes of ruins of the ancient world and has played a key role in the study of archaeology for over a century.

⊚ World Heritage Site inscribed 1982
http://whc.unesco.org/en/list/190

OPPOSITE PAGE: Cyrene suffered a massive revolt in AD 115, two earthquakes, barbarian raids in late antiquity and deliberate destruction in 1978. Many tombs line the slopes around the site (bottom left). With their burials long destroyed, they are littered with graffiti and even used as animal stalls. Vegetation has invaded exposed walls and mosaics (top right).

ABOVE RIGHT: The Temple of Zeus (c. seventh century BC and rebuilt three centuries later), the largest Greek Pantheon outside of Athens, is deteriorating; its 1960s concrete-and-iron restoration is crumbling.

Cyrene thrived on the export of wheat, vegetables, fruit, sheep and goat products, horses and the highly sought-after herb silphium.

Cyrene's wealth was tied to trade in silphium, a medicinal plant and seasoning that grew only in this coastal area. Believed to have been a relative of giant fennel, it featured on the city's coins and was a widely sought after herbal contraceptive, especially in ancient Egypt. Its heart-shaped seed has been linked to the traditional symbol of love. Its extinction may be related to grazing, overharvesting or desertification – according to Pliny, the last known stalk was presented to Emperor Nero.

Eratosthenes, the Greek mathematician and third librarian at Alexandria, famous for his work on prime numbers and for measuring the diameter of the Earth, was born here in 276 BC.

Excavations of just a portion of the sanctuary of Demeter and Persephone have yielded 4500 terracotta figurines, 750 marble and limestone sculptures and reliefs, as well as high-quality pottery, votives, jewellery, glass, lamps, gold and coins.

Located in eastern Libya, 13 km (8 miles) inland from the Mediterranean on a plateau near the Sahara, Cyrene's remains are witness to the wealth of its agricultural civilization. At the site's centre is the ancient walled town, which includes the temple of Zeus, the agora, theatre and the baths and sanctuary of Apollo around an ancient spring. The city spread onto two massive hills – the southwest, with the acropolis, agora and forum is free of modern buildings, while the northeast is largely covered by fields and the old Arab village of Shahat. Tombs are cut into the surrounding slopes. The hillside sanctuary of Demeter and Persephone, one of the best preserved in the eastern Mediterranean, covered over 9000 sq m (97,000 sq feet) at its peak.

Plundered by Antiquity

Bisected by several roads, this site is vulnerable to theft and vandalism. Largely unfenced and poorly documented, the site is rich with unexcavated remains. In 2005 Italian archaeologists discovered seventy-six second-century AD statues intact under a collapsed wall. The necropolises are particularly vulnerable and are stained with smoke and graffiti from visitors. Key tombs have been walled off and a bunker built to protect historic items, but there remains little funding for guards and conservation. An international search continues for important statues stolen in 2000 from the site. Archaeological work is suffering from lack of maintenance and sewage flows in a wadi through the site. Encroachment from farms and the burgeoning town of New Shahat are also a problem, although authorities are attempting to relocate locals.

Serengeti National Park
United Republic of Tanzania

Home to the highest concentration of large mammals on Earth and site of the greatest land migration, the vast plains of the Serengeti are arguably the world's most famous wildlife sanctuary. One of the last uninterrupted migrations, the annual circular pilgrimage of some two million herbivores (wildebeest, zebra and Thomson's gazelle) followed by their predators, is one of nature's most impressive spectacles.

GUARDED

KEY THREATS Conflict | Theft | Development | Tourism | Pollution | Disasters | Constraints | Changing Uses | Invaders | Climate

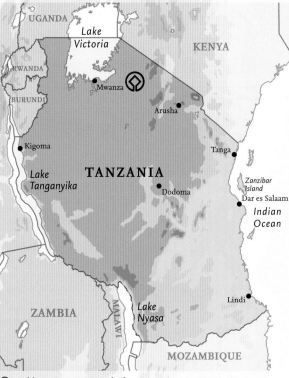

⊙ World Heritage Site inscribed: 1981
http://whc.unesco.org/en/list/156

Derived from the Masaai word "siringitu" meaning "endless plains", Serengeti is a fitting description of the dry and tree-less sunburned central plains of the park.

Five little Serengeti creatures who share names with the famous "big five" mammals once sought by game hunters include the: ant lion (larval stage of a flying insect which catches its prey in sand pits), rhino beetle (who deftly rolls dung into balls upon which to lay its eggs), elephant shrew (miniscule and with a long snout), buffalo weaver (a white-headed bird), and leopard tortoise (a black and orange flecked land turtle that can live for up to seventy-five years). The rhino beetle, unlike its namesake, is far from endangered, with more than 100 species present.

OPPOSITE PAGE: Stretching across shimmering plains as far as the eye can see, millions of wildebeest, zebra and gazelle voyage over 1600 km (1000 miles) every year in the world's greatest migration, moving along a circular route from the northern hills to the southern plains and back.

ABOVE RIGHT: During the 1960s and 1970s, much of the acacia forests was devastated by fire but stricter controls have allowed the habitat to recover.

Located in northern Tanzania on the Kenyan border and surrounded by reserves and conservation areas, Serengeti National Park encompasses 15,000 sq km (5700 sq miles) of protected savanna – an area roughly the size of Northern Ireland or the US state of Connecticut. One of the Earth's oldest ecosystems and Africa's most complex and least disturbed, the Serengeti's plains were created 3 to 4 million years ago from ash blown down from the volcanic highlands. Ranging from the savanna studded with symbolic kopje (weathered granite outcroppings), to light woodland and riverine forest, the flora and fauna here have changed little in millennia.

The park is home to magnificent wildlife: in addition to the migrant grazers, elephants, hippopotamuses, giraffes, elands, topis, kongonis and impalas roam. From prides of lions to solitary leopards, cheetahs, spotted hyenas and all three African jackal species, as well as the crocodiles which infest the waters in the north, predators seek their prey. Numerous smaller species, including beautiful serval cats, aardwolves, otters, baboons, mongoose and rock hyraxes are also to be found. More than 500 bird species from ostrich to flamingo are present, including 34 raptors, 6 vultures and aggregations of more than 20,000 wildfowl and waders.

Wildlife Under Pressure

Although the Serengeti was initially spared the wildlife decimation that other African countries suffered (due in part to the presence of tsetse-conveyed sleeping

sickness), by 1929 when the Seronera Valley was declared a game reserve, much of the fauna had succumbed – to both mechanized hunting and an Asian rinderpest epidemic in 1880.

Illicit trade has long been the Serengeti's greatest threat. During Tanzania's depression in the 1960s poaching halved the buffalo population, reduced the elephants to a few hundred and slashed the once thriving rhino herds to two. With a recovering economy, international support and the 1989 worldwide ivory ban, the park's wildlife has made a remarkable comeback. Yet commercial meat poaching is rife: hunting, snares and pitfall traps kill more than 40,000 animals annually. Wildebeest, zebra, giraffe, buffalo and impala are the prime targets, but endangered species are also at risk.

BELOW LEFT: Although fire forms an integral part of the Serengeti ecosystem, fires set off in the dry season by pastoralists, farmers, beekeepers and poachers have a devastating impact on both plants and animals.

BELOW RIGHT: Lions and other predators come under threat through poaching of their prey species, competition and diseases carried by livestock. In 1994 a distemper virus epidemic killed 30 per cent of the lions in the park.

OPPOSITE PAGE: Hippopotamuses are among the abundant and spectacular wildlife of the Serengeti. However, with the human population around the park growing at a rate of 4 per cent a year, this wildlife is at risk from poaching and from competition for scarce water resources.

"The survival of our wildlife is a matter of grave concern to all of us in Africa. These wild creatures amid the wild places they inhabit are not only important as a source of wonder and inspiration but are an integral part of our natural resources and of our future livelihood and well-being. In accepting the trusteeship of our wildlife we solemnly declare that we will do everything in our power to make sure that our children's grandchildren will be able to enjoy this rich and precious inheritance."

FROM THE ARUSHA MANIFESTO, DELIVERED BY TANZANIA'S FIRST PRESIDENT, MWALIMU JULIUS K. NYERERE, SEPTEMBER 1961

DEVELOPMENT

As the world becomes more crowded and land for farms, cities, industry, and infrastructure more scarce, once isolated and pristine World Heritage Sites are facing growing pressure from development. From forests cleared for pasture and crops, to historic monuments dwarfed amongst skyscrapers, or great wonders lost in rising waters behind massive dams, development presents a serious and increasing threat. Since World Heritage Sites by definition are areas of outstanding beauty or interest, the integral or neighbouring land and resources are often a tempting prospect for developers, whether rural or urban, industrial or commercial.

Encroachment is difficult to police and prevent. From the vast scale of many natural sites, to the layers of ownership and control in historic centres, managing growth and protecting against incursion into World Heritage Sites and their buffer zones is a challenge. Rapid economic growth puts additional demand on a region's resources, and when the financial lure is high, short term interests can overshadow the longer term value of preservation as pressures are brought to bear, nationally, provincially and locally, to ignore conservation issues. International big business is also sometimes a powerful force in these circumstances. Sufficient budgetary support for effective management for many protected areas is often lacking, while overlapping administrations make continuity difficult, in particular with regard to management authority and responsibility.

In the countryside, destruction of the environment through increasing population constitutes a major threat, especially by way of farming. The conversion of forest to agriculture fragments habitats and can create landslides on slopes, and overstocking of pasturelands, leading to overgrazing. Elsewhere rising water tables, caused by farmers' irrigation methods, frequently damage foundations of ancient and historic sites nearby.

Rural development can also encompass mining. The escalating prices commanded worldwide for ores and minerals are an attractive proposition to large mining conglomerates. Even the once-protected Guinean area of the Mount Nimba Strict Nature Reserve, on the Côte d'Ivoire, is now under threat because of its rich deposits of high-grade iron ore, a potentially lucrative source of revenue for the country. A mining operation needs roads, wells, workshops and mineshafts, not to mention dwellings for miners and their families, all of which lead to further destruction of the area. During the mining large amounts of rock and soil are removed over large areas, often resulting in serious erosion and water pollution.

Although most historic cities are an amalgam of centuries of growth, the rapid pace and scale of modern development frequently threatens to drown out the historic character and obscure scenic vistas. In London and Cologne, debate rages over modern high-rise buildings which increasingly dwarf centuries-old stone monuments. Particularly striking is the incongruity of the once remote Pyramids at Giza, near Cairo, which today stand opposite hotels, apartment blocks and houses.

The increasing pace of life results in demands for the shortest, quickest route, and in many areas uncontrolled development leads to the construction of roads, bridges and dams. Highways are hacked through conservation areas, and bridges built without thought to the visual impact on the area. Dams constructed to provide irrigation and power can cause increased humidity and rising water tables, putting at risk any ancient buildings or archaeological sites in the vicinity.

As World Heritage Sites receive publicity more people want to see them, with the result that overall visitor numbers rise steadily, increasing the need for more infrastructure and improved access to the areas.

In order to lessen the impact of development, UNESCO and the international community work with the host country in many ways. Often, rural populations from areas with vulnerable ecosystems are relocated to regions where there is more farmland and higher population-carrying capacity. Water tables can be lowered by means of drainage ditches and pipes, inside and around sites of historic interest. Strict controls are exerted over illegal construction in the area at risk, and zoning and land-use regulations are put in place and enforced, as are traffic regulations to ban heavy-duty vehicular traffic from World Heritage areas.

IN DANGER

KEY THREATS Conflict | Theft | Development | Tourism | Pollution | Disasters | Constraints | Changing Uses | Invaders | Climate

Mount Nimba Strict Nature Reserve
Côte d'Ivoire / Guinea

The highest point in Guinea and the Ivory Coast, Mount Nimba towers 1752 m (5750 feet) over the corner of Guinea, Côte d'Ivoire and Liberia. Rising abruptly above the surrounding lowlands and savanna, its slopes are covered by dense forest at the foot of grassy mountain pastures. They harbour a rich variety of plant and animal life, with 200 endemic species, including endangered stone tool-using western chimpanzees, nocturnal semi-aquatic Nimba otter-shrews and the unique Mount Nimba toad. The range is home to more than 2000 species of vascular plants including a unique orchid, Rhipidoglossum paucifolium.

⊛ World Heritage Site inscribed 1982
Inscription on the List of World Heritage in Danger: 1992
http://whc.unesco.org/en/list/155

OPPOSITE PAGE: The iron ore-rich Mount Nimba dominates the landscape of the Reserve (above). Signs around the perimeter of the Reserve do little to deter poaching and exploitation of its forest resources (below).

ABOVE RIGHT: Although part of Mount Nimba is protected, the site is in urgent need of stricter protection and improved management, to safeguard the Nimba toad and several other threatened species in the area.

The chimpanzee shares 98 per cent of our genes. Once found in twenty-five African countries they are now extinct in some and critically at risk in others because of deforestation and hunting for bushmeat. They can walk on just their legs for more than 1 km (0.6 miles). Young individuals sometimes swing from branch to branch. Chimpanzees eat with their hands, which they also use to throw objects at enemies and to create tools. Notably, they will poke a stick into a termite mound to extract the insects, and crack nuts open with stones.

The critically endangered Mount Nimba toad (Nimbaphrynoides occidentalis) belongs to the only type of toads that give birth to live young after an extended gestation period. Unique to the montane grasslands of Mount Nimba, they are threatened by habitat loss and degradation because of the mining of iron ore and bauxite.

Quarried from 1963–83, the Liberian half of the mountain remains unprotected. Its mine was once deemed commercially exhausted, but its estimated 450 million tonnes of 53–63 per cent grade ore make renewed exploitation at today's prices worthwhile.

Part of the Nimba Massif (the "Guinean Backbone"), the Guinean portion has been a strict nature reserve, closed even to tourists, since 1944. It is home to at least twenty-five species of rodents, fifteen of insectivores, sixty-five of reptiles and over forty-three of amphibians (including endangered Ivory Coast and Guinea screeching frogs and the goliath which can weigh as much as 3 kg [6.6 lb]). There are seventy-two species of birds and ninety of mammals, including several duikers and big cats, among them civets and the leopard which is almost extinct here.

Ore versus Animals

Site of one of the largest deposits of high-grade iron ore ever discovered, Mount Nimba is continually threatened by large-scale mining. In the last few years mining has accounted for 80 per cent of Guinea's exports and 25 per cent of government revenues. Soaring global metal prices, and over a billion tons of 63–68 per cent grade iron ore, make mining Mount Nimba tempting. In 2003 Guinea signed an exploration licence with a multinational consortium including BHP Billiton (UK), Newmont Mining (US) and Areva/Cogema (France). Since the 1990s, the site has been invaded by waves of refugees from Liberia and Sierra Leone, and now by Côte d'Ivoire rebels, making it unsafe to enter. With mineral exploration, limited management capacity, vague boundaries, poaching, encroachment and deforestation, the site remains in danger of losing not just the Nimba toad but many other species.

République de Guinée
Réserve de la Biosphère des Monts Nimba
Site du Patrimoine Mondial
STATION CENTRALE DE SURVEILLANCE

Pnud   Don de la Société Nimco

Fort and Shalamar Gardens in Lahore
Pakistan

IN DANGER

KEY THREATS Conflict | Theft | Development | Tourism | Pollution | Disasters | Constraints | Changing Uses | Invaders | Climate

These two masterpieces of the great Mughal civilization, which reached its height during the reign of the Emperor Shah Jahan, together illustrate the complete history of its architecture and landscape design. The red sandstone and cut-brick fort contains marble palaces and mosques decorated with glazed tile and mosaics, and pietra-dura and gilding. The elegance of the splendid gardens, built near the city of Lahore on three terraces with lodges, waterfalls and large ornamental ponds, is unequalled.

⊚ World Heritage Site inscribed: 1981
Inscription on the List of World Heritage in Danger: 2000
http://whc.unesco.org/en/list/171

OPPOSITE PAGE: The second level terrace, with the east end red pavilion in the background. This terrace was called Faiz Baksh – Bestower of Goodness.

ABOVE RIGHT: The south wall pavilion at the end of a long line of fountains on the lower terrace, which was called Hayay Baksh – Bestower of Life.

A 161-km (100-mile) long "Royal Canal" was built to bring water to the gardens. A series of hydraulic tanks fed over 400 fountains, which helped to cool the spot in the extreme summer heat.

The garden courtyards of Lahore Fort were largely rebuilt with every change in rule. The best preserved, built during the reign of Shah Jahan, faces the Shish Mahal (Hall of Mirrors). A square, marbled enclosure open to the sky, it is the most elaborate and beautiful courtyard in Lahore.

At the northwest edge of the walled city, the huge fort contains twenty-one monumental buildings spanning the history of the Mughal empire. There is evidence of a structure predating Mahmood of Ghazni (AD 1025), but it was not until the reign of the third Mughal emperor, Akbar, that the fort came to prominence. Lahore became his capital and he rebuilt the old mud structure in brick adding a wall and the Masti Gate.

The Shalamar, commissioned by Shah Jahan in 1637, is in the old village of Baghanbura. It embodies the Mughal concept of a perfect garden. Laid out on three terraces, it is surrounded by a high red sandstone wall with turrets. Calm canals, thirty-one tanks, 414 fountains and four rippling and singing cascades, interspersed with roses and cypresses among 4785 m (15,700 feet) of walkways, create an ensemble which is the stuff of legend.

Lost in a Sprawling Metropolis
The fort and gardens are today mired in the city sprawl, crowded by stalls and stands. With limited resources, and showing the wear of time and post-Mughal interventions, the fort and gardens are collapsing. They were placed on the list of World Heritage in Danger in 2000 after the 375-year-old water tanks were demolished for an adjacent road. In addition, termites, woodworm, fungi and corrosion are eating away what man has not damaged. The government has asked for help to safeguard the site – UNESCO and donors have assisted with more than US$1 million in aid and expertise, but much remains to be done if these vast gems of the Mughal civilization are to survive for future generations.

Dresden Elbe Valley
Germany

IN DANGER

KEY THREATS Conflict | Theft | Development | Tourism | Pollution | Disasters | Constraints | Changing Uses | Invaders | Climate

A crossroads of culture, science and technology in the eighteenth and nineteenth centuries, the cultural landscape of the Dresden Elbe Valley contains exceptional examples of court architecture and festivities, as well as renowned examples of middle-class architecture and industrial heritage representing European urban development into the modern era. Integrating celebrated Baroque art, architecture and gardens into an artistic whole within the river valley, the site extends some 18 km (11 miles) along the Elbe from the Übigau Palace and Ostragehege fields in the northwest through Dresden to the Pillnitz Palace and the Elbe River Island in the southeast.

◎ World Heritage Site inscribed 2004
Inscription on the List of World Heritage in Danger: 2006
http://whc.unesco.org/en/list/1156

OPPOSITE PAGE: Many of the historic sites were affected by the 2002 floods, but the current threat is from a proposed bridge across the Elbe in one of the most sensitive areas.

ABOVE RIGHT: At its height at the turn of the twentieth century, Dresden was considered to be one of the most beautiful cities in the world.

Dresden already has eight bridges across the Elbe for its half a million residents, a capacity deemed adequate by some, as the city also features one of Germany's best tram systems.

Although heavily damaged by allied bombing in February 1945, the historical area of the city has become a symbol of peace and resurrection. With donations from across Germany and the world, the Frauenkirche was painstakingly pieced back together and rebuilt. Its golden cross was donated by the diocese of Coventry.

Like the World Heritage Site of Prague, Dresden was badly hit in 2002 by the floods that inundated large areas of Europe. The Elbe climbed over its banks and flooded many low-lying areas of the city and cultural landscape. With a changing climate, many fear flooding will become more frequent here.

The site is crowned by the historic area of Dresden with its numerous monuments and parks from the sixteenth century to the twentieth, as well as the Pillnitz Palace. The landscape also features nineteenth- and twentieth-century suburban villas and gardens, low meadows and valuable natural features. Some terraced slopes along the river are still used for viticulture and several old villages have retained their historic structure and elements from the industrial revolution: notably the 147-m (482-foot) Blue Wonder steel bridge (1891–1893), the single-rail suspension cable railway (1898–1901) and the funicular railway (1894–1895). Passenger steamships (the oldest from 1879) and shipyard (c. 1900) are still in use.

A Bridge over Troubled Water

The Dresden Elbe Valley is caught between development and conservation. In 2005, residents voted for a new traffic bridge at the widest and most sensitive point of the Elbe Valley, potentially seriously threatening the pristine views of the city and environment. In a tug of war with the State of Saxony, conservation groups and the city council have repeatedly challenged the plan, arguing that the project should be rethought, perhaps with a tunnel instead of a bridge. But in 2007 the German Constitutional Court agreed with the voters, saying that their voice overrode international commitments under the World Heritage Convention and that the US$220 million project must go ahead. The World Heritage Committee has placed the site "In Danger" and threatened to take the step of removing it from the list if the bridge proceeds as planned.

Tower of London / Palace of Westminster
United Kingdom of Great Britain and Northern Ireland

AT RISK

KEY THREATS Conflict | Theft | Development | Tourism | Pollution | Disasters | Constraints | Changing Uses | Invaders | Climate

Two world heritage sites are situated in the heart of London, the capital of the United Kingdom. One of these is the fortress of the Tower of London – an impressive complex of several buildings set within two parallel rings of defensive walls and a moat. The second site comprises Westminster Palace, Westminster Abbey, and Saint Margaret's Church. These sites represent the history of Britain and its government, from Norman stronghold to coronation and burial place of kings and queens and seat of government. On the banks of the River Thames these two famed groups of monuments are recognized the world over.

In approximately 1080 William the Conqueror began construction of a massive stone tower at the heart of his London fortress.

An architectural masterpiece of the thirteenth to sixteenth centuries, Westminster Abbey sits on the site of King Edward the Confessor's western "minster" (as opposed to St Paul's the church on the eastern side of London). This original church was largely replaced by the current Gothic structure, begun in the middle of the thirteenth century by King Henry III.

⊚ **World Heritage Sites inscribed 1988 and 1987**
http://whc.unesco.org/en/list/488 + http://whc.unesco.org/en/list/426

OPPOSITE PAGE: The Tower in all its splendour. This fine example of Norman military architecture is threatened in the long term by climate change, as it is expected that there will be more frequent and intense flooding of the River Thames on the banks of which it sits.

ABOVE RIGHT: An aerial view of the World Heritage Site of the Palace of Westminster (the Houses of Parliament), Westminster Abbey and St Margaret's Church, with Big Ben and Westminster Bridge to the right.

The Tower of London, an imposing fortress with many layers of history, has become one of the symbols of royalty. Built at the southern edge of the Roman city by William the Conqueror to protect London and assert his power, the original massive White Tower is a typical example of Norman military architecture. Its influence was felt throughout the country and helped to secure the kingdom.

The Palace of Westminster, rebuilt from 1840 onwards on the site of important medieval remains, is a fine example of neo-Gothic architecture. More commonly known as the Houses of Parliament, the waterfront palace is the seat of government today. With the small medieval church of St Margaret, built in a perpendicular Gothic style, and the prestigious Westminster Abbey, on a site where all the English sovereigns since the eleventh century have been crowned, the collective group is of great historic and symbolic significance.

The Palace, the Abbey and St Margaret's illustrate in stone the nature of the country's rulers over nine centuries. Whether one looks at the royal tombs of the chapter house, the remarkable vastness of Westminster Hall, the House of Lords or the House of Commons, art is everywhere present and harmonious, making a veritable museum of the history of the United Kingdom.

A Tower Dwarfed

Symbolizing the conflict between preservation and development, and historic versus modern, London and its heritage are increasingly threatened by the high-rise building boom of the city's success. From the eleventh century to the twentieth, the 27.5-m (90-foot) White Tower dominated the skyline, a symbol of royal power meant to strike awe and respect in rebellious Londoners. But today the Tower and Westminster are increasingly lost in the sea of buildings and noise of traffic. From Norman Foster's hypermodern rounded-glass Swiss Re building (known as the Gherkin) to the 310-m (1020-foot) "Shard of Glass" (due to be completed in 2011), more than eight skyscrapers endanger the views of and from the city's heritage. At the heart of the issue is the Mayor

BELOW LEFT: Modern buildings crowd right up to the edges of the Tower of London — at one time an imposing fortress.

BELOW RIGHT: In the foreground the Tower of London, which once dominated the skyline. Today it is overshadowed by Norman Foster's "Gherkin."

OPPOSITE PAGE: One predicted scenario of climate change is sea level rise which will put low-lying settlements under huge risk. This computer-generated image depicts a scenario where the Thames flood barrier is breached during a higher than average high tide and storm surge. (From the film Flood)

and Greater London Development Authority's tall buildings strategy: without a clear management plan, the original idea of clustering in and around the financial district and transport hubs has given way to planning consent for skyscrapers across the entire city.

Climate change in turn presents a longer term, but quite tangible threat, as it is expected to lead to more frequent and intense flooding of the River Thames next to which both sites sit. A combination of high tides and storm surges from low pressure systems funnelling water from the southern end of the North Sea into the Thames Estuary, compounds the risk of rising global sea levels to both these sites.

Ancient Thebes with its Necropolis
Egypt

AT RISK

KEY THREATS Conflict | Theft | Development | Tourism | Pollution | Disasters | Constraints | Changing Uses | Invaders | Climate

Home to some of the most spectacular wonders of ancient Egypt, Thebes has been called the world's greatest open-air museum. Located on the upper Nile, 675 km (420 miles) south of modern Cairo, this city of the god Amon was the capital of Egypt during the Middle and New Kingdoms. Including the temples and palaces at Karnak and Luxor, and the necropolises of the Valley of the Kings and the Valley of the Queens, Thebes is a striking testimony to Egyptian civilization at its height.

⊛ World Heritage Site inscribed 1979
http://whc.unesco.org/en/list/87

Although most estimates put the population of ancient Thebes at 50,000 to 80,000 some think it could have ranged as high as 1 million. In any case, it was one of the largest cities of the ancient world.

To date, sixty-three tombs have been located in the Valley of the Kings. Despite the name, not all are of kings however. The most famous perhaps is the sixty-second found, that of Tutankhamun, which was discovered almost intact in November 1922 by Howard Carter after an extensive search. In 2006, a sixty-third tomb was discovered nearby.

Thebes rose to become the capital of Egypt during the eleventh dynasty (twenty-first century BC) and continued (with a brief interruption in the fourteenth century BC) until it was sacked in 661 BC by the Assyrians. Spanning both sides of the Nile, it includes the temple complexes of Luxor and of Amon at Karnak on the east. Once linked by a 3-km (2-mile) avenue flanked with perhaps 2000 sphinxes, the vast temple ruins and their massive colonnades still inspire awe. On the west bank, an area of 9 sq km (3.5 sq miles) holds: the vast necropolises in the valleys of the Kings and Queens, the village of Dayr al Madinah, the palace of Malkata, more than 5000 nobles' tombs and some forty temples and their remnants. These include the colossi of Memnon, the Ramesseum of Ramses II and the temples of Ramses III and Queen Hatshepsut. Among the most famous tombs is that of Tutankhamun.

OPPOSITE PAGE: On the west bank, Queen Hatshepsut stands guard at the entrance to her temple at Dayr al Bahri.

ABOVE RIGHT: Hatshepsut's mortuary temple. She is one of only a few women to rule Egypt in her own right.

Flooded by Water, People and Pollutants

Thebes is under threat from a mix of factors including encroaching farms, rising water tables, pollution, urban development, uncontrolled tourism, limited resources, looting and occasional terrorism. The basis of the problem is a soaring population. At Luxor and Karnak, modern buildings now encircle the temples, while across the river, farms extend right up to the steps of others and homes are interspersed among the tombs. As farms encroach, traditional irrigation by flooding from the Nile brings the rising water table ever closer. Water, wicked up by the porous sandstone temples evaporates from the surfaces, leaving behind salts which crystallize, causing spalling and flaking. Chemical fertilizers add to the problem and stagnant water brings bacteria and

fungi which also harm the stones. Damage is already visible at Luxor and at the Mortuary Temple of Amenhotep III, while the Ramesseum and the massive temple complex of Karnak are under imminent threat. The government is trying to persuade farmers to switch to drip irrigation and to enact stronger legal protections for heritage lands, yet problems mount. At some temples, gravel-filled trenches have been dug to keep water away from the foundations, but this solution is expensive and potentially damaging in its own right. If action is not taken soon, experts warn, reliefs, subsurface archaeology and even whole monuments dating back thousands of years could be gone in a decade.

Kathmandu Valley
Nepal

AT RISK

KEY THREATS Conflict | Theft | Development | Tourism | Pollution | Disasters | Constraints | Changing Uses | Invaders | Climate

At the crossroads of the great civilizations of Asia, the historic brick and carved-timber palaces, temples, stupas and houses of the Kathmandu Valley illustrate the heights of Nepalese culture. Seven groups of monuments make up the protected area: the three Darbar palaces, squares and residential areas of the royal cities of Kathmandu, Patan and Bhaktapur (Bhadgaon); the two Buddhist stupas of Swayambhu and Bauddhanath and the two Hindu temple complexes of Pashupati and Changu Narayan.

Kathmandu Darbar Square is the most extensive of the three royal palace squares in the valley with sixty important structures. Although most date from the seventeenth and eighteenth centuries, Taleju Bhawani Temple was commissioned in 1576.

Patan, famous as the oldest city in the Kathmandu Valley, is also known as the "City of Fine Arts." The exquisite art and architecture in and around the Patan Darbar Square date from the sixteenth century on, but the history of Patan goes as far back as AD 570.

Among the 130 listed structures are places of veneration to both Hindus and Buddhists: pilgrimage sites, temples, shrines, bathing areas and gardens.

◎ World Heritage Site inscribed 1979
http://whc.unesco.org/en/list/121

OPPOSITE PAGE: In the thirty-year period from 1969, when the top photograph was taken, the population of Kathmandu increased five-fold due mostly to migration from the countryside. This resulted in the built-up area of the city expanding outwards to swallow up rural communities. The photograph below, taken from the same location, shows a dramatic change in the landscape in this relatively short period of time.

ABOVE RIGHT: Patan's Sundari Chowk contains superb examples of artistic achievement including the Tusha Hiti in the middle of the square.

High in the foothills of the Himalaya, this legendary valley has been a political hub for close to 2000 years. In the fourteenth century, with the arrival of the Mallas, the region experienced a flourishing of Nepalese art and architecture. By the mid-eighteenth century, competition among the valley's three rival kingdoms brought artistic expression to a peak.

An Urban Explosion

Rapid and largely uncontrolled urban development in Nepal in recent years has put great strain on the unique architectural heritage of the Kathmandu Valley. With a population growing at an annual rate of 6 per cent—more than three times as fast as in many western countries—the urban fabric is under threat of progressive destruction. Six of the seven protected areas have already been altered. Although there has been progress in developing a management plan and reining in some of the development around the historic sites, the aesthetic appeal of the ancient temples and other treasures is disappearing as modern concrete structures rise around the periphery. Pollution adds to the problem, blocking scenic views of the great mountains around the valley. Conflict and disasters also loom in the background—catastrophic earthquakes in 1833 and 1934 caused widespread destruction and many monuments had to be rebuilt. The possibility of another quake in this now crowded metropolis is high. While the site is still at risk, the progress that has been made led to its removal from the List of World Heritage in Danger in 2007.

Three Parallel Rivers of Yunnan Protected Areas
China

AT RISK | KEY THREATS Conflict | Theft | Development | Tourism | Pollution | Disasters | Constraints | Changing Uses | Invaders | Climate

In the high Hengduan Mountains in southwestern China are the upper reaches of the Yangtze (Jinsha), Mekong (Lancang) and Salween (Nujiang). Originating on the Qinghai-Tibet Plateau they plummet from glaciated peaks more than 6000 m (19,685 feet) high, through steep gorges as deep as 3000 m (10,000 feet) and run roughly parallel from north to south for more than 300 km (190 miles). The site is amongst the most biologically diverse temperate regions on earth. Its 17,000 sq km (6500 sq miles) support a quarter of the entire planet's animal species, in fifteen protected areas in eight clusters, in a region bordering on Myanmar and the Tibet autonomous region in the Three Parallel Rivers National Park.

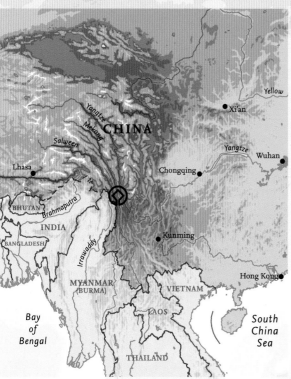

⊚ World Heritage Site inscribed 2003
http://whc.unesco.org/en/list/1083

OPPOSITE PAGE: Tiger Leaping Gorge, the world's deepest and part of the World Heritage Site has been cut in the soft rock by the fast-flowing Yangtze.

ABOVE RIGHT: Proposed dams in China, Thailand and Myanmar would adversely affect the site.

In January 2006 Yunnan Province was declared the destination of choice for Chinese tourists – visits to the region soared from 15,000 in 1994 to 2.65 million in 2005, and are expected to exceed to 4.5 million by 2010, which will put new pressures on the protected areas.

Although the area covers less than 0.5 per cent of Chinese territory, it contains more than 20 per cent of the higher plants and 25 per cent of the animal species of the country. Thirty-four species of rare plants under state-class protection here include the Chinese fir, spinulose tree fern and the yew. Some 200 species of rhododendrons and nearly 100 species of rough gentians are also to be found.

The Mingyongqia Glacier is a notable natural phemonenon, descending to 2700 m (8860 ft) from Mount Kawagebo (6740 m [22,110 ft]). It is said to be the lowest-altitude glacier for such a low latitude (28°) in the northern hemisphere.

This area contains virgin forests and more than 6000 plant species, of which 2700 are endemic to China. Records list 173 mammals (81 endemic), 417 birds (22 endemic), 59 reptiles (27 endemic), 36 amphibians (25 endemic), 27 swallowtail butterflies (8 endemic) and 76 fish (35 endemic). Seventy-nine rare or endangered animals include the Chinese shrew-mole, Yunnan snubfaced monkey, red panda, Bengal tiger, black-necked crane, takin and snow leopard.

Southeast Asia's last Great Undammed River

China's rapidly growing economy and population are putting enormous pressure on this wilderness as mines, hydroelectric plants, roads and bridges, and tourist infrastructure extend into once pristine areas. In 2003, the Yunnan provincial government was preparing plans for a large copper mine nearby and thirteen dams on the Nujiang that would have affected the ecosystems of the gorges. Following national and international outcry, on 1 April 2004 China's premier suspended plans for dams on the Nujiang, pending research and scientific analysis. Non-Governmental Organizations report that work on four dams is going ahead, although national authorities have yet to issue permits. Some claim the site boundaries are being redrawn, reducing the area by 20 per cent, in order to put the dams outside the protected area. Until the issue is resolved, this fragile and globally crucial ecosystem remains at high risk. In October 2006 China's water resources minister indicated disapproval for the thirteen dams originally planned on the Chinese side, but also implied that some dams would be built.

Memphis and its Necropolis
Egypt

AT RISK

KEY THREATS Conflict | Theft | Development | Tourism | Pollution | Disasters | Constraints | Changing Uses | Invaders | Climate

The capital of ancient Egypt for more than 2000 years, Memphis and its necropolis are marked today by vast pyramid fields and the iconic Sphinx. The three pyramids at Giza are the sole survivors of the original Seven Wonders of the World. The capital and royal residence during the proto-dynastic and Old Kingdom (3100–2184 BC) periods, Memphis was the heart of unified Egypt and was at its peak the world's largest city. Stretching for 30 km (19 miles) along the west bank of the Nile, the site includes extraordinary funerary monuments, from rock tombs to ornate mastabas (in which nobles were buried), temples and numerous pyramids.

◎ World Heritage Site inscribed: 1979
http://whc.unesco.org/en/list/86

OPPOSITE PAGE: The aerial view of the plateau shows the advancing edge of Cairo's sprawl.

ABOVE RIGHT: The pyramids and sphinx spent thousands of years isolated in the desert, but are now threatened by tourism, development and pollution.

One of the world's oldest tourist attractions, the pyramids are the sole survivors from Antipater of Sidon's original list of the Seven Wonders of the World.

Recent findings indicate that the pyramids were built by skilled workers rather than slaves or foreigners. 20,000–30,000 artisans worked at the Giza Plateau over a period of eighty years and their community boasted bakers, butchers, granaries, cemeteries and even primitive health care.

As well as the three pyramids of Khufu, Menkaure and Khafre, the site includes the pyramid fields at Saqqara, Dahshur, Helwan, Abusir, Zawyer and Abu-Rawash. The step pyramid of Djoser (2630 BC) at Saqqara is the earliest of ninety-seven known edifices. The Great Pyramid (the Pyramid of Khufu, c. 2550 BC) is the largest ever built. Measuring 263.4 m (755 feet 9 inches) on each side, it is made up of roughly 2.3 million blocks of stone, weighing from 1.5 to 75 tonnes each. Because of the loss of its facing stone, it is 9 m (30 feet) shorter than its original height of 147 m (481 feet). It was built by 20,000–30,000 workers over a period of thirty-five years. Still relatively intact after 4500 years but with little written evidence about their symbolism and their burials long gone, the pyramids remain shrouded in mystery.

A Crowded Desert

A hundred years ago, the pyramids were still in the desert. Today, the site is at risk from the continued advance of urban sprawl. Without clear site boundaries or a buffer zone, these great monuments stand unprotected from one of the world's largest cities. Hotels and stalls ring the site, and buildings grow closer, and higher, every year. For over a decade plans for a road across the plateau have been under debate. Opposed by the World Heritage Committee, archaeologists and Egypt's president, this project is being considered once more. Development and tourism have brought rising groundwater, pollution, theft and damage to the site. With limited capacity, this vast complex has suffered for more than fifteen years with no management plan.

Pasargadae
Iran (Islamic Republic of)

GUARDED

KEY THREATS Conflict | Theft | Development | Tourism | Pollution | Disasters | Constraints | Changing Uses | Invaders | Climate

Founded by Cyrus the Great in the sixth century BC, Pasargadae was the first capital of the Persian empire. This dynastic seat's palaces, gardens and mausoleum are outstanding examples of the first phase of royal Achaemenid art and architecture and exceptional testimonies to Persian civilization. Particularly noteworthy vestiges in the 1.6-sq-km (0.6-sq-mile) site include the Mausoleum of Cyrus II (the Great), the fortified terrace of Tall-e Takht and an ensemble of royal gatehouse, audience hall, residential palace and gardens. Pasargadae was the capital of the first multicultural empire in western Asia, spanning from Egypt to the Indus valley, and is considered the first to respect the cultural diversity of its peoples.

According to the Roman geographer Strabo of Amasia, Pasargadae was built on the site where Cyrus defeated the leader of the Medes, Astyages, in 550 BC.

The "Four Gardens" type of royal ensemble, which was created in Pasargadae, became a prototype for Western Asian architecture and design.

World Heritage Site inscribed 2004
http://whc.unesco.org/en/list/1106

OPPOSITE PAGE: At the head of the Tang-e-Bolaghi Gorge, Pasargadae is only one of the many important archaeological sites in the area (above). Below is the Sivand Dam prior to it being filled with water in March 2007. The dam has become the centre of global concern with many archaeologists saying flooding will cause harm to the nearby World Heritage Sites of Pasargadae and Persepolis.

ABOVE RIGHT: Pasargadae is one of the earliest examples of cultural conservation – Alexander the Great ordered restoration of Cyrus' tomb in 324 BC. Preservation work continues to this day.

Pasargadae's architecture, which is a synthesis of different styles and building types, reflects its cultural diversity. Left unfinished after Cyrus' early death in battle, it was replaced shortly after by Darius' new seat at Persepolis, 87 km (54 miles) to the southwest.

Rising Waters

Pasargadae is situated at the end of a growing lake being formed by the Sivand Dam. Begun in 1992 to provide power and irrigation in this parched region, the dam has sparked international concern for this ancient capital. The site is above the planned high-water mark, but experts agree that increased humidity will accelerate decay (as lichen eats away at the 2500-year-old ruins). The rising water table may also damage archaeological evidence and threaten foundations as portions of the site's buffer zone will be inundated. Other sites throughout the 13-km (8-mile) gorge are at greater risk.

In 2004 UNESCO and the Iranian authorities issued an appeal for archaeological missions, estimating that more than 129 sites from the prehistoric period to Qajar monarchy (which fell in 1925) would be at risk. Rescue work has found fifteen important sites dating from the Elamite (pre-4000 BC) to the present, including three Achaemenid palaces, portions of ancient Persia's imperial road from Persepolis to Pasargadae, a fire temple and 9.5 km (6 miles) of rock-cut water channels. These, and twenty unexcavated Sassanid-dynasty sites (AD 224–651), are all expected to be lost. Despite years of lobbying, a 60,000-signature petition, and protests to the Iranian Parliament, the dam began to be filled on 15 March 2007.

UNSUSTAINABLE

Some of the best-known World Heritage Sites are also those attracting the largest numbers of tourists – the spectacular wildlife, geology and archaeology lure people from all over the world. Angkor in Cambodia, Machu Picchu in Peru and Petra in Jordan are just three areas which have seen visitor numbers rise each year. Although tourism is not at all bad, if not well-managed it can adversely impact monuments and ecosystems.

Tourists bring revenue, but in the twenty-first century they want a degree of comfort often unrealistic in the area to which they have come. The temptation to capitalize on the visitors all too often proves irresistible to developers, with the result that luxury hotel resorts, golf courses, shops and all the other trappings of modern-day living spring up in an uncontrolled fashion. Many once remote sites are now "islands" in a sea of development and increasingly removed from their historic context. When owned or funded by outside investors, these developments seldom leave revenue with the local population, further reducing their benefit.

Any site of interest will inevitably develop to some extent. What was once a remote and peaceful location, can suddenly grow to encompass ticket kiosks, shops, restaurants, confusing signposts, information panels, camp and picnic grounds, toilets and rubbish bins. Instead of being welcomed at sites by the grand vistas of the past, many visitors now arrive in noisy, dusty and overcrowded car parks. Peripheral activities, such as balloon rides, scenic flights, bungee jumping, off-road vehicle rentals and camel rides, can adversely impact sites with obstructed views, noise, smells, and trash. Tracks, trails and paths from the feet of many tourists tramping across a site are often unwittingly carved through vulnerable locations. At Machu Picchu, for example, landslides on fragile slopes are becoming more common, threatening monuments and whole villages.

Where there are tourists there often follow souvenir stalls, hawkers, beggars and food stalls. The vendors may have little understanding of the cultural, historic or ecological importance of the area, but know there is money to be made. People from further afield also move into the area, attracted by the revenue the tourists bring, putting more pressure on the infrastructure. Incompatible satellite "towns" have sprung up alongside sites of interest, bringing additional pressures upon fragile properties. To meet the needs of new inhabitants, wood is foraged, lands plowed, and vast quantities of water are drawn or diverted from streams, often to the detriment of the local flora and fauna and the foundations

TOURISM

of ancient monuments and buildings.

Cruise liners, ferries, aeroplanes, coaches, buses, jeeps and taxis service the incoming tourists, while inappropriate vehicle use often leads to damaged roads, and vehicle-tracks becoming excessively enlarged.

The damage inflicted by uncontrolled numbers of tourists can be considerable, and lack of management resources and funds to properly plan paths and routes or to guard sites make it difficult to physically control these increasing numbers. Soft stone stairs that have lasted a thousand years can be ground down in a few seasons by hundreds of thousands of feet and hard-soled shoes. Some carry off what they consider to be "insignificant" souvenirs – a rock, a plant, a shell – ultimately weakening the infrastructure. Others climb over ancient buildings, putting friable sandstone and rocks at risk, or walk and cycle through protected areas – the wear and tear caused by visitors has a cumulative effect, often invisible to the individual, but nonetheless significant. Although tourists bring money to the region, they can also bring hostile bugs, litter, pollution, graffiti and crime.

In national parks and reserves, local wildlife become acclimatized to humans, with all the dangers that this entails. Hides and viewing platforms are built close to watering holes or near nesting sites, while roads and buildings encroach on habitats. Scavenging animals become fearless in their hunt for the food carelessly disposed of wherever areas are colonized.

At the other extreme, in an effort to protect fragile sites, sometimes tourists are kept at bay, an area is enclosed and fenced off, and becomes remote or derelict, detracting from its natural beauty and limiting the public's care and understanding

To protect World Heritage from the worst excesses, and harness the positive energy of tourism, UNESCO, the UN World Tourism Organization, a growing number of Non-Governmental Organizations and responsible corporations are promoting sustainable tourism practices. Clear regulations and effective enforcement can direct tourism's potential to conservation. From low-impact facilities, to non-polluting transportation, carbon-offsets against travel, and measures to ensure that entry fees go back to the sites where they are collected, progress is being made. Efforts are underway at a growing number of sites to protect local ecosystems and promote preservation and awareness through responsible, sustainable and community-based tourism.

Historic Sanctuary of Machu Picchu
Peru

Hidden for centuries deep in the tropical forest of the high mountains of Peru, Machu Picchu, "the Old Peak", rises majestically on a sheer ridge 2430 m (7970 feet) above sea level. One of the most spectacular urban creations of the Incas, this legendary site's exact role, 100 km (60 miles) from the capital, Cuzco, is shrouded in mystery. Dating from the Inca Empire's height, Machu Picchu's Cyclopean stone walls, terraces and ramps seem as if they were cut into the continuous rock escarpments by the gods. The pristine natural setting, on the eastern slopes of the Andes, encompasses the upper Amazon basin with its rich diversity of flora and fauna.

The city consists of approximately 200 structures and may have sheltered a population of about 1000 inhabitants, including priests and administrative officials.

Machu Picchu was abandoned as a city when the Spanish overthrew the empire in 1534, escaping detection by the outside world for centuries. There are also signs it may have been hastily deserted after a destructive fire some time before the Spanish conquest.

Around Machu Picchu and within the area of the historic sanctuary are many other subsidiary sites with homes and cultivated terraces, including Inkaraqay, Chachabamba, Sayacmarka, Puyupatamarka, Winay Wayna and Choquesuysuy.

Overlooking the Vilcanota river, the fabled "Lost City" was revealed to the outside world in 1911 when Yale University historian, Hiram Bingham, with the aid of the National Geographic Society and a nineteenth-century map, arrived at the overgrown site. The fortified mountaintop retreat was built by the Pachacutec Inca Yupanqui (1438–1471) and his descendants. It was used for two centuries after the fall of the Inca as a safe haven for forces fighting Spanish rule.

The complex was planned with a clear separation between farming and residential areas, with a typical large plaza between the upper and lower sections of the site. The buildings include a supposed "farmers" quarter near the colossal terraces and hanging gardens, as well as "industrial", "royal" and "religious" ones. Noble structures include the Temple of the Sun, the so-called Room of the Three Windows, and the unique Intihuatana, a large monolithic stone altar or sundial.

⊛ World Heritage Site inscribed 1983
http://whc.unesco.org/en/list/274

OPPOSITE PAGE: Once thought to have been a defensive "citadel", experts now argue that the remote ridge was more likely an exclusive royal retreat. While the sheer slopes helped keep the site hidden, earthquakes and mudslides, such as the deadly one that hit Aguas Calientes in 2004, are a growing concern.

ABOVE RIGHT: Constructed in the classic Inca architectural style, buildings and walls are mortarless and feature tightly fitting irregular stone. Many features, including staircases, are carved directly from the bedrock.

Aguas Calientes – Heritage in Hot Water

Virtually unknown 100 years ago, Machu Picchu is today a major tourist destination and important component of the Peruvian economy. Once accessible to only backpackers and archaeologists, the site has gone from 9000 visitors in 1992, to more than 300,000 in 2006, with more than 4000 entering on some days. At Machu Picchu's base, Aguas Calientes (named for its hot springs), the terminus of the private rail line to the site, has become a harrowing obstacle course of vendors and detritus. The surge of visitors, and those seeking to capitalize on them, has brought US$40 million in annual revenue to the economy but also litter, erosion up on the mountain, wear and tear and the threat of large tourist infrastructure projects. Proposals to build an

amusement park at the base were eventually thwarted, but plans for a tram continue. In defiance of the national government and a court order, a local mayor eager to cash in on the boom has built an 80-m (262-ft) bridge over the Vilcanota river nearby, opening a new access route to the site and threatening to increase the flood of visitors. Landslides and earthquakes are a very real danger, having struck frequently in the past. With uncontrolled development, and national authorities losing control over the site, Machu Picchu is in trouble.

Iguazu National Park & Iguaçu National Park
Argentina and Brazil

AT RISK | KEY THREATS Conflict | Theft | Development | Tourism | Pollution | Disasters | Constraints | Changing Uses | Invaders | Climate

Two World Heritage Sites, one in Argentina and the other in Brazil, come together at the famous Iguazu Falls to protect 2250 sq km (868 sq miles) of rushing water and southwestern Atlantic rainforest. One of the world's largest and most spectacular waterfalls, this huge break in the Iguazu river measures an incredible 2.7 km (1.6 miles) along its horseshoe rim. Pouring through as many as 275 separate cataracts at an average rate of 1.7 million litres (373,950 gallons) per second, its waters thunderously plunge 82 m (269 feet) – or the height of a 24-floor building – into the gorge below.

⊕ World Heritage Sites inscribed 1984 (Argentina) and 1986 (Brazil)
http://whc.unesco.org/en/list/303
http://whc.unesco.org/en/list/355

OPPOSITE PAGE: The lush green rainforest through which the river flows is threatened by both tourism and development.

ABOVE RIGHT: Squeezed at its edges by massive growth, the site is threatened from within by tourism. With more than 1 million coming every year to the small area around the falls, traffic, noise from helicopters and the building of facilities all pose a threat.

The Portuguese word Iguaçu and the Spanish Iguazú both mean big water, stemming from the Amerindian Guaraní words y (large) and guasu (water). According to native legend, the falls were created by an angry and jealous god to split the beautiful maiden Naipú from her mortal lover Tarobá after they tried to elope in his canoe.

The first westerner to see the splendour of the falls was Spanish explorer, Álvar Núñez Cabeza de Vaca, in 1541.

Bisected by the river, these adjoining national parks form one of the last green islands of wilderness in the rapidly developing region at the border of Argentina, Brazil and Paraguay. The subtropical rainforest has more than 2000 species of vascular plants and is home to numerous endangered and vulnerable species. Jaguars, ocelots, tiger-cats, giant anteaters, coati, tamandua, tapirs, giant Brazilian otters, black-capped capuchin and howler monkeys, and endangered broad-nosed caimans call this lush reserve home. Rare bird species include the purple-winged ground dove, glaucous macaw, black-fronted piping guan, harpy eagle, vinaceous-breasted parrot and saw-billed duck.

A Last Island of Atlantic Rainforest

Tourism, development and a lack of coordination threaten the habitat and splendour of both parks. Over 1 million visitors a year on the Brazilian side and close to 600,000 in Argentina are taking their toll. In a rush to capitalize on the tourists, uncoordinated and uncontrolled development is destroying the exceptional natural beauty and integrity of the site. Concrete walkways are left collapsed in the river bed, large hotels disrupt views, countless stalls haphazardly congest the rim and helicopters disrupt the tranquility.

While tourism is eating away at the heart of the site, development is, in addition, attacking its borders on all sides. The three surrounding cities have seen population explosions: the Brazilian Foz do Iguaçu, a small town with a population of 30,000 in the 1960s, may already have surpassed 300,000 inhabitants. The region's rivers

are peppered with dams, and despite assurances by both Argentina and Brazil that new works are not planned, many others remain on the cards. The new Yaciretá hydroelectric complex will come onstream in 2008, and will undoubtedly affect the region. Argentina and Paraguay may move forward with the Corpus Christi hydroelectric project, while on the Brazilian side the Lower Iguaçu Hydroelectric project is also proving a cause for concern.

Agricultural land now runs up to the park boundaries on all sides, and although an attempt by locals to reinstate the old Estrada do Colono Road was averted by the 1999–2001 placement of Iguaçu on the List of World Heritage in Danger, some still dream of opening a route through the Brazilian side.

BELOW: Some of the most spectacular waterfalls in the world, the Iguaçu, lie at the junction of Argentina, Brazil and Paraguay. The isolation of this region gave rise to the Paranaense rain forest ecosystem which supported thousands of species unique to the region. This satellite image taken in early 1973 shows early evidence of deforestation, with patterns of tree felling following lines of communication.

OPPOSITE PAGE: This satellite image taken in May 2003 illustrates the dramatic changes that have taken place in this region. Vast areas of forest have been cleared for agriculture, particularly in Paraguay on the left of the image. This process was accelerated by the creation of a huge new reservoir, following the construction of the Itaipu Dam and reservoir (top centre) on the Paraná River in the early 1980s. Some forest on the right of the image lies within the Iguaçu National Park and has been protected from destruction.

Petra
Jordan

AT RISK

KEY THREATS Conflict | Theft | Development | Tourism | Pollution | Disasters | Constraints | Changing Uses | Invaders | Climate

The "Lost City" of Petra is one of the world's most famous archaeological sites. Half-built and half-carved in the walls of a richly hued sandstone valley, this hidden world is ringed by mountains riddled with passages and gorges. It has been inhabited since prehistoric times and was at its peak as capital of the Nabataean kingdom from the second century BC to the fourth century AD. Situated in Jordan, not far from the tip of the Red Sea, Petra was the heart of a trading empire which brought gums, spices, silks and other riches up from the Gulf of Aqaba to Sinai, Dead Sea, Syria and beyond. At an important crossroads between Arabia, Egypt and Syria-Phoenicia, its architecture blends eastern traditions with the Hellenistic.

There are more than 1000 burial monuments in Petra.

The semi-desert climate led to the invention of a sophisticated early hydraulic engineering system, with an ingenious network of channels, basins, cisterns and chamfered clay pipes, to capture the meagre annual precipitation of just 50–250 mm (2–10 in).

The collapse of the elaborately channelled ancient waterworks threatens the site, as without the sophisticated system of collection and redirection, water comes down over structures and façades wearing away carved surfaces.

Several projects to resurrect Nabataean dams and catchment systems have been launched, but the task is enormous.

Ⓧ World Heritage Site inscribed 1985
http://whc.unesco.org/en/list/326

OPPOSITE PAGE: The scale of the Al-Dayr temple, at 47-m (154-ft) wide and 48.3-m (158-ft) high, one of the largest monuments in Petra, can be judged from the tourists below the entry.

ABOVE RIGHT: Best known for its palatial carved tomb façades, Petra was an extensive city with a main open area, a pre-Roman theatre for 3000 people, a colonnaded street and large civic buildings.

Accessed through a 2-km (1.2-mile) long narrow, twisting gorge called the Siq, the city was naturally protected from the pillage of battle, only to fall to a massive earthquake in AD 363. Lost to the western world for hundreds of years, Petra remains clouded in mystery today. Although there are many tombs, few residential structures survive. Did the inhabitants live on the outskirts or in long-gone houses in the middle?

With less than one-fifth of the site unearthed, new findings continue to challenge conventional thought. In 1998, an immense pool was found near the Great Temple, in 2000, a Nabataean villa was discovered outside the Siq, and in 2003, rock-cut tombs were revealed beneath the "Treasury" causing some to rethink its interpretation.

A Risk of Being Worn Away

The richly hued sandstone which makes the site so appealing is also its weakest point: it is soft, vulnerable and easily eroded. Petra has survived 2000 years, but the elements and increasing tourism are taking their toll. Ever since its "rediscovery" in 1812, people have been going to see Petra. Visitor numbers have climbed at a rapid rate in recent years, reaching 500,000 in 2000 (up from 41,000 a decade earlier). Horses are now banned, but the hooves of donkeys and camels continue to wear away Nabataean stonework, especially on the paths up to the higher points. In only a decade, 40 mm (1.5 in) of the surface of Khazne has vanished, worn down by tourists touching, leaning on, and rubbing it. In 1990, 15–20 per cent of the stonemasonry markings in the Theatre could still be seen. Less than 5–10 per cent of them are now visible.

second century BC — inhabited since Neolithic times, Petra was chosen by King Aretas of the Nabataeans to be his royal seat.

first century AD — by the first century, Petra was a thriving capital with more than 20,000 inhabitants.

twelfth–thirteenth centuries — a small Crusader fortress is housed here.

| 0 | AD 500 | AD 1000 | AD 1500 | AD 2000 |

AD 106 — on the death of King Rabbele II the city came under Roman administration, presumably by agreement.

19 May AD 363 — an earthquake hits, damaging nearly half of the city including many free-standing structures. No longer a key link in the caravan trade, the city cannot be rebuilt and falls into decline.

AD 747 — during Byzantine occupation a second earthquake hits, further damaging the now largely empty city.

1812 — Swiss explorer Johannes L. Burckhardt 'rediscovers' the city after hearing rumours of it among local Bedouin.

1984 — the government relocates local B'doul people from the historic caves to a new town.

1985 — it is inscribed on the World Heritage List.

The explosion in tourism has in turn led to a boomtown on the edges of the site. Numerous hotels have sprung up, many built over areas where vestiges of Nabataean dwellings are thought to exist. Water tables are rising, causing efflorescence (powdery encrustations on the rocks), while vendors crowd the site, hawking their wares. Careless visitors leave litter, scrawl graffiti and can cause damage by climbing over the carved rock. Despite progress on several fronts, Petra still lacks a management plan to link archaeological and tourist needs, and the financial and human resources to implement it. Ongoing talk of electrification of the park, construction of an open-air theatre, visitor centre and campsites all pose further risks. A temporary restaurant, built of concrete, recently dodged rules and became permanent.

BELOW LEFT: Eroded statues stand guard alongside an ancient water channel.

BELOW RIGHT: Wind and water are slowly eroding away once grand façades carved from solid rock. The collapse of the water system means that water now washes down over façades instead of through the network of Nabataean channels, increasing erosion.

OPPOSITE PAGE: The richly striated walls of the narrow Siq give way to the so-called Treasury, one of the most extraordinary buildings of antiquity. Cut from solid rock, it is 40 m (131 ft) tall and 28 m (92 ft) wide. A suicidal route for taking the city, the narrow entry canyon helped to protect Petra from conquest for hundreds of years. The Siq has been carved by waters over centuries and flashfloods still occur: in 1963 one carried a group of tourists away.

"... match me such a marvel, save in Eastern clime,
A rose-red city, half as old as time."
"Petra" BY JOHN BURGON

Uluru-Kata Tjuta National Park
Australia

AT RISK · KEY THREATS Conflict | Theft | Development | Tourism | Pollution | Disasters | Constraints | Changing Uses | Invaders | Climate

Home to Australia's most famous natural landmark, Uluru-Kata Tjuta National Park is 450 km (280 miles) southwest of Alice Springs. The park's two spectacular rock formations dominate the flat, sandy centre. Uluru (Ayers Rock), an immense rounded red sandstone monolith, is 9.4 km (5.8 miles) in circumference and rises to a height of 340 m (1115 ft) above the plain. Kata Tjuta (the Olgas), the rock domes 32 km (20 miles) to the west, reach 500 m (1640 ft). They form part of the belief system of one of the oldest human societies. Covering 1326 sq km (511 sq miles) of arid ecosystems in the traditional lands of the Anangu, the park was the second cultural landscape to be inscribed on the World Heritage List.

World Heritage Site inscribed 1987, extended 1994
http://whc.unesco.org/en/list/447

OPPOSITE PAGE: Uluru (Ayers Rock) appears a more subdued orange-red than the surrounding desert soils in this satellite image. The vegetation around the iconic landmark is under threat from both reduced water supplies and invasive species such as camels and rabbits.

ABOVE RIGHT: The rock has been tilted on its side, so its sedimentary layers are easily eroded. Erosion caused by people walking on the rock is a more immediate worry.

Uluru is an inselberg, an "island mountain", the isolated remnant of an ancient formation which has eroded away. An arkose sandstone (dotted with granite), it is tilted on its side, revealing the ancient sedimentary layers. Kata Tjuta comprises thirty-six steep-sided rock domes of varying sizes, the largest of which is Mount Olga.

Climbing Uluru has become a point of contention between the traditional land owners and visitors. Scaling the 1.6-km (1-mile) steep ascent is frowned upon by the Anangu who do not climb the rock and ask visitors not to. The trail has left a deep scar on the rock.

Gullied and worn by water flowing down their sides, the rocks' waterholes have been a gathering point for Aboriginal people for thousands of years. Rock art on the caves and walls around its base is evidence of the enduring traditions.

Inalienable freehold title to Uluru-Kata Tjuta National Park was handed back to the traditional owners in 1985. They lease the land back to Parks Australia and a joint board manages the site.

For thousands of years the Anangu have managed the landscape, keeping it healthy by using fire in a mosaic of burned and unburned areas to allow species to rejuvenate. More than 400 plant species are found here – the landscape is dominated by spinifex and low shrubs and dotted with large desert oaks. At the base of the rocks, water holes support bloodwoods, acacias and native grasses as well as rare and unique plant species. Twenty-one native mammals and 170 bird species have been recorded. Reptiles are reportedly found in unparalleled numbers. The rare giant desert skink and Australia's largest lizard, the perentie, are present.

Water Worries

Uluru is challenged by its popularity. Not seen by westerners until the 1870s, the arrival of a road in 1948 allowed visitor numbers to soar. Water for the 400,000 tourists, who have been arriving since 2000, is pumped up from the ancient dune plains aquifer far below the surface. Too deep to be recharged by the rare rains, it is estimated to be more than 80,000 years old. No one is sure how long this source will last or how its loss may affect the surface, but half of the boreholes have already dried up. Tourism is climbing by 10 per cent per year, causing concern because of the extra wear and tear.

Invasive species disrupt the natural balance. Rabbits, foxes, cats, dogs, house mice and camels are eating the plants, while weeds such as perennial buffel grass choke out native species. Although progress has been made, especially against the invasion of rabbits, some 40 per cent of native plants have become extinct.

Angkor
Cambodia

AT RISK

KEY THREATS Conflict | Theft | Development | Tourism | Pollution | Disasters | Constraints | Changing Uses | Invaders | Climate

Once tucked away in the Cambodian rainforest, the world-renowned ruins of Angkor are among the most important archaeological sites in Southeast Asia. Stretching over some 400 sq km (150 sq miles) near Tonle Sap lake, Angkor Archaeological Park contains the magnificent remains of successive capitals of the Khmer Empire, dating from the ninth century to the fifteenth. These include the world's largest temple, Angkor Wat, and, at Angkor Thom, the Bayon Temple with its countless sculptural decorations. More than seventy major temples and buildings dot the landscape, while the remains of a vast and complex irrigation system are visible in two great reservoirs, or "barays."

◎ World Heritage Site inscribed 1992
http://whc.unesco.org/en/list/668

OPPOSITE PAGE: Sunrise over the largest temple complex in the world. This photograph is taken by thousands of tourists every day.

ABOVE RIGHT: Many answered UNESCO's call for international assistance. Sophia University has been working with local craftsmen to restore the ancient causeway using traditional stone and building methods, conducting scientific research and creating sustainable jobs.

Angkor Wat is said to be the world's largest religious monument. Built between 1113 and 1150, its outer wall is 1025 × 802 m (3363 × 2632 ft) and is surrounded by a wide moat. Dedicated to Vishnu, the temple embodies Hindu cosmology in the measurements and symbolism of its structures. The mausoleum of Suryavarman II features a vast bas-relief of his victories.

The citadel of Angkor Thom is ringed by an 8-m (26-ft) high, 12-km (7.5-mile) long wall and contains the impressive Bayon temple. Dedicated to Buddha, this features 144 gigantic stone faces, which gaze out in all directions from its spires, and superb bas-reliefs with more than 11,000 figures.

Angkor, from the Sanskrit "nagara", literally means city or capital.

The last remnant of a vast civilization which played a formative role in the political and cultural development of the entire region, Angkor's intricate art and striking architecture are still "an amazing sight", 700 years after being chronicled as such by a Chinese emissary. Once covered in gold, the central temple of Angkor Wat was built at the beginning of the twelfth century. Ringed by a 174-m (570-ft) wide dyke and successive outer and inner walls, its long processional causeway symbolizes the voyage through the Hindu cosmos from the outer oceans to Mount Meru, the home of the gods at the centre of the universe. The central temple-mountain of sandstone and laterite towers three floors over the 1500 × 1300-m (4800 × 4200-ft) rectangular complex. More than 500 m (1800 ft) of bas-reliefs line the walls, including the famous "churning of the great sea of milk" in which eighty-eight devils and ninety-two gods turn the waters to butter to extract the elixir of immortality.

In 1992, as peace dawned, UNESCO and the international community launched a major safeguarding campaign. A model of the good that can come out of darkness, the overgrowth has been cleared, tourists have returned and scholars and conservationists are actively working to understand and protect the site.

A Victim of Its Own Success

Having overcome centuries of obscurity and more recent conflict, looting and neglect, Angkor has finally recovered only to be a victim of its own success. Today tourists have returned in droves: from zero during the dangerous 1970s and 1980s, to more than 900,000 in 2006. Visitors are expected to reach 3 million in 2010.

1181–1201 — Jayavarman VII restores order and launches a massive building programme. He constructs the state temple of Bayon, dedicated to Buddha, at the walled citadel of Angkor Thom. Ta Prohm, Preah Khan and others are also built.

sixteenth century — Portuguese travellers visit the site.

1907–1931 — the Ecole Française d'Extrême-Orient (EFEO) manages the site without major intervention, shoring up buildings with wood and clearing vegetation. Conservation enters a new phase of anastylosis (or reconstruction), and EFEO begins rebuilding the site with concrete and iron, and fabricating replacement blocks from old stones.

1960s — The Indochina conflict brings unrest and Angkor becomes increasingly unsafe.

1970s–1980s — war consumes the site. Conservation halts and vegetation quickly takes over.

AD 1000

AD 1500

AD 2000

c. 1000 — the Western Baray is added.

c. 889 — Yashodapura or Angkor (from the Sanskrit "nagara" for city or capital) becomes the seat under Yashovarman. The Bakong, Preah Ko and Eastern Baray are built In the ensuing years the capital shifts around the region as a number of temples and fortified palaces are built by successive rulers.

c. AD 800 — the Angkorian period begins as Jayavarman II unifies the region to create the Kingdom of Kambudja. He establishes the first capital 29 km (18 miles) northeast of Angkor.

1113 — Suryavarman II accedes to the throne and builds Angkor Wat.

1177 — Angkor is sacked by the Chams and the wooden city burned.

1220 — Angkor's long decline begins, as the Thai empire rises at Ayutthaya.

1296 — the Chinese diplomat Zhou Daguan pens a fascinating account of life here, providing a detailed record of Angkorian society.

1431 — Angkor is sacked for a third time by Thai invaders and the Khmer empire fades away.

c. 1850 — the forgotten city, still occupied by roughly 1000 monks, is chronicled by French missionary Bouillevaux, followed by Henry Mouhot.

23 October 1991 — Paris Accord brings peace at long last, but there are few resources or capacity for conservation in the decimated country.

1992 — the World Heritage Committee inscribes Angkor under emergency circumstances and UNESCO launches a major international safeguarding campaign.

Every evening, over 3000 tourists climb the narrow stone stairs of Phnom Bakheng, wearing away the sandstone steps and carvings, to capture the sunset views. The site will collapse under this load unless things change. Just beyond Angkor's gates lies Siem Reap, the boom town which serves this growing flood of visitors. Part Las Vegas, part Wild West, Angkor is under threat as Siem Reap's shopping malls, karaoke bars, sex tourism and amusement parks sprawl towards it. Less visible is what is happening beneath the surface. The World Bank has warned that a number of temples, including the spectacular Bayon, are sinking into the ground as the town pumps away the underlying water to feed and bathe its guests. Sadly, the locals see minimal gain from all the growth, as foreign cartels siphon off profits.

BELOW LEFT: Tourists now flood the site in droves to experience its magic. Sunrise and sunset can feel like a Tokyo train ride, with thousands squeezing and jostling for the perfect view.

BELOW RIGHT: The fast-growing roots of a banyan tree slowly pry apart the ancient stones at Ta Prohm. If the tree is cut down, the shifted structure will collapse; if it is left, the walls will eventually be pushed apart.

OPPOSITE PAGE: The sprawling town of Siem Reap has exploded on the edges of the archaeological park as seen in this satellite image of 12 April 2004. Unplanned luxury hotels, golf courses and shopping malls are spreading across the fields, threatening to turn this magical complex into just another urban amusement, while beneath the surface the water which supports the foundations of the temples is being siphoned away. Angkor Wat and its blue moat are visible in the middle of the view, with Siem Reap below.

"More magnificent than any building left by the Greeks or Romans."
HENRY MOUHOT'S DESCRIPTION OF ANGKOR WAT FOLLOWING HIS TRAVELS IN INDOCHINA IN THE 1860S

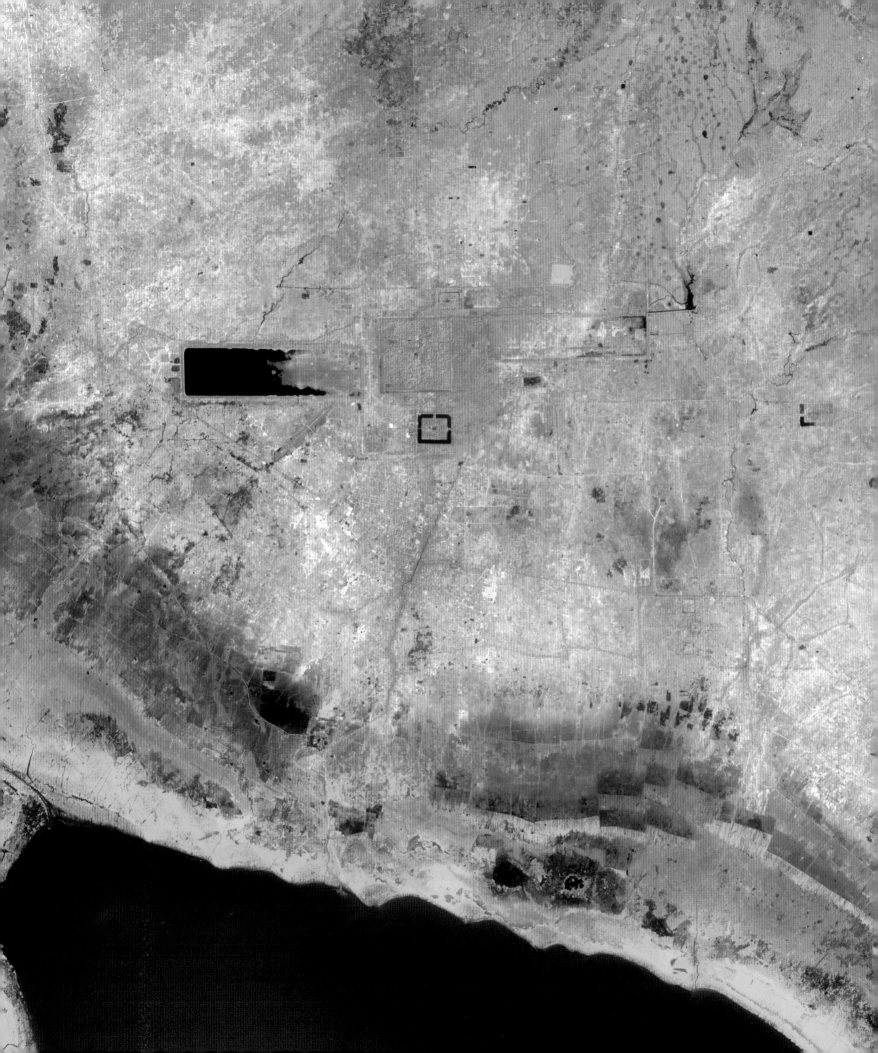

Old Town of Lijiang
China

AT RISK

KEY THREATS Conflict | Theft | Development | Tourism | Pollution | Disasters | Constraints | Changing Uses | Invaders | Climate

A political and cultural city since the time of Emperor Kublai Khan, Lijiang's historic Old Town has been a major commercial hub for more than 800 years. Once a key stop on the old tea-horse road trading route, this provincial capital near the border with Myanmar in southwest China's ethnically diverse Yunnan province is notable for its harmonious fusion of different cultural traditions. Set in a dramatic mountain landscape, Lijiang is perfectly adapted to the uneven topography of its strategic setting. With its coordinated urban form, spacious homes, water system and unique artistic style, this picturesque city has retained a historic townscape of high quality and authenticity.

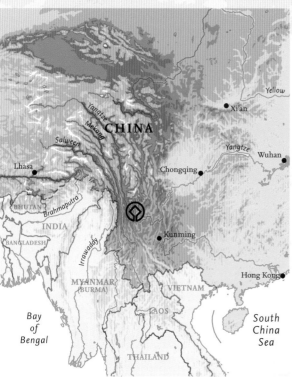

Ⓦ World Heritage Site inscribed 1997
http://whc.unesco.org/en/list/811

The Old Town of Lijiang is the only imperial city in China to possess neither a regular street pattern nor city walls.

Known for its beautiful mountainous landscape, Yunnan province is home to twenty-five of China's fifty-five recognized minority groups.

There are 354 bridges in Lijiang's Old Town.

It is famed for its network of water channels and bridges and the intricate and ingenious water-supply system which still functions today.

OPPOSITE PAGE: The combination of its scenic mountain location and picturesque old town buildings make Lijiang a "must see" for millions of tourists.

ABOVE RIGHT: Various architectural styles and the fusion of cultures and art give Lijiang its unique historic townscape.

Illustrating the unique style of the Naxi group, the Old Town is a condensation of the architecture of China's Han, Bai, Yi and Zang nationalities in both its overall layout and specific buildings. The city's houses, streets, squares, courtyards, arches, inscribed boards and carved tablets embody the cultural and artistic achievements of the Naxi. The Baisha murals of the Dongba culture constitute a brilliant chapter in the history of human civilization.

A Tourist Takeover

Lijiang suffered badly in a magnitude-seven earthquake on 3 February 1996 and in the aftermath the Old Town was rebuilt, keeping the traditional fabric but adding modern conveniences. As a result, this once remote town has become one of China's top tourist attractions, with more than 3 million visitors a year. Most tourists (90 per cent in 2004) come from within China, eager for a glimpse of "tradition" and disappearing culture.

But Lijiang's rebirth has come at a price. On major holidays the Old Town is impossibly crowded. Local authorities rush to build new "old houses" on the edges of the historic area. Locals have moved out, the open-air market sells souvenirs not food and traditional dances and activities are now staged. The real winners are not the locals, but the big hotels and tourist facilities, owned by outside investors. Some argue the positives outweigh the negatives and that tourism has brought a revival to a poor and neglected spot, creating jobs and renewing interest in local culture and traditions. But the Lijiang of old is gone forever, having given way to a facsimile.

Ngorongoro Conservation Area
United Republic of Tanzania

AT RISK

KEY THREATS Conflict | Theft | Development | Tourism | Pollution | Disasters | Constraints | Changing Uses | Invaders | Climate

Called "Africa's Eden", the Ngorongoro Conservation Area contains a natural paradise within the protective rim of the world's largest unbroken volcanic caldera. It is home to Africa's highest density of mammalian predators and extraordinary fossil evidence of man's origins at Olduvai and Laitoli. Covering 8094 sq km (3125 sq miles), the World Heritage Site stretches from the Serengeti's plains in the northwest to the volcanic highlands and wall of the Great Rift Valley in the south and east. Split from Serengeti National Park in 1959 as a multi-use conservation zone, the site is Tanzania's leading tourist attraction, host to spectacular wildlife and the continuing home to indigenous pastoral people including the Masaai.

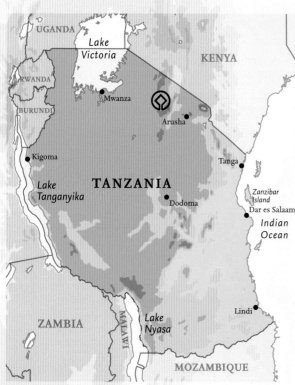

World Heritage Site inscribed 1979
http://whc.unesco.org/en/list/39

OPPOSITE PAGE: Lions on the floor of Ngorongoro Crater. The crater is home to the world's highest density of lions – sixty-two were recorded here in 2001.

ABOVE RIGHT: The crater is 22.5 km (14 miles) across at its widest and roughly 610 m (2000 ft) deep. One of the activities which put it at risk is the uncontrolled grazing by cattle.

Ngorongoro Crater is part of the Great Rift Valley, a geological fault system which extends for about 4830 km (2995 miles) from Syria to central Mozambique.

The word Olduvai comes from the Masaai "oldupaai", the wild sisal plant which grows in the steep ravine. Once the crater formed the shores of a salt lake between 1.9 million and 1.2 million years ago, the area is rich in fossil deposits, including mammals, many hominid remains and items belonging to one of the oldest stone tool technologies, called Olduwan. The recovered objects date from 2.1 million to 15,000 years ago.

Tanzania's national parks, reserves and conservation areas cover 14 per cent of the total land area – a higher percentage than for any other nation.

At Olduvai Gorge excavations have resulted in the discovery of one of our distant ancestors, Homo habilis, while the Laitoli site is one of the main localities of early hominid footprints, dating back 3.6 million years.

The remnant of a massive volcano which once rivalled Kilimanjaro, Ngorongoro Crater formed 2 million years ago when the cone collapsed. Some 25,000 large animals live in the crater, from the critically endangered black rhino to lion and numerous ungulates.

Too Many Tourists?

An experiment in multiple land use, the conservation area was created to balance the needs of the wild with development of resources, promotion of tourism and interests of local people. Caught in a tug of war between man and nature, the site is at risk from human activity. In 2002, there were 250,000 visitors and numbers are increasing. Tourists put pressures on the ecosystem, from booming border populations drawn by the prospect of work to the push to develop more accommodation. The site management plan sets a limit of fifty vehicles per day in the crater zone, but the restriction has been greatly exceeded as tour operators push to get in.

Grazing by livestock is on the rise, despite rules intended to limit it to subsistence levels. Access to the crater for salt and water for livestock requires a permit but this has not been enforced. Beyond the crater, the highland forest has suffered loss of migration routes and habitat from illegal logging, cultivation and grazing, forcing the animals elsewhere and leading to tourist viewing points being built farther into the conservation area. In the pastoral zone, the government's development of health and social services, and livestock facilities, has led to an influx of Masaai from outside – the population rose from 9000 in 1959 to more than 60,000 in 2002.

Borobudur Temple Compounds
Indonesia

AT RISK

KEY THREATS Conflict | Theft | Development | **Tourism** | Pollution | Disasters | Constraints | Changing Uses | Invaders | Climate

One of the world's greatest Buddhist monuments, this magnificent temple complex in central Java dates from the eighth and ninth centuries. It was built in three tiers: a pyramidal base with five concentric square terraces, the trunk of a cone with three circular platforms and, at the top, a monumental stupa. The walls and balustrades are decorated with fine reliefs, covering a total surface area of 2500 sq m (26,900 sq ft). Around the circular platforms are seventy-two openwork stupas, each containing a statue of the Buddha. Another 432 statues grace the lower levels.

⊛ World Heritage Site inscribed 1991
http://whc.unesco.org/en/list/592

OPPOSITE PAGE: Built as a single large stupa, Borobudur measures 118 m (387 ft) on each side and in plan takes the form of a giant tantric mandala.

ABOVE RIGHT: Efforts to protect the reliefs, from steam cleaning to epoxy injection and silicone-based water repellents, have led to faster deterioration: in the last few years experts have advised a rethinking of conservation practices.

The monument once had 504 statues of the Buddha on its many levels: 300 of them are mutilated and 43 are completely gone.

The site includes two smaller temples, Pawon and Mendut. Although found to be in a line with Borobudur, their relation is still clouded in history.

Once a year Indonesian Buddhists still make a pilgrimage to the monument to celebrate Vesak.

Carved gargoyles once channelled water off the platforms through their mouths. The failure of the drainage system has led to water infiltration, spalling and salt efflorescence on the reliefs.

Borobudur is also threatened by disaster as it sits in the shadow of one of Indonesia's most active volcanoes, Mount Merapi. An earthquake on 27 May 2006 caused some damage – a reminder of the site's vulnerability.

Built on an artificial mound on a natural rise, the nine platforms are constructed with 55,000 cubic m (almost 2 million cubic ft) of mortarless stone, joined with knobs, dovetails and indentations. There are approximately 2670 reliefs, of which 1460 are narrative and illustrate the different phases of the soul's progression as well as episodes from the life of the Buddha. Abandoned presumably between the eleventh and fourteenth century, the temple was gradually hidden under layers of volcanic ash and vegetation and not rediscovered until the nineteenth century. After an appeal from the Indonesian government, the temple was restored, with UNESCO's help, in a US$7 million international project between 1973 and 1982.

Tourist Development at the Doorstep

Indonesia's most visited tourist attraction, Borobudur is caught between preservation and development. Although the 1970s restoration was state of the art at the time, it isolated the monument from the greater cultural landscape. As a result, some have seen the temple only in the context of selling goods to tourists. Overrun by crowds, stalls and hawkers, the sacred site's value is threatened. With 2.5 million visitors a year by the mid-1990s, the pressure to capitalize on the influx has grown even more. Plans to develop a major commercial complex and road next to the site are currently on hold, although with no clear legal or institutional framework there is a risk that they may re-emerge.

Stonehenge, Avebury and Associated Sites
United Kingdom of Great Britain and Northern Ireland

GUARDED **KEY THREATS** Conflict | Theft | Development | Tourism | Pollution | Disasters | Constraints | Changing Uses | Invaders | Climate

Among the most famous and impressive megalithic monuments in the world, Stonehenge is symbolic of Britain. Located on Salisbury Plain in southern England, Stonehenge and Avebury, 17 miles (28 km) to the north, consist of circles of menhirs arranged in a pattern whose astronomical significance is still being explored. These holy places and the nearby Neolithic sites are an incomparable testimony to prehistoric times.

Stonehenge is often erroneously attributed to the druids – the monuments predate the forest temples of these Celtic people by more than 2000 years. Although the actual builders are unknown, current theories support construction by a late Neolithic people known as the Beaker people.

In the twelfth century Stonehenge was already being called one of the wonders of the world by the chroniclers Henry de Huntington and Geoffrey of Monmouth. In the seventeenth century it was the focus of study by Inigo Jones.

Controversy surrounds some of the stellar alignments at Stonehenge, but it is clear that on the longest day of the year the rising sun does align behind the "Heelstone", casting a shadow into the heart of the five interior "Sarsen" stones.

⊙ World Heritage Site inscribed 1986
http://whc.unesco.org/en/list/373

OPPOSITE PAGE: Although Stonehenge is not the largest stone circle in the world, it is the only one which has lintels.

ABOVE RIGHT: The world-famous stone circle at Avebury in Wiltshire has been voted the country's third most spiritual place.

Stonehenge was built in several distinct phases from 3100 to 1100 BC. The sheer size (with some blocks weighing 50 tonnes), height, perfection of the plan, use of large lintels on vertical blocks and the 200 km (125 miles) the bluestones were carried, all continue to amaze thousands of years later. Avebury, although not as well known, is Europe's largest circular megalithic ensemble with 100 stones covering a 1.3 km (0.8 mile) circle. In all, 180 standing stones were put in place before the beginning of the third millennium BC.

The World's Oldest Tourist Attraction

For more than 5000 years these stone circles have drawn visitors in. Although well protected from development and the hordes of vendors which crowd sites in many parts of the world, Stonehenge has lost its magic, fenced off and surrounded by massive numbers of onlookers. Although seemingly necessary to protect the stones from vandalism and the wear and tear of thousands of feet and hands, the protective fencing disrupts the aesthetic appeal. At Avebury, on the other hand, access has resulted in damage to stones and prehistoric earthworks. For several decades the A344 road, which bisects the site has been the subject of controversy. Although plans to close this road and reroute the main A303 or move it underground have been proposed, the project seems caught in perpetual delays. Each scheme would affect the landscape and monuments. In the meantime, cars continue to traverse this ancient space.

POLLUTION

Pollution is defined as an undesirable state of the natural environment through contamination with harmful substances, usually as a consequence of human activities. These activities may be the release of substances that are toxic to one or more species of animal, plant or marine life, to fresh- or seawater, or to buildings; or they can be the release of energy (heat, light, radiation, or sound), which interferes with the development of animals or plants.

Contaminated water, whether in a stream, river or sea, can rapidly harm aquatic life with devastating consequences for whole ecosystems. In addition to lethal matter, polluted rivers draining into larger bodies, such as the pristine waters of Lake Baikal, can carry concentrated nutrients, leading to algal blooms that choke out aquatic plant and animal life. On land, the causes of water pollution include toxins irresponsibly discharged into water systems from industrial factories or plants; nutrient-rich waste water from sewer pipes, purification plants, or irrigation channels; pesticide- and fertilizer-laced agricultural runoff; eroded sediments from clearcut forests, and careless disposal and illicit dumping of potentially toxic substances, such as used motor oil, food waste and animal faeces into drains.

Agricultural waste water is of particular concern because of the fertilizers, herbicides and pesticides it contains. Releasing raw sewage into waterways provides a source of food for bacteria and fungi, which then thrive and consume oxygen in the water, depriving other creatures living there. The spectacular Ha Long Bay in Vietnam is particularly at risk, given the growing human population around its shores.

At sea, ships discharge their garbage and bilge water into the ocean, while things lost or thrown overboard wash up on the shore, sometimes many months later. Oil spills are distressingly common, as happened in the waters off Dorset and the East Devon Coast, England, in 2007. Moreover, frequent anchoring and the dredging of shallow waters for the development of ports and harbours disrupts the seabed, resulting in loss of habitat for the creatures that live there, and leads to sedimentary pollution – which has an especially detrimental effect on coral reefs.

Although motor vehicles are increasingly using cleaner fuels, ships are still major contributors to air pollution. The harmful pollutants in the gases emitted by large ships contribute to acid rain and smog, as well as to health problems. Acid rain eats away at ancient stones and harms vegetation. It can run into lakes and rivers, changing water chemistry and making them uninhabitable to some species of flora and fauna. On land, hazardous air pollutants (HAPs) are released by power, chemical and printing plants, dry cleaners and motor vehicles, and can cause serious health and environmental effects. In many urban World Heritage Sites, air pollution is etching away the details of buildings, monuments, statues, and other structures. The increasing emissions are also a growing threat to rock carvings, textiles, works of art and archaeological monuments. In China, for example, where coal is the principal energy source, corrosion rates are substantially greater than the worst levels in Europe, while incinerated waste from industrial furnaces and boilers releases into the air toxins which can be carried for many thousands of miles. Measures being undertaken to reduce the damage done by pollution include monitoring the pollution risks and identifying potential "hot spots"; planting green buffer zones, as has been done at the Taj Mahal in India, to protect monuments from encroaching development; and working with local agencies to oppose any potential pollution-causing proposals. Pollution is a worldwide problem that is being tackled on many fronts.

Everglades National Park
United States of America

AT RISK | KEY THREATS Conflict | Theft | Development | Tourism | Pollution | Disasters | Constraints | Changing Uses | Invaders | Climate

"A river of grass flowing imperceptibly from the hinterland into the sea", the Everglades are a river like no other. This vast sheet of water flowing from Lake Okeechobee is a subtle mosaic of surprising diversity. The World Heritage Site is the largest subtropical wilderness in continental North America, yet protects just a fifth of the Everglades' original extent. This paradise is a sanctuary for numerous birds and reptiles, from frogs to herons, egrets, spoonbills, pelicans, wildcats, lizards and bottlenose dolphins. It is refuge for fifty-six threatened and endangered animal species, including the American alligator and crocodile, Florida panther, Key deer, Cape Sable seaside sparrow, wood stork and West Indian manatee.

⊕ World Heritage Site inscribed 1979
http://whc.unesco.org/en/list/76

Numbers of waders have declined by 93 per cent since the 1930s, from 265,000 to just 18,500.

As the human population in the vicinity has exploded from 500,000 in 1945 to many millions today, water has been diverted for the growing cities and agriculture. Some 900 new residents come to Florida every day, requiring an extra 757,080 litres (166,530 gallons) of fresh water.

Of the twenty-seven species of snakes in Everglades National Park, only four are venomous – the cottonmouth, diamondback rattlesnake, dusky pygmy rattlesnake and coral snake.

Every year 1.2 million people visit the park.

OPPOSITE PAGE: It is estimated only thirty to fifty Florida panthers still survive here. In 1989 the threat of mercury to panthers became apparent when a female was found dead in Everglades National Park with lethal levels of mercury, as well as PCBs and pesticides in her liver.

ABOVE RIGHT: An atmospheric mercury monitoring tower looks out over the Everglades. Mercury is released into the air from power stations, incinerators and mines, then washed down to ground level by rain as the highly toxic methylmercury which builds up in the ecosystem.

Overlaying porous limestone bedrock, the highest point in the park is a mere 2.5 m (8 ft) above sea level. Its many distinct ecosystems include sawgrass prairies, pinelands, hammocks, cypress swamps, mangroves, saltwater marshes and the waters of Florida Bay at its tip. The park is known for its flora – among its more prominent plants are bromeliads and epiphytic orchids. As many as twenty-five varieties of orchids are found, in addition to more than 1000 other kinds of seed-bearing plants and 120 species of both tropical and temperate trees (including some sixty which are endemic to southern Florida). More than 350 species of birds have been recorded, seven of which are rare or endangered. Forty species of mammals are also present.

Dredged, Drained and Diverted

Years of draining, dyke-building, digging and construction have destroyed more than half of the historic Everglades. What remains has become polluted with nutrient-rich nitrate-laden agricultural runoff, stormwater contamination and even mercury. Today this is North America's most endangered park, despite the world's largest restoration plan – a 30-year, US$10.5 billion effort launched in 2000. Although no longer on the List of World Heritage in Danger, great challenges remain as the park's water catchment lies far to the north amid central Florida's growing population, farms, cities and flood control canals.

For more than 150 years, especially since the 1950s, man has been trying to "clean up" the Everglades, draining the swamps to eradicate mosquitoes, by reclaiming farmland and controlling flooding. As cattails spread in the phosphorus-rich waters, species disappeared, wildfires threatened and – without the protective buffer of the wetlands – hurricane damage increased. The park is also threatened by alien species. Brazilian pepper plants and melaleuca tree are among the worst of 140 invaders. Burmese pythons are now reproducing here, endangering even the alligators. Eradication of tilapias, oscars and Mayan cichlids, which threaten native fish, has so far proved impossible. A huge budget for research, a massive land purchase fund and the largest scientific staff in the US park system offer hope.

BELOW LEFT: Distinguished by its short, blunt rounded snout, the American alligator was threatened with extinction in the 1960s. This is the only place in the wild that alligators and crocodiles co-exist. Mercury contamination was first seen in fish but has since been found in raccoons, alligators and panthers.

BELOW RIGHT: It is hoped that some 30–40 per cent of the Everglades natural habitat can be saved and restored to its former state.

OPPOSITE PAGE: Whooping cranes were extinct in the Everglades by the 1940s but there is hope that habitat restoration and breeding and reintroduction programmes, will bring about their return. At nearly 1.5 m (5 ft) tall with a wingspan of 2.3 m (7.5 ft), it is the tallest bird in North America. Fewer than 500 are left, and the International Whooping Crane Recovery Team has taken innovative measures, including using ultralight aircraft to guide young cranes on migration to new areas.

"Here are no lofty peaks seeking the sky, no mighty glaciers or rushing streams wearing away the uplifted land. Here is land, tranquil in its quiet beauty, serving not as the source of water but as the last receiver of it. To its natural abundance we owe the spectacular plant and animal life that distinguishes this place from all others in our country."
PRESIDENT HARRY S. TRUMAN'S ADDRESS AT THE DEDICATION OF THE EVERGLADES NATIONAL PARK ON 6 DECEMBER 1947

Belize Barrier Reef Reserve System
Belize

AT RISK

KEY THREATS Conflict | Theft | Development | Tourism | Pollution | Disasters | Constraints | Changing Uses | Invaders | Climate

One of the world's most pristine reef ecosystems, the Belize Barrier Reef Reserve System is home to a vast array of plants and animals and spans an outstanding collection of offshore atolls, sandy cays, mangrove forests, coastal lagoons and estuaries. The World Heritage Site's seven separate protected zones illustrate the evolutionary history of reef development and are a significant habitat for threatened species including the West Indian manatee, Nassau grouper, green, loggerhead, and hawksbill turtles and American crocodile.

Gulf of Mexico

Caribbean Sea

MEXICO

Belmopan • • Belize

BELIZE

• Dangriga

GUATEMALA

HONDURAS

EL SALVADOR

Pacific Ocean

NICARAGUA

World Heritage Site inscribed: 1996
http://whc.unesco.org/en/list/764

OPPOSITE PAGE: A haven for divers, the 318 m (1040 ft) diameter Boca Ciega or "Blue Hole" is believed to have formed when the ceiling of a large cavern collapsed over 18,000 years ago. This rare sinkhole's walls and stalactites contain a fascinating record of climatic conditions from the last ice age onwards.

ABOVE RIGHT: Idyllic white sandy beaches may appeal to tourists, but cleared of protective grasses and mangroves, these unnatural scenes increase the area's vulnerability to hurricanes and erosion.

Jacques Cousteau called for protection of the reef in 1970 when he visited in his research ship Calypso and filmed a television documentary.

The reef was first used for fishing some 2500 years ago. Lobster and conch are the principal fishery products and contribute most of the value of seafood exports to the economy.

The Mayans dug the Bacalar Chico channel to allow transshipment of their trade goods more than 1000 years ago, while in the seventeenth century the reef was a haven for pirates and buccaneers who preyed upon Spanish and British shipping.

The reef is thought to be home to the largest population of West Indian manatees (approximately 300–700) as well as a population of American crocodiles. It is also home to major colonies of seabirds including red-footed boobies, brown boobies, common noddies, magnificent frigatebirds and laughing gulls, which sadly no longer breed on Laughing Bird Caye because of visitor numbers.

Perhaps best known for the striking "Blue Hole" which pierces the shallow waters around it to drop more than 125 m (410 ft) down through the ocean floor, the reef has been dubbed one of the "Seven Wonders of the Underwater World" by recreational divers. Second in size only to Australia's Great Barrier Reef, and the largest reef in both the northern and western hemispheres, the Belize submarine shelf and its barrier extend nearly 260 km (160 miles) from the Mexican border to that with Guatemala. It ranges from a few hundred metres offshore in the north to more than 40 km (25 miles) offshore in the south. The World Heritage Site includes three large atolls outside the reef itself. Unlike atolls in the Pacific, these are not volcanic but are instead formed over igneous and metamorphic rock. Most of the cays are covered with mangroves, but some include sand and shrub vegetation. The site has 178 species of terrestrial plant and 247 taxa of marine flora. The waters are rich with life, including more than 500 known species of fish, 65 scleritian corals, 45 hydroids and 350 molluscs, as well as a great variety of sponges, marine worms and crustaceans. The red-footed booby nests on Half Moon Caye, the brown booby on Man O'War Caye and the common noddy on Glover's Reef.

A Reef at Risk

A complex ecosystem, the Belize reef is at risk from interlinked factors. According to a study by the World Resources Institute, one-third of the reef is at high risk from land-based pollution: nutrient-rich effluents from booming settlements and agrochemicals from rapidly expanding banana, coconut and citrus plantations cause algal blooms, while eroded sediments washed down from cleared land smother ocean life. As tourism has tripled in the last decade, coastal development has led to the cutting of protective mangroves (see pages 254–7), further increasing sedimentary pollution, while on the reef dredging and dynamite have been used to clear channels for deep-water marinas. Offshore, sand mining and anchors rip up the fragile floor and choke the corals.

BELOW LEFT: A queen conch takes a look around. Together with lobsters, conches are one of the two main commercial catches. Sadly, overfishing and poaching have caused a dramatic decline in the population.

BELOW RIGHT: As with coconut and banana plantations, citrus plantations are on the increase and the chemicals used can cause pollution, and algal blooms.

OPPOSITE PAGE: Plastic jettisoned from ships litters the waters around mangroves on Glover's Reef. A typical cruise ship generates large amounts of oily bilge water and garbage every day. Cruises in the Caribbean have quadrupled in the last twenty years, and an enormous amount of garbage, legally disposed 7 km (4 miles) offshore, is now washing up. In addition, unseen pollutants in the form of nutrient-rich effluents from growing coastal developments, as well as sediments from erosion and sand from dredging, are killing the coral.

"The most remarkable reef in the West Indies."
CHARLES DARWIN, 1842

Pollution stresses corals, and may increase their susceptibility to disease and bleaching. In the past thirty years, the Caribbean reefs have seen reduced numbers of long-spined black sea urchin, losses of staghorn and elkhorn corals from white-band disease, fungal attack on sea fans, black band disease and white plague. Weakened, the reef is at risk during tropical storms and hurricanes.

Over-harvesting and cross-border poaching have taken their toll – conch and lobster catches have halved in just the last few years. Nassau grouper levels at Glover's Reef have dropped from 15,000 in 1970 to just 3000 in 2002. Manatee and marine turtles have also been affected.

As oil prices have increased, so has interest in offshore exploration and with it the threat of spills. To date, there have been no major finds here, but the threat remains.

Native species are being squeezed out by newcomers – the great-tailed grackle and bronze cowbirds are more tolerant of humans and are encroaching on indigenous birds' colonies. Finally, sea-surface temperatures here are already at the upper limits at which coral can survive, and scientists expect bleaching (see pages 262–5) to be an annual event by 2020. Although part of the natural cycle in the Caribbean, the increasing number and severity of hurricanes in recent years (with the highest number on record in 2005) are giving the reef little chance to recover.

BELOW LEFT: The reef is the site of one of two Atlantic nesting colonies of the rare white morph of the red-footed booby. Picked on for centuries, it may abandon Half Moon Caye much as the laughing gull has left Laughing Bird Caye in the wake of pressure from too many visitors.

BELOW RIGHT: Although development within the site is strictly controlled, growth is booming on its fringes. Here, an island is being cleared for a massive planned development and deep-water harbour close to the protected "Blue Hole."

OPPOSITE PAGE: Dead coconut palms, stripped of their fronds, stand bare silhouetted against the sunset. Under attack from an introduced virus, without costly antibiotic injections, the symbolic coconuts are dying. Native birds and sealife are also under attack from introduced species.

Historic Cairo
Egypt

AT RISK

KEY THREATS Conflict | Theft | Development | Tourism | Pollution | Disasters | Constraints | Changing Uses | Invaders | Climate

Tucked away amid the modern urban area of Cairo lies one of the world's oldest Islamic cities, with its famous mosques, *madrasas*, *hammams* and fountains. Founded in the tenth century, the "City Victorious" became the new hub of the Islamic world, reaching its golden age in the fourteenth century.

Mediterranean Sea

ISRAEL
WEST BANK
GAZA

Alexandria

JORDAN

Giza Cairo

SAUDI
ARABIA

Nile

LIBYA

EGYPT

Luxor

Red Sea

Aswan

Lake Nasser

SUDAN

The colossal granite statue of Ramses II which once graced Cairo's Ramses Square was recently moved back to the Giza plateau, out of the corrosive air and away from the traffic which encircled it for fifty years.

Several modern development projects, including a massive complex next to the citadel have raised concern in recent years as they threaten to dwarf and overshadow the historic structures that define the city.

⊕ World Heritage Site inscribed 1979
http://whc.unesco.org/en/list/89

OPPOSITE PAGE: The historic structures of Cairo are threatened by pollution which eats into the materials from which they are made.

ABOVE RIGHT: The population of Cairo is growing rapidly and because the city cannot easily expand into the desert, new buildings crowd toward the older areas.

There are few cities in the world as rich in old buildings filled with significance and formal beauty as Cairo. Spanning an area 8 km by 4 km (5 miles by 2.5 miles) on the eastern bank of the Nile, the historic area includes no fewer than 600 classified monuments dating from the seventh century to the twentieth. Among its focal points are al-Fustat, including the AD 641 mosque of Ibn al-Is and Roman fortress; the mosque of Ibn-Tulun (876) and the surrounding area with its Mamluk monuments; the environs of the citadel with the surrounding palaces and mosque of Sultan Hasan (1356–1359); the Fatimid nucleus from Bab Zuwaila to the north wall with the city gates Bab al-Futuh and Bab-an-Nasr, as well as major Ayyubid and Mamluk monuments and the necropolis; from al-Fustat to the northern limits of Fatimid Cairo, with its many mausoleums and funerary complexes.

Choking in its Success

Cairo today is increasingly lost in a haze of pollution. Already one of the world's largest cities, this ancient capital is rapidly expanding, putting extreme pressure on its environment. More than 2 million cars are on the streets, 60 per cent of which were manufactured before modern emission controls were introduced. The air, already clouded at times with windborn sand from the desert, is today laced with high levels of volatile organic hydrocarbons as well as dangerous quantities of lead and other pollutants. This toxic haze is eating away the buildings, while rampant development threatens the urban fabric.

Ha Long Bay
Vietnam

Ha Long Bay, on the Gulf of Tonkin in northern Vietnam, includes some 1600 islands and islets, forming a spectacular seascape of limestone pillars. Because of their precipitous nature, most of the islands are uninhabited and unaffected by human presence. The site's outstanding scenic beauty is complemented by its great biological interest. The stable climate and warm sea temperature support a proliferation of life forms: 163 species of coral cover 30 per cent of the bay's floor, and 107 varieties of fish swim in the waters. One of the finest examples of a karst landscape, the site is fundamentally important to the study of limestone geomorphology.

There are four fishing communities with more than 1600 people inhabiting the bay, living on floating houses and boats and making their livelihood from fishing and aquaculture.

"Ha Long" is literally translated as "Bay of Descending Dragons."

◎ World Heritage Site inscribed 1994, extended 2000
http://whc.unesco.org/en/list/672

OPPOSITE PAGE: Until recently the few people who lived and worked here had little impact on the ecology of the bay. Today, the floating communities are disturbing the natural ecosystem through everything from shrimp farming to sanitation.

ABOVE RIGHT: Ha Long Bay's limestone pillars form a spectacular seascape. The bay's outstanding natural beauty is both its greatest asset and its own worst enemy.

In the south, the islands rise to 100–200 m (330–660 ft) with smaller islets of only 5–10 m (16.5–33 ft) between them, while in the east, the medium-sized islands have almost vertical slopes. There are numerous caves and grottoes throughout.

Tourists and Turbidity

The calm clear water of the bay is also its greatest threat. Its beauty has lured hundreds of thousands of tourists, while its natural protection has brought ports and greater number of ships. The increased usage has brought pollution and sediment which are intensifying turbidity and choking the life. Visitor numbers exploded from 236,000 in 1996 to more than 2 million today; by 2010, 2.5–3 million tourists are expected to arrive, with a corresponding increase in infrastructure to support them. Already, the flow of visitors has brought newcomers, eager to make a living, to the floating communities. These burgeoning villages on the water are disturbing the natural ecosystem through everything from shrimp farming to sanitation. Logging has caused erosion and increased sedimentation. Beyond the World Heritage Site but close enough to have an effect, a coal mine, port and cement plant are potential threats. Cai Lan, a deep-sea port with seven wharves and a capacity of 14 million tonnes will be completed by 2010, bringing with it risks of spills and pollution in this pristine environment. Although water conditions have been improving and turbidity has declined recently, the site remains at risk as the growth could easily turn the tide against it at any point.

Imperial Palaces in Beijing and Shenyang
China

AT RISK

KEY THREATS Conflict | Theft | Development | Tourism | Pollution | Disasters | Constraints | Changing Uses | Invaders | Climate

The seat of power for more than five centuries, Beijing's Forbidden City is a priceless testimony to Chinese civilization during the Ming and Qing dynasties. Begun in 1406, it took more than 100,000 skilled craftsmen sixteen years to build. Added to and enhanced throughout its 560-years, its landscaped gardens and structures housed twenty-four emperors, their families and concubines, eunuchs and guards. Reflecting the height of Chinese architectural art, design and layout, the walled Crimson City measures 960 by 760 m (3150 by 2493 ft) and is organized around a grand central axis. More than 9000 rooms contain furniture and works of art, exceptional evidence to the living traditions and customs of the period.

The Imperial Palace is the largest and most complete group of ancient wooden architecture in the world today, occupying an area of 720,000 sq m (7,750,015 sq ft) with more than 9000 rooms, which are divided into two sections, the official and the residential.

The entire complex is encircled by a wall 8 m (26 ft) high and 3 km (1.9 miles) long which has exquisitely styled watch towers at its corners. A 52-m (170-ft) wide moat surrounds the palace fortress.

⊗ World Heritage Site inscribed 1987, extended 2004
http://whc.unesco.org/en/list/439/

OPPOSITE PAGE: The walled Forbidden City of Beijing (above) and the same view (below) during a sand storm. The Gobi desert has expanded and when the Spring winds blow they often carry large amounts of sand and dust eastward toward Beijing. The sky turns yellow with the dust in the atmosphere, visibility is greatly reduced and the inhabitants have to wear masks to aid with breathing.

ABOVE RIGHT: The nine dragon screen facing Huangi Gate is one of three such elaborate Qing dynasty glazed-tile screens in Beijing.

The Imperial Palace of the Qing Dynasty in Shenyang, 500 km (300 miles) northeast of Beijing, consists of 114 buildings, erected between 1625 and 1783. It contains an important library and was the capital of the last dynasty to rule China before it expanded its power to the centre of the country and moved to Beijing. This palace then became auxiliary to the Imperial Palace in Beijing. Its structures document the cultural traditions of the Manchu and other tribes in the north of China.

Smog, Sand and Acid Rain

Beijing's massive growth has brought with it great challenges. Profound modifications to the age-old urban fabric surrounding the Forbidden City have obscured the strict hierarchical plan, as skyscrapers and roads have obliterated the orthogonal network. Of greater concern is the pollution. Overfarming in the west of China has caused the desert to expand and advance. Massive dust storms and pollution from industry, coal soot and the recent rapid rise in the use of cars, have combined to endanger these monuments. Acid rain is damaging roofing tiles, marble and polychrome. Although restorations in the twentieth century (repainting in the 1920s and poor reconstructions in the 1970s) did not meet current conservation standards, an extensive effort to address the problems of some of the structures most at risk began in 2002 and is continuing. In addition to pollution and development, earthquakes also pose a risk in this seismically active region – thirteen of magnitude six or above have hit the city since its construction. Major ones in 1679, 1730, 1748 and 1976 all caused damage.

Old Town of Segovia and its Aqueduct
Spain

AT RISK

KEY THREATS Conflict | Theft | Development | Tourism | Pollution | Disasters | Constraints | Changing Uses | Invaders | Climate

Known for its soaring ancient Roman aqueduct, the historic walled city of Segovia is located in central Spain, roughly 90 km (56 km) north of Madrid. Probably built around AD 50, the aqueduct's impressive, freestanding stone arches carried water for almost nineteen centuries. Other notable features include the fairytale eleventh-century Alcázar, or royal castle, the soaring sixteenth-century Gothic cathedral and the highest concentration of Romanesque churches anywhere in Europe.

⊚ World Heritage Site inscribed 1985
http://whc.unesco.org/en/list/311

OPPOSITE PAGE: Traffic fumes, other pollutants and water damage are eating into the stones of Segovia's 2000-year-old aqueduct.

ABOVE RIGHT: The stones of the city's monuments, such as the Alcázar and the Gothic cathedral are also suffering damage.

It was at the Alcázar that Queen Isabella promised Christopher Columbus the financial backing he needed to see if he could find a westerly route to the Indies: on the voyage, he discovered the Americas instead.

Famous in the fifteenth century for its wool production, Segovia is also home to a 1583 mint, claimed to be the world's oldest surviving industrial manufacturing plant.

A testament to Roman engineering, the aqueduct is 813 m (2670 ft) long and 28.5 m (94 ft) tall. It is built without mortar, and its 20,000 granitic ashlar blocks, in two stacked tiers of arches with 128 pillars, are held together by their own weight. The last leg in a system that carried water from the Frío River 18 km (11 miles) away, the aqueduct brought water in a channel along its top to the highest point in the city. It was in active use until the end of the nineteenth century.

Ancient Stones Destabilized by Modern Pollution

Listed on the 2006 World Monuments Watch of the 100 Most Endangered Sites, Segovia's ancient aqueduct is at risk from modern pollution. After surviving for almost 2000 years, its stones are being eaten away by traffic fumes and other pollutants. The ashlar masonry blocks are particularly vulnerable – exposed to accelerated weathering because of pollution, their once flat sides and tight joints erode and become rounded, destabilizing the mortarless structure. Additionally weakened by vegetation and the constant vibration of traffic and water leaking from the upper channel (which is no longer maintained), the entire structure is at risk. Segovia's challenge is not unique. Ancient stone structures across the world are seeing accelerated decay in the face of modern pollution.

Taj Mahal
India

AT RISK

KEY THREATS Conflict | Theft | Development | Tourism | Pollution | Disasters | Constraints | Changing Uses | Invaders | Climate

An immense mausoleum of white marble, the Taj Mahal is the jewel of Muslim art in India and one of the universally admired masterpieces of the world's heritage. Built between 1631 and 1648 by order of the Mughal emperor Shah Jahan in memory of his favourite wife, Arjumand Banu, it sits on the right bank of the Yamuna River in Agra, not far from Fatehpur Sikri and the Red Fort. It is equally famous for both its architecture and serene aesthetic beauty.

⊕ **World Heritage Site inscribed 1983**
http://whc.unesco.org/en/list/252

OPPOSITE PAGE: The charbagh garden was originally filled with fruit trees, and flowering plants such as daffodils and roses. The current planting scheme was laid out centuries later by the British, in a manner reminiscent of the formal gardens of London.

ABOVE RIGHT: As many as twenty-eight different varieties of semiprecious and precious stones were used in the inlay work, including jasper from the Punjab, jade and crystal from China, turquoise from Tibet, sapphire from Sri Lanka, lapis lazuli from Afghanistan and carnelian from Arabia.

Some 7 million tourists a year now visit the site.

The sarcophagus at the centre was once fenced off with a screen of gold studded with gems but this was replaced with the present marble screen in 1642. Two silver doors once graced the entrance but these were looted and melted down by the Jats in 1764.

The charbagh garden, which is 300 m (1000 ft) square, is an aesthetic departure from early garden tombs.

It stands majestically at the water's edge in a compound of 170,000 sq m (1,830,000 sq ft) and framed by four outward tilting minarets at the corners of the plaza, the central octagonal structure features a bulbous dome sitting on a tall drum. This is embellished with a fairy-like décor of floral arabesques and decorative bands inlaid with semi-precious stones in polychromatic pietra dura. The interior consists of a two-storey octagonal hall with a vaulted ceiling comprising the lower shell of the beautiful double dome. The interior is lined with white marble of pure texture and delicate grain. It is embellished with artistic pietra dura ornamentation in floral and arabesque patterns, elegant marble carvings in low relief, marble railings with delicate tracery and beautiful inscriptions in black marble inlay.

White Marble and Black Air

Air pollution has led to deterioration of the marble, inlays and sandstone walls. Panels have been cleaned and replaced in recent decades, but air quality remains a problem. The Indian Supreme Court has imposed limits on industry, reducing the acid rain from refineries and a new manufacturing complex was successfully blocked a number of years ago. However, massive population growth in the region and the rise in the number of vehicles continue to endanger the stone. The site is also threatened by landfill in the river and plans for major tourist facilities on its periphery. Research is underway to allow better understanding of the pollution's impact, but in the meantime the beautiful stones of this temple to enduring love are being eaten away.

Lake Baikal
Russian Federation

AT RISK

KEY THREATS Conflict | Theft | Development | Tourism | Pollution | Disasters | Constraints | Changing Uses | Invaders | Climate

Situated in southeastern Siberia, the 31,500-sq-km (12,100-sq-mile) Lake Baikal – the "Sacred Lake" – is the oldest (25 million years) and deepest (c. 1637 m, 5369 ft) lake in the world. Containing 20 per cent of the planet's total unfrozen freshwater reserve, it is also the largest freshwater lake on Earth in volume. It is known as the "Galápagos of Russia" – its age and isolation have produced one of the world's richest and most unusual freshwater faunas, which is of exceptional value to evolutionary science.

RUSSIAN FEDERATION

Lena

Lake Baikal

Irkutsk

Ulan-Ude

Chita

Amur

Blagoveshchensk

MONGOLIA

CHINA

NORTH KOREA

◎ World Heritage Site inscribed 1996
http://whc.unesco.org/en/list/754

OPPOSITE PAGE: Lake Baikal, seen here from space, is the world's oldest, largest, and deepest freshwater lake. It is nearly a 1.6km (1 mile) deep and holds over 23,000 cu km (5518 cu miles) of water.

ABOVE RIGHT: The nerpa of Lake Baikal is the world's only freshwater seal. In summer, they lounge on the lake's islands and islets.

The 636-km (400-mile) crescent-shaped expanse holds more water than all of North America's Great Lakes combined and 90 per cent of Russia's freshwater resources.

It is said that all the rivers on Earth would take a year to fill Lake Baikal. It takes 383 years for the water in Baikal to be exchanged.

The lake is fed by up to 336 rivers but only one, the Angara, flows out.

In an active rift valley, the lake's underwater hot springs harbour unique life.

With the construction of the Trans-Siberian railway at the end of the nineteenth century, the lake was discovered by visitors.

Baikal harbours more than 1500 animal species of which 80 per cent are endemic, including the Baikal seal, or nerpa. There are more than 1000 plant species, 150 of which are endangered. With a low mineral content and saturated with oxygen, the water is very pure. The tiny endemic Baikal crayfish – epishura – help to maintain a visibility that can reach 40 m (130 ft).

People, Pulp, Pipelines and Pollution

The pristine waters of Baikal are at risk from pollution. Several million people live in the basin and effluent from cities and factories winds its way into the lake. Opened in 1957, the Baikalsk Pulp and Paper Mill on the south shore is one of the greatest concerns. It poisoned 200 sq km (80 sq miles) of the lake with dioxin, chlorine and other chemicals and caused some of the worst air pollution in Russia. After many years of effort, it is due to switch to a closed-water cycle in 2007. In 2006, Russian President Vladimir Putin ordered the Transneft Siberia–Pacific oil pipeline to be rerouted away from the lake – originally planned to be 800 m (0.5 miles) from the shore, it was moved 40 km (25 miles) north to avoid a potentially catastrophic spill in the seismically active region.

However, tainted water from the Baikalsk sewage system, as well as from the Selenga river which drains Ulan Ude and several cities in Russia and Mongolia, still brings pollutants, despite the installation of more than 100 waste-water treatment plants in the past decade. Adding to the problem, every summer fires rage across Russia's boreal forests. This results in erosion, which brings more sediment into the clear water.

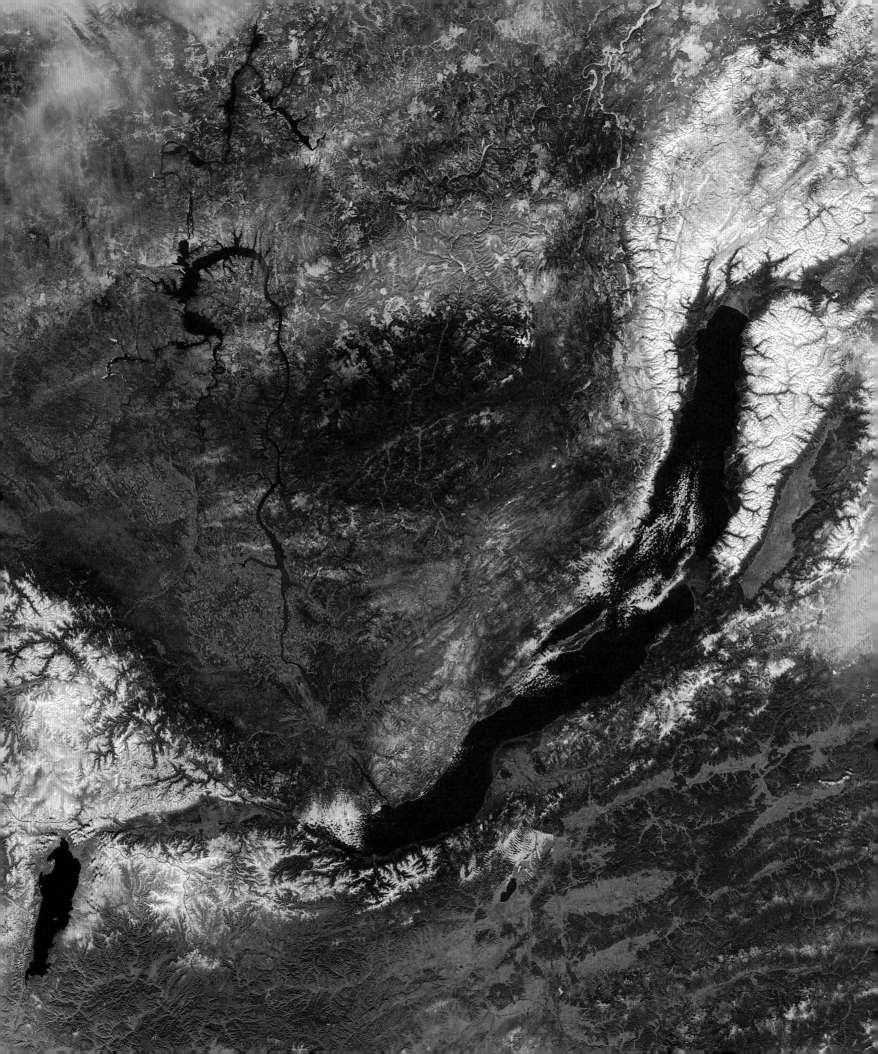

Historical Monuments of Mtskheta
Georgia

AT RISK

KEY THREATS Conflict | Theft | Development | Tourism | Pollution | Disasters | Constraints | Changing Uses | Invaders | Climate

An outstanding example of medieval religious architecture in the Caucasus, the richly decorated Historical Monuments of Mtskheta illustrate the high artistic and cultural level attained by this ancient Georgian capital. At the confluence of the Kura and Aragvi rivers, just northwest of the present-day capital of T'bilisi, Mtskheta was the seat of Georgian kings (the Iverian kingdom) from the third century BC to the fifth century AD. The birthplace of Christianity in the region, Mtskheta became a major pilgrimage site and remains the spiritual centre of the country to this day.

Built on the site where one of the first crosses in Georgia was erected, the Jvari ("holy cross" in Georgian) Monastery marks the spot where in the fourth century AD the female evangelist St Nino converted King Mirian and Queen Nana to Christianity. The Great Church is still used for major celebrations, and part of St Nino's cross remains visible to this day.

The eleventh-century Svetitskhoveli Cathedral (meaning "Column of Life") houses a relic said to be from the robe of Christ and is among the most significant monuments of Georgian Renaissance architecture. The Samratovo Convent stands on the site of Georgia's first church and contains the tombs of King Mirian and Queen Nana.

⊛ World Heritage Site inscribed: 1994
http://whc.unesco.org/en/list/708

ABOVE RIGHT: Like the other monuments at Mtskheta, the Jvari Monastery is at risk because of pollution and lack of resources.

Many of Georgia's oldest and most beautiful religious monuments are here, including the sixth–seventh-century Jvari Monastery and eleventh-century Svetitskhoveli Cathedral and Samratovo Convent. On a hilltop overlooking the old city, the Jvari complex includes the Small Church of AD 545 and the Great Church, which was begun in AD 586 and is a medieval domed masterpiece housing St Nino's cross. Representative of the tetraconch architectural type that became popular in the Black Sea region, the Great Church served as a model for many others. With a splendid decorated interior and unusual and varied relief sculptures on its façade, the monastery is an important example of early Christian architecture.

Future generations may never see Jvari. Suffering from harsh climate conditions and limited resources, the ancient masonry is being eaten away by acid rain. Weakened by centuries of inadequate maintenance, the buildings have during the past thirty years suffered significant erosion because of pollutants. Poor conservation work has only contributed to the damage. Part of the roof of the Small Church has collapsed, and the interior mosaics and frescoes have been largely destroyed by the elements. The government has proposed a conservation plan, but without adequate resources these monuments are at risk of total destruction.

Dorset and East Devon Coast
United Kingdom of Great Britain and Northern Ireland

An area of outstanding natural beauty and great value to earth science, this unspoiled length of stunning coastline stretches along 150 km (95 miles) of the English Channel. The cliff exposures, running from East Devon to Dorset, provide an almost continuous sequence of rock formations spanning the Mesozoic Era, or some 185 million years of the Earth's history. The area's important fossil sites and classic coastal geomorphologic features have been important to the study of earth sciences for more than 300 years.

GUARDED

KEY THREATS Conflict | Theft | Development | Tourism | Pollution | Disasters | Constraints | Changing Uses | Invaders | Climate

Inscribed in 2001 as England's first natural World Heritage Site, its value was first pointed out in 1673 by the early naturalist John Ray, who recognized the importance of the fossil wealth at Lyme Regis.

The work of the amateur Anning family of Lyme Regis advanced science in the early nineteenth century in a way without parallel in Europe. They found the first ichthyosaur specimen to come to the attention of scientists as well as the world's first complete plesiosaur, and numerous other fossils including the first British pterosaur.

Atlantic Ocean

NORWAY

Edinburgh

Belfast

UNITED KINGDOM

North Sea

NETHERLANDS

IRELAND

Cardiff   London

BELGIUM

FRANCE

◎ World Heritage Site inscribed: 2001
http://whc.unesco.org/en/list/1029

ABOVE RIGHT: Durdle Door, towards the eastern end of the Jurassic Coast, is formed of limestone that has taken longer to erode than the weaker rocks that lie around it. Like all of this coast, it is at risk from maritime environmental disasters such as oil spills.

Commonly known as the Jurassic Coast, the tilted sequence of layers here allows a walk through the geological record from west to east. Marching from the Triassic through the Jurassic and Cretaceous, the sequence is the finest and most accessible in one place anywhere in the world. Nine internationally important fossil groups are found here, from Triassic terrestrial fauna at East Devon, to the Fossil Forest on Portland and the Lower Cretaceous Purbeck Beds at Durlston Bay. The site is the best source of Lower Jurassic marine reptile, fish and insect fossils anywhere, and the Late Jurassic Fossil Forest site is unique. Also at Durlston can be found the richest group of Lower Cretaceous reptiles, fish, insects and early mammals known.

On 18 January 2007, the container ship MSC Napoli ran into trouble in good weather in the English Channel. In an effort to minimize damage to the vessel and any environmental impact, it was beached two days later in Lyme Bay, within the World Heritage Site. By the end of the incident, 103 containers and 200 tonnes of heavy fuel oil had been spilled, littering beaches and waters. Authorities described the emergency preparedness as "model", but when looters began combing the coast and ripping cargo apart, it was, in reality, chaotic. Although disaster was averted (3500 tonnes of oil were safely removed and the weather was good), the accident illustrates the ongoing risk to coastal heritage sites, especially those close to busy shipping routes. One suggested solution is that such important sites could be designated as Particularly Sensitive Sea Areas or Areas to Be Avoided under international maritime rules.

DISASTERS

Some disasters are preventable, others are not. Natural disasters can result from fire, earthquake, volcano, climate change, flood or war, while disasters occurring as a result of preventable causes include carelessness, vandalism, arson, conflict and illegal occupation.

Destruction by fire is an ongoing concern, especially since significant wooden buildings, with their ancient timbers, are particularly vulnerable – the Historic City of Ayutthaya, in Thailand, and the Ancient Building Complex in the Wudang Mountains, in China, have both suffered incalculable damage through fire at various times in their history. In addition to accidental fires and fire as a result of a volcanic eruption or an earthquake, fires are often deliberately set to clear land for other uses, but then get out of control, precipitating other natural disasters such as landslides and erosion, flooding and the silting of rivers. And it's not only buildings that are at risk – fire destroyed thousands of valuable and irreplaceable paintings, drawings and books in Weimar, Germany, just a few years ago. Additionally, the water used to put out a fire does itself cause damage.

The preservation of World Heritage in locations prone to earthquakes is also a challenge. In regions where tremors are common, strategies and response plans may be in place, but often, a quake can come as a surprise, as it did in the ancient city of Bam in Iran several years ago when an unknown and inactive fault came to life with devastating consequences. Restoration work at some sites in the last century replaced traditional materials such as massive walls with thin blocks, and soft lime mortar with stiff concrete. Although seemingly insignificant, such changes can be the difference between a structure flexing in a quake and being so rigid that it literally gets torn apart, as with the top-heavy 20th century concrete cathedral spires which came down during the recent tremor in Arequipa, Peru.

Elsewhere, normal seasonal river overflows have been compromised by deliberate diversion of streams and dams, making them more severe and resulting in flooding and mudslides. The money needed in vulnerable areas to build water barriers such as dykes and flood controls and to provide pumps is not always available, thus putting sites at risk.

Disasters often also have indirect effects – in Indonesia, after the 2004 tsunami, wood for rebuilding was illegally taken from tropical rainforests, endangering not only the flora, but tree-dwelling animals and birds.

After a disaster, the priority is to locate survivors, and this often causes further damage to sites as lifting machinery and emergency crews struggle to free trapped people. The proper removal of debris is also critical, since it will often contain important archaeological remains, from which may come evidence and fragments to help rebuild structures that have been damaged or destroyed.

Sometimes, despite all the preparation and prior knowledge, simply because of the location and fragility of the site, there is little that can be done except to hope that a disaster doesn't happen. In the event of a volcanic eruption, for example, with the rapid raining down of lava, ash and gas, evacuation of people is achieved far more easily than the conservation of buildings and works of art. However, in many places throughout the world some of the structural damage that occurs during a natural disaster is caused by the lack of observance of building regulations, inconsiderate changes to existing structures and lack of maintenance.

"Be prepared" is the best maxim, and custodians of World Heritage, especially within disaster-prone regions, are encouraged to give consideration to the impacts of disasters on cultural and natural heritage when designing their strategic goals and plans.

Action which can be taken includes anti-flood measures, continuous monitoring of earthquake, volcanic and tsunami risk, safe removal and storage of portable items, and vigilance by agencies such as the fire service and the police to strengthen fire protection and security measures. In some cases new laws and regulations to help reduce dangerous human practices, such as preventing shipping near coastal protected areas, or transporting hazardous materials through historic centres, may be an option.

When a disaster does occur, UNESCO and other UN and international organizations provide technical, financial and emergency assistance to those affected, and support the efforts of local authorities and the people in their rehabilitation and restoration work.

IN DANGER

KEY THREATS Conflict | Theft | Development | Tourism | Pollution | Disasters | Constraints | Changing Uses | Invaders | Climate

Bam and its Cultural Landscape
Iran (Islamic Republic of)

Located in an oasis on the southern edge of the Iranian high plateau, the ancient mud-brick fortress complex at Bam has been called the world's largest adobe structure. The origins of this desert settlement can be traced back to the Achaemenid period (sixth to fourth centuries BC). Destroyed and rebuilt a number of times during its history, the fortified city developed at the crossroads of the old spice routes. Life in the oasis was based on underground irrigation canals, known as qanats, of which Bam has some of the oldest surviving in Iran. The citadel is the most representative example of a fortified medieval town built in vernacular technique using mud layers (Chineh) combined with mud bricks (Khesht).

The Bam fault, which lies along the town had not been known to be active until 2003. The fissure was known, however, and had been utilized for centuries as part of the qanat system of underground water channels.

A pilgrimage point during Sassanid times, Bam's Zoroastrian fire temple was replaced during the Saffarid period (AD 866–903) with the Jame Mosque.

⊛ World Heritage Site inscribed 2004
Inscription on the List of World Heritage in Danger: 2004
http://whc.unesco.org/en/list/1208

OPPOSITE PAGE: Bam's citadel has been stormed, destroyed and restored on several occasions.

ABOVE RIGHT: The mud-brick construction of Bam makes it vulnerable to earthquakes.

In its heyday from the seventh to the eleventh century AD, Bam was known for the production of silk and cotton garments. As well as the citadel, the town contained a bazaar, caravanserai and one of the oldest mosques in Iran, dating from the eighth or ninth century. During the Safavid period (1502–1722) the city grew to span 6 sq km (2.3 sq miles) and housed 10,000 people. An outer wall and thirty-eight watchtowers protected the four fortified areas, including government quarters, stables and the historic town.

Earthquakes and Adobe

On 26 December 2003 a devastating twenty-second earthquake of magnitude 6.5 ripped through the area. In its wake 26,000 of the greater city's 100,000 inhabitants were dead (some estimates were as high as 43,000), another 40,000 were homeless and 70 per cent of the structures were destroyed. The Iranian government, the UN and some sixty nations responded with emergency teams and relief supplies. It is estimated the reconstruction will total a billion US dollars.

Earth-built structures are particularly susceptible to seismic events – few other mud-brick settlements in the region survive as most have been previously damaged in earthquakes. In Bam, the disaster severely damaged the urban area, walls and fortress, as well as ancient irrigation systems.

sixth–fourth centuries BC — there is evidence of early settlement in the Achaemenid period.

second century BC — first signs of the use of *qanats* for irrigation.

third century AD — a city grows under the Sassanids and is a centre of cotton and silk weaving.

tenth century — Islamic writers mention a well-established trading place with three mosques, a strong fortress and busy bazaars. It is known for its palm trees, its inhabitants' elegant garments and the use of the *qanats* to provide drinking water and irrigate the fields.

sixteenth–eighteenth centuries — under the Safavids (1502-1722) Bam is a trading hub for silk and cashmere and experiences a period of calm and prosperity. The main 65-m (210-ft) observation tower and governor's palace area of the citadel are built and the 6-sq-km (2.3-sq-miles) area is ringed by a wall and thirty-eight towers.

nineteenth century — the city expands outside the walls and residential quarters in the fortified area fall into ruin.

1948–1993 — a restoration campaign is undertaken, including extensive repairs of the citadel which begin in the mid-1970s.

BC 500	0	AD 500	AD 1000	AD 1500	AD 2000

1179 — the Turkish Ghoz nomads invade the area and take Bam.

1213 — Bam is conquered by the Great Lord Master of Zuzan and its walls are destroyed.

1220 — the Mongol invasion in the north spares Bam and the walls are rebuilt.

c. 1408 — the Timurids occupy Bam, restoring the citadel and housing in the fortified enclosure.

1342 — Bam is recaptured by Amir Mobarez al-Din and the walls are restored.

1719–1730 — the city is twice occupied by the Afghans and falls into decline.

1810 — Invaders from the Shiraz region take the city.

1841 — the Ismailis briefly gain control.

1930s — the army, which had occupied the citadel, moves out and it is abandoned.

1993 — a massive earthquake on the Bam fault levels the town and citadel, killing thousands.

The tower and higher structures of the citadel (including the upper levels of the garrison and stables) and the south-western side, were reduced to rubble. The main south gate was considerably damaged, as were the yakhadan (ice house) and large portions of the enclosure walls. In the town, many houses and buildings were shattered including the mosque, religious theatre, caravanserai, bazaar, alleys and a portion of the school. In the aftermath and rush to clear debris and locate survivors, some residual damage to structures and historical traces inevitably occurred. But overall the emergency measures have helped to save what remains through bracing, strapping and stabilizing fractured monuments. Nonetheless, a massive amount remains to be done.

BELOW: Referred to as the world's largest adobe structure, the ancient mud-brick fortress complex at Bam is seen here prior to the devastating earthquake of 2003.

OPPOSITE PAGE: The citadel suffered particularly badly in the earthquake, with large parts of its walls and towers simply shearing off the mound on which it had sat for hundreds of years.

Tropical Rainforest Heritage of Sumatra
Indonesia

AT RISK

KEY THREATS Conflict | Theft | Development | Tourism | Pollution | Disasters | Constraints | Changing Uses | Invaders | Climate

Home to the disappearing orang-utan, this expanse of 26,000 sq km (10,000 sq miles) of equatorial rainforests is made up of three different Indonesian national parks on the island of Sumatra: Gunung Leuser National Park, Kerinci Seblat National Park and Bukit Barisan Selatan National Park. From the highest lake in southeast Asia to magnificent volcanoes, waterfalls, caves and lush high and lowland forest, it is an area of outstanding beauty. This once vast area of tropical habitat has been reduced to isolated remnants in just fifty years. The site holds great potential for the conservation of the distinctive flora and fauna of Sumatra, and is critical to a number of species on the brink of extinction.

⊚ World Heritage Site inscribed 2004
http://whc.unesco.org/en/list/1167

OPPOSITE PAGE: A satellite view of the flattened communities and forest on the northern edge of Gunung Leuser. On 26 December 2004, a magnitude 9.1 earthquake off Sumatra's western coast generated a tsunami, which devastated coastal regions around the Indian Ocean. Northwest Sumatra suffered extensive damage and great loss of life.

ABOVE RIGHT: This site represents the most important block of forest on the island of Sumatra for the conservation of the biodiversity of both lowland and mountain forests.

After the Congo and the Amazon, Indonesia's tropical rainforests are the third largest in the world. But with illegal logging, conversion to palm-oil and sugar-cane plantations and forest fires, Indonesia is losing its forests at an estimated rate of 15,380–26,500 sq km (5940–10,230 sq miles) annually.

Indonesia was once inhabited by three sub species of tiger – Javan, Balinese and Sumatran – but today only the Sumatran survives. With fewer than 500 left in the wild, experts estimate that fifty are being lost a year to illegal trade, and the species is in critical danger. Although its use is banned internationally, tiger bone is sadly still sought for traditional Asian medicine.

The illegal logging is an international problem – the valuable tropical hardwood from these protected forests can fetch US$300 per cu m (35 cu ft) in overseas markets, for which workers can make US$7 a day, which is a small fortune in this hard-hit region.

At-risk fauna includes the critically endangered: Sumatran orang-utan, tiger, rhinoceros, hare and Sumatran ground-cuckoo, as well as the Rueck's blue-flycatcher and leatherback turtle. Other animals here are the endangered Sumatran elephant, Asian tapir, otter civet, Beccari's shrew, white-winged duck, green turtle and Borean river turtle.

The protected area is home to an estimated 10,000 plant species, including seventeen endemic genera, 180 species of mammals and some 580 birds of which 465 are resident and 21 are endemic. The World Conservation Union (IUCN) has red-listed fifty-eight of the birds. Of the mammal species, twenty-two are Asian and are not found elsewhere in the archipelago and fifteen are confined to the Indonesian region, including the endemic Sumatran orang-utan.

Located on the prominent main spine of the Bukit Barisan Mountains, the "Andes of Sumatra", these three parks provide prominent mountainous backdrops to the settled and developed lowlands of Sumatra. The site includes the spectacular Lake Gunung Tujuh; giant Mount Kerinci volcano; numerous small volcanic, coastal and glacial lakes in natural forested settings; fumaroles belching smoke from forested mountains; and waterfalls and cave systems in lush rainforest. It also provides biogeographic evidence of the evolution of the island.

A Tsunami and its Impact

Among the last and largest sources of valuable tropical hardwood in Asia, the rainforest has been badly impacted by the 2004 Asian tsunami. Although the tsunami caused minimal direct damage to the natural habitat, the northern portion, Gunung Leuser, was not spared the massive loss of life and possessions – several staff members were killed and the park's headquarters was washed away. In the wake of the tsunami, wood, to help replace thousands of destroyed homes, was taken from the park. Many Non-Governmental Organizations unknowingly contributed to the practice in the months following the disaster. Today knowledge and stricter controls have limited this, but the demand for ancient hardwoods continues to fuel large-scale illegal logging.

BELOW LEFT: Valuable and threatened hardwoods float away offering short term gain but long term loss as the island's heritage is sold off.

BELOW RIGHT: With limited resources to control illegal logging, especially in the wake of the devastation of the tsunami, wood was taken first for rebuilding and later for international markets.

OPPOSITE PAGE: Indonesia's rainforests are rapidly disappearing as encroachment for new family farms and palm and sugar cane plantations eat away at the edges of protected areas.

The World Wildlife Fund estimates that Aceh province will require at least 860,000 cu m (30.4 million cu ft) of sawn timber for the construction of 200,000 homes over the next five years. Road construction has had the unfortunate side-effect of allowing illegal loggers easier access and, with limited resources in the wake of the tsunami, enforcement of regulations has been difficult. As conflict in the region has wound down and growth has returned after the tsunami, encroachment (largely for sugar-cane fields) has become a major concern. By 2005, in one of the three sections of the park, more than 1577 sq km (609 sq miles) had been encroached upon by roughly 40,000 families.

Classical Weimar
Germany

AT RISK

KEY THREATS Conflict | Theft | Development | Tourism | Pollution | Disasters | Constraints | Changing Uses | Invaders | Climate

In the late eighteenth and early nineteenth centuries, the small Thuringian town of Weimar, in the middle of present-day Germany, witnessed a remarkable cultural flowering, attracting many great writers and scholars, including Goethe, Schiller, Herder and Wieland. This development is reflected in the rich public and private buildings and parks in and around this classical town.

Ⓖ World Heritage Site inscribed 1998
http://whc.unesco.org/en/list/846

OPPOSITE PAGE: The interior of the Duchess Anna Amalia library before it was hit by fire in 2004. The library originally housed more than 1 million volumes.

ABOVE RIGHT: Memorial statues of Goethe and Schiller in front of the National Theatre in Weimar.

Formerly a palace, the Duchess Anna Amalia Library, which dates back to 1691, is one of the oldest public libraries in Europe. Its collection of more than 1 million volumes focuses on German literature from 1750 to 1850.

More than thirty rococo paintings and a death mask of the German poet Schiller were destroyed in the fire of 2004. Another hundred paintings, eighty sculptures, and twenty drawings were damaged. More than thirty-seven tonnes of severely burned or waterlogged books were taken to a special deep-freezing and restoration facility.

Enlightened ducal patronage by Anna Amalia and her son, Duke Carl Augustus, made Weimar the cultural focus of the Europe of the day. The World Heritage Site includes Goethe's house, Schiller's house, the town church of St Peter and St Paul (with Herder's house and the old high school), the Residential Palace, the Widow's Palace, the Duchess Anna Amalia Library, the ducal crypt and historic cemetery, the Park on the Ilm (with the Roman House and Goethe's garden house), the Tiefurt Palace and Gardens, the Belvedere Palace, Orangery and Park and Ettersburg Palace and Park.

The Duchess Anna Amalia library is particularly noteworthy, housing more than 1 million volumes from the period. Before it was hit by fire in 2004, its collection included 3900 works by Goethe (including the world's largest collection of editions of Faust), Nietzsche's private library, 2000 manuscripts from the Middle Ages and 8400 historic maps as well as an important collection of Bibles and volumes of music. In addition to its literary prominence during the era of Goethe, Weimar later became a hub for musicians including Liszt, Wagner and Berlioz (following in the footsteps of early resident Johann Sebastian Bach). Literary societies sprang up in the late-nineteenth century, and in the twentieth century art and architecture took off with the birth of the Bauhaus movement in Weimar under the leadership of Walter Gropius (1883–1969). Other prominent artists include Klee, Kandinsky, Feininger, Itten, Muche, Moholy-Nagy and Schlemmer. The Weimar Bauhaus sites are part of an adjoining World Heritage Site, the "Bauhaus and its Sites in Weimar and

Fire and the Threat to Books

Numerous great libraries have burned at times through the ages and despite today's rapid response and advanced detectors, many aging sites remain at high risk from fire. On the evening of 2 September 2004 disaster struck Weimar's Anna Amalia Library, as flames engulfed the upper floors. In the words of German State Secretary for Culture, Christina Weiss, it was a "national cultural catastrophe and a great loss for the world's heritage" – the attic and third floor of the oldest section, the sixteenth-century rococo Green Palace were destroyed. Some 50,000 volumes were lost and another 62,000 were damaged, in particular by the water used to extinguish the fire. More than 900 volunteers helped to evacuate tens of thousands of books from the building

BELOW LEFT: Taken in January 2001, this picture shows the Anna Amalia library before the fire. Thousands of priceless books were destroyed by the fire that swept through this 300-year-old building.

BELOW RIGHT: A skilled painter works on the historic rococo hall of the library.

OPPOSITE PAGE: Part of the roof and the top floor of this seventeenth-century library have been painstakingly rebuilt and renovated after the fire in a €12 million effort. However, the lost volumes have proven much harder to replace.

and the rubble, saving many great works including a 1543 Martin Luther Bible and travel papers by the naturalist Alexander von Humboldt. Some damaged books were meticulously restored in a painstaking process which involved freeze-drying them. Replacements were donated or bought where possible, but countless irreplaceable volumes were lost. Just months before the fire the library was due to be closed for renovation and the books moved to a new fireproof underground storage facility. The timing of the fire was particularly unlucky.

Development of a ring road and the risk from a changing climate (the 2002 floods that caused extensive destruction across Europe affected the site) are also factors here.

Historical Centre of the City of Arequipa
Peru

AT RISK

KEY THREATS Conflict | Theft | Development | Tourism | Pollution | Disasters | Constraints | Changing Uses | Invaders | Climate

The historic centre of Arequipa, built from a white volcanic stone known as "sillar", represents an integration of European and native building techniques and characteristics, expressed in the admirable work of colonial masters and Criollo and Indian masons. This combination of influences is illustrated by the city's robust walls, semicircular arches and vaulted roofs, courtyards and open spaces, and the intricate Baroque decoration of its façades.

Known as the "White City" because of the pearly (or occasionally pinkish) local volcanic stone (sillar) used in their construction, Arequipa's historic buildings feature massive earthquake-resistant stone walls— 1–1.5 m (3–5 ft) thick in domestic buildings and more than 2 m (6.5 ft) thick in the churches.

The historic area contains some 500 casonas, the characteristic well-proportioned vernacular houses, of which more than 250 are listed for protection. They were generally built in the nineteenth century on the sites of earlier colonial buildings destroyed in the 1868 earthquake.

⊚ World Heritage Site inscribed 2000
http://whc.unesco.org/en/list/1016

OPPOSITE PAGE: The sun shines on the cathedral, in the Plaza de Armas, which is in the middle of Arequipa. The cathedral is deemed to be the most important neoclassical structure in Peru.

ABOVE RIGHT: The monastery of Santa Catalina, now a convent, was built in 1580 and enlarged in the seventeenth century. It is regarded as one of the most fascinating of the colonial churches.

Situated in the high Andean foothills of southern Peru some 2300 m (7740 ft) above sea level, Arequipa sits in a fertile valley in the shadow of the snow-capped 5822-m (19,100-ft) El Misti volcano. The modern city was founded in 1540 by emissaries of the Spanish conquistador, Pizarro, although there is evidence of more than 7000 years of inhabitation. In its middle is the Plaza de Armas, which is flanked on three sides by archways and on the fourth by the cathedral. The most important neoclassical structure in Peru, it was constructed in the mid-nineteenth century on the ruins of an earlier Baroque church.

The remarkable Santa Catalina monastery, covering some 20,000 sq m (216,000 sq ft), was established at the end of the sixteenth century. Damaged many times by earthquakes, it has been successively rebuilt over three centuries, presenting a unique blend of architectural styles. It houses many paintings from the so-called Cuzco school, a mix of Spanish and Inca styles developed between the sixteenth and eighteenth centuries. Forty-nine central city blocks were built in the seventeenth and eighteenth centuries: they form a uniform ensemble in carved stone with vaults and domes.

On the Rim of Fire

Peru's second largest city, Arequipa, with its 1 million-plus inhabitants, sits on the seismically active Pacific Rim of Fire, in the Valley of the Volcanoes. On 23 June 2001 a magnitude 7.9 earthquake struck the region with devastating force, killing more than 70, injuring almost 3000, destroying or damaging 58,000 dwellings and

leaving 200,000 homeless. Originating under the Pacific Ocean 190 km (120 miles) offshore where the Nazca plate subducts under the South American, the earthquake razed seventy per cent of homes in Arequipa and badly damaged the historic buildings.

Arequipa sits in the shadow of two active volcanoes (El Misti "the mountain" and Chachani "the beloved") and one dormant one (Pichu Pichu "top top"). El Misti last erupted with explosive force in the late fifteenth century, but has released smoke, ash and poisonous gas in the early sixteenth century, in 1577, 1677, 1787, 1831, 1869, 1870, 1948-49, 1984-85 and 1997. Earthquakes add to the risk: in addition to outright destruction they could trigger a massive eruption. Earthquakes have struck throughout Arequipa's history: destroyed in Inca times, it was

BELOW LEFT: Residents of Arequipa clearing the debris in the aftermath of one of the many earthquakes which have struck the city throughout its history.

BELOW RIGHT: Snow-capped El Misti, an active volcano, dominates the skyline to the north-east of the city posing a continuous threat to its inhabitants.

OPPOSITE PAGE: The seventeenth-century Jesuit church of La Compania has withstood the earthquakes which destroyed the cathedral and many other buildings.

flattened again in 1687 and 1868. In 1958, a magnitude 7.3 event killed twenty-eight, injured 133 and damaged many older homes. Just two years later a magnitude 7.5 earthquake killed sixty-three, injured hundreds and triggered mudslides on El Misti. It is only 13 km (8 miles) from the volcano's summit to the million people living in Arequipa, and a large eruption would be devastating to the population and its heritage. A thorough disaster plan needs to be implemented urgently.

Mount Athos
Greece

A focus of Orthodox Christianity for more than 1000 years, the monastic community of Mount Athos is a living vestige of the Byzantine world. It is in northeastern Greece on a narrow leg of the Chalcidice Peninsula jutting into the Aegean Sea. Its rugged seclusion has helped to protect it since AD 963. Its twenty monasteries, twelve smaller communities (*sketae*) and many hermitages are home to a rich collection of Byzantine art and impressive fortress-like architecture, with influences from as far afield as Russia. Granted self-rule by Byzantine Emperor Tsimiskis in AD 972 and declared a World Heritage Site in 1988, the world's last Autonomous Monastic State enjoys special independence under the Greek constitution.

⊛ World Heritage Site inscribed 1988
http://whc.unesco.org/en/list/454

The chief standard-bearer of Orthodox Christianity, Mount Athos bows to the Patriarch of Constantinople on religious matters and the Greek State on political ones.

The community only allows males over the age of eighteen to enter. To prevent temptation among the monks, women remain banned from the peninsula, although the European Union has pushed for access for them. Even female animals are barred, although cats and chickens appear to be flouting the rules.

The Athonian monasteries hold numerous invaluable medieval treasures, from icons to holy relics, vestments and chalices, as well as written codices and texts.

OPPOSITE PAGE: The ornate "katholikon" of Chilander monastery (above) escaped damage in the fire but is at risk from a similar catastrophe in the future. The photograph below shows the monastery before the fire of 2004.

ABOVE RIGHT: On 4 March 2004 a fire broke out in the Chilandar monastery, destroying more than half of the medieval fortress. The blaze, which took sixty firefighters a day to put out, destroyed a 1598 residence, guest quarters and four chapels with seventeenth- and eighteenth-century frescoes.

With records of Christian worship here dating back to the time of Constantine (r. AD 306–377), the peninsula's natural beauty and calm have made the it a religious haven for centuries. Home to its namesake 2033-m (6670-ft) peak, and covered in evergreen chestnut trees, the peninsula contains the last extensive forest in the Mediterranean area. With no road links and accessible only by sea, Mount Athos continues to enforce a strict ban on women and children. Although populations declined in the last century, the community survives, and has grown again to roughly 2500 inhabitants today.

A Continuing Battle Against Fires

Over the centuries almost every monastery has been struck by fire at some point – only the Great Lavra has been spared, although it was hit by an equally destructive earthquake in the sixteenth century. Hit by devastating fires twice in the last twenty years, Mount Athos' rugged seclusion, forested hills, ancient structures and steep slopes make it especially vulnerable. A dispersed population, limited fire-fighting equipment, and the use of open flames have not helped. A large wildfire in 1990 was followed with a huge blaze at the Chilandar monastery in 2004. Although relics and key structures were saved, the blaze illustrates the high ongoing threat of fire on the remote peninsula.

Additional threats include the lack of proper waste management on the peninsula, from solid and liquid waste to old vehicles. There is also a potential risk of logging in the forests.

Historic Centre of Prague
Czech Republic

One of Europe's most beautiful cities, Prague has been the political, cultural and economic heart of the Czech state for more than 1000 years. Located on the Vltava river in central Bohemia, this "City of a Hundred Spires" was twice capital of the Holy Roman Empire and played an important role in the development of Christianity in central Europe. Its Old Town (Staré Mesto), Lesser Town (Malá Strana) and New Town (Nové Mesto), built between the eleventh and eighteenth centuries, display the great architectural and cultural influence enjoyed by the city since the Middle Ages.

In August 2002 massive flooding in Europe hit Prague as the Vltava river broke its banks and flooded historic areas. Many libraries were affected including the Architecture Archives at the National Technical Museum.

Disaster has struck the city many times before. In 1689 a great fire devastated it, and in 1890 a huge flood caused extensive damage.

Having largely survived the destruction of World Wars I and II, Prague contains one of the world's most pristine and varied collections of architecture, from Romanesque to baroque, Renaissance, cubist, Gothic, neo-classical, Art Nouveau and the modern. Its many magnificent monuments span all periods and include the Hradcany Castle, the eleventh-century Romanesque St Vitus Cathedral, the 1357 Charles Bridge across the Vltava, Gothic churches and palaces built in the fourteenth century under the Holy Roman Emperor Charles IV, baroque structures from the eighteenth century and relics from the industrial revolution in the nineteenth century.

The establishment in 1348 of the Charles University, said to be the first in central or eastern Europe, made the city an important seat of learning. Famous names associated with the city include Johannes Kepler, Franz Kafka and Wolfgang Amadeus Mozart.

Baltic Sea

POLAND

GERMANY

Prague
CZECH
REPUBLIC
Plzeň
Ostrava
Brno

Danube

SLOVAKIA

AUSTRIA

HUNGARY

SLOVENIA

CROATIA

ITALY

Adriatic Sea

World Heritage Site inscribed 1992
http://whc.unesco.org/en/list/616

OPPOSITE PAGE: In 1357, the Charles Bridge was built across the Vltava river to connect the Old Town and Malá Strana. Baroque statues (a total of 30) began to be placed on either side of the bridge in the seventeenth century. Now many of them are copies and the originals can be seen in the Lapidarium.

ABOVE RIGHT: Prague is the City of a Hundred Spires. These are the spires of St Vitus Cathedral – the seat of the Archbishop of Prague. The cathedral is located within Prague Castle and contains the tombs of many Bohemian kings. It is an excellent example of Gothic architecture.

1340s – under Charles IV Prague becomes capital of the Holy Roman Empire and its university is founded.

1000   1500   2000

870 – Hradcany castle founded.

1085 – Prague becomes a capital under Vratislaus II.

1538 – under Rudolf II Prague becomes capital of the Holy Roman Empire for a second time.

1689 – fire devastates the city.

1890 – major flood hits the city.

1918 – Prague becomes capital of Czechoslovakia.

1618 – the second defenestration of Prague sparks the Thirty Years War.

1948 – Prague becomes capital of communist Czechoslovakia after a coup.

1968 – the Soviet army invades to stamp out the liberalization of the "Prague Spring."

1989 – the Velvet Revolution marks the fall of communism. Prague becomes capital of the new Czech Republic in 1993.

2002 – Prague is hit by another major flood.

The Flood of the Century

In August 2002, after more than a week of heavy rains, massive floods swept across Europe, inundating the Historic Centre of Prague with water. The World Heritage Sites at Dresden, Weimar, Dessau-Wörlitz, Budapest, Cesky Krumlov, Salzburg, Vienna, Eisleben and Wittenberg, and Wachau were also affected.

In Prague, the "stoleta voda", or flood of the century, submerged theatres, concert halls and even the metro. In some structures waters reached up to 2 m (6.5 ft) above ground level and many waterlogged buildings collapsed. According to the Director of the National Library, about 1 million books, including several incunabula (books printed before 1501) and early prints and books from rare collections, were damaged. Losses

BELOW LEFT: The fourteenth-century Charles Bridge, a major tourist attraction, links historic sites on both sides of the Vltava river.

BELOW RIGHT: Many of the buildings in the middle of Prague are beautifully decorated. Those closest to the river are particularly at risk, as flood waters can weaken lower levels and lead to collapse, especially if water is not fully removed from the walls before the winter freeze.

OPPOSITE PAGE: In 2002 the Vltava river burst its banks, flooding much of historic Prague and damaging buildings and their contents.

at museums and archives were even greater. Climate change is thought to be a contributor – the UN Intergovernmental Panel on Climate Change has found that average rainfall and frequency have risen in the last 100 years and warns that instances of extreme precipitation events are likely to increase. In 2005 and 2006, floods struck the Danube and Elbe, threatening the World Heritage Site of Budapest and causing extensive destruction.

Coupled with the risk of disasters, Prague is facing renewed growth and the threats of development – two proposed high-rise towers may soon loom over the historic skyline. The site is already facing challenges as tourists flood into the sixth most-visited city on the continent.

Ancient Building Complex in the Wudang Mountains
China

AT RISK

KEY THREATS Conflict | Theft | Development | Tourism | Pollution | Disasters | Constraints | Changing Uses | Invaders | Climate

The palaces and temples which form the nucleus of this group of secular and religious buildings exemplify the architectural and artistic achievements of China's Yuan, Ming and Qing dynasties. Masterpieces of ingenious planning, the buildings are spread across the scenic valleys and on the slopes of the Wudang Mountains in Hubei Province in central China. Built as an organized complex during the Ming dynasty (1368–1644), the site also contains Taoist buildings from as early as the seventh century. It represents the highest standards of Chinese art and architecture over a period of nearly 1000 years.

Some 200,000 workmen and soldiers were said to have toiled for twelve years to complete the massive project.

The Wudang Mountains are a series of ranges stretching over 400 km (250 miles). The 1612-m (5290-ft) Sky Pillar peak at its core is surrounded by seventy-two lesser peaks and twenty-four ravines. Its impressive setting led to it becoming a major religious site.

⊗ World Heritage Site inscribed 1994
http://whc.unesco.org/en/list/705

ABOVE RIGHT: A road leading to the ancient building complex in the Wudang Mountains.

The site includes nine palaces, nine temples, thirty-six convents and seventy-two cliff temples. On Sky Pillar peak at its core is the Golden Shrine. Shipped to the site for assembly via the Grand Canal and rivers, it was cast in large bronze pieces in Beijing. Made to resemble wood, the shrine's lost-wax castings and elaborate gilding represent the pinnacle of the technology of the period. The shrine is ringed by a Forbidden City and wall of rectangular stones 345 m (1130 ft) in circumference, 1.8 m (6 ft) thick and up to 10 m (33 ft) high.

Centuries of History Lost in Hours

On 20 January 2003, a fire broke out in one of the complex's groups of structures. Two-and-a-half hours later, the Yuzhengong Palace was burned to the ground. No-one was injured in the fire but many Ming dynasty structures were destroyed or damaged. The 600-year-old palace, which covered an area of over 50,000 sq m (540,000 sq ft), was typical of late imperial Yuan (1271–1368) and early Ming Dynasty architecture. Since its inscription on the World Heritage List, this complex has suffered from lack of a clear management plan and policies. Two people were eventually convicted for the fire, which broke out from a lamp in an "illegal" school operating in one of the many structures. The other wooden structures here, many on much higher and less accessible slopes, remain at risk from fire. Although there is a commitment to rebuild the lost structures, their location in the valley presents a new challenge as a dam downriver means that the site will soon be flooded, and the reconstruction may need to move to higher ground.

Historic City of Ayutthaya
Thailand

Founded in 1350 on the site of an earlier Khmer city in a bend in the Chao Phraya river, Ayutthaya was the second capital of Siam (Thailand) after Sukhothai. For 412 years Ayutthaya, "the Invincible", was the royal seat and the most powerful and prosperous city in southeast Asia. At its peak, it had more than 1 million inhabitants, and accounts from foreign ambassadors compared it to Paris in splendour. Set in a vast floodplain in central Siam, it grew rich from the fields and provinces around it, extending its rule into Laos, Cambodia and Burma (now Myanmar). It was sacked by the Burmese in 1767, and its remains today, characterized by the prang (reliquary towers) and gigantic monasteries, give an idea of its past magnificence.

AT RISK

KEY THREATS Conflict | Theft | Development | Tourism | Pollution | Disasters | Constraints | Changing Uses | Invaders | Climate

Of the 400 wats (temples and monasteries) that once graced the city, only the remains of 211 are still visible today, with the most important in the oval loop in the river. Remnants of the 12-km (7.5-mile) wall that ringed the city are also visible.

The brick structures seen today were once covered in a white lime plaster and ornately decorated. More than 1 million visitors a year come to the ruins.

Although a Disaster Preparedness Plan is in place and barriers have been constructed to protect the historic site, the embankments and levees corralling the river, and the more frequent and powerful storms brought by climate change, mean that Ayutthaya remains at risk.

⊚ World Heritage Site inscribed 1991
http://whc.unesco.org/en/list/576

ABOVE RIGHT: On 16 October 2006, workers rushed to patch a leak in the storm barrier built to keep the floodwaters of the Chao Phraya river (right) from entering the historic area. Water levels were not expected to recede until the end of the month because of the seasonal high tides.

With the exception of religious structures made of stone and brick, most of the architecture was wooden, elevated on stilts above the reach of the annual floods. The largest surviving temple, Wat Phra Si Sanpet, was part of the royal palace and once contained a 15-m (50-ft) tall gold leaf Buddha. After its sacking, the city fell into disrepair – its buildings, art treasures and libraries were almost all destroyed by fire. From 1854–1910, restoration campaigners worked on many of the surviving structures.

In the past, annual inundations spilled over the land bringing silt and replenishing the soil. But modern waterworks and levees have slowly boxed in the river along its length, giving it nowhere to go. In 1995, flooding eroded the foundations of many temples. In August 2006, heavy rains following Typhoon Xangsane caused more floods. By 15 October, twenty-five temples, forts and pagodas in historic Ayutthaya were inundated and thirteen more at risk as the Chao Phraya broke its banks. Some monuments, such as Wat Chai Pattanaram, which had already been damaged in 1995, were even at risk of being washed away. Much of the region was under 30–120 cm (1–4 ft) of water as authorities rushed to build and reinforce dykes and pump it out.

Historic Centre of Naples
Italy

AT RISK

KEY THREATS Conflict | Theft | Development | Tourism | Pollution | Disasters | Constraints | Changing Uses | Invaders | Climate

From the Neapolis founded by Greek settlers in 470 BC to the city of today, Naples has retained the imprint of the successive cultures which emerged in Europe and the Mediterranean basin. Twenty-five centuries of growth have left a unique site, with numerous outstanding monuments such as the Church of Santa Chiara and the Castel Nuovo. The city's street pattern, wealth of historic buildings and setting on the Bay of Naples give it an outstanding universal value without parallel and one that has had a profound influence in many parts of Europe and beyond.

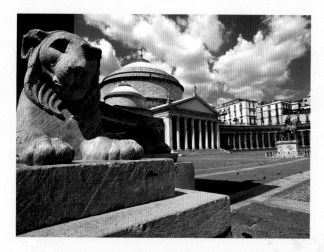

⊚ World Heritage Site inscribed 1995
http://whc.unesco.org/en/list/726

Frederick II founded a university in Naples in 1224 which boasted St Thomas Aquinas among its students.

The domestic architecture from the eighteenth century is noteworthy for its "open stair", an original solution to the problems of limited space.

Closely associated with the early history of Christianity, the site is home to the second-century AD catacombs of San Gennaro (Januarius) and San Gaudioso, with their remains of many saints and holy men.

OPPOSITE PAGE: Looming over the Bay of Naples, Vesuvius is the greatest threat to the city and people of Naples. Its last major eruption was over 1900 years ago, but this is of little comfort as it appears to undergo a 2000-year cycle of activity and may be due to erupt again at any time.

ABOVE RIGHT: The heart of old Naples has been subject to rebuilding works over the centuries, such as the Piazza del Plebiscito, which was driven through the area in the early nineteenth century by the French. Now it is also under threat from encroaching development.

Neapolis, literally the New City, was established in the fifth century BC by Cumaean colonists next to a seventh-century BC town after they defeated the Etruscan fleet and took control of the region. Enclosed by defensive walls, its ancient rectangular grid is still visible today.

In the Shadow of a Slumbering Giant

At the foot of Mount Vesuvius, best known for the eruption in AD 79 that buried Herculaneum and Pompeii, Naples has had a restless existence for millennia. In 2006, researchers found that a Bronze-Age eruption 4000 years ago completely covered the site of the modern city in up to 3 m (10 ft) of ash and lava. Heavily damaged in the earthquake of AD 62, and the one which preceded the eruption of AD 79, the city was shaken by smaller eruptions in 1631 and 1944, and an earthquake in the 1980s. Experts warn that Naples is at high risk from a major eruption, especially as the volcano has an apparent 2000-year cycle. Although it is constantly monitored, and plans exist for the evacuation of 600,000 people away from a pyroclastic flow and rain of hot ash, a major event would devastate the monuments and 3 million-plus residents. Of more immediate concern, the city is suffering from a changing population, poverty and sanitation problems and unauthorized development in its core. Attempts to revive the dilapidated historic area have had little impact, while illegal construction work has threatened ancient structures and buried remains.

Historic Monuments of Ancient Kyoto
Japan

GUARDED | KEY THREATS Conflict | Theft | Development | Tourism | Pollution | Disasters | Constraints | Changing Uses | Invaders | Climate

Built in AD 794 on the model of the capitals of ancient China, Kyoto was the imperial capital of Japan from its foundation until the middle of the nineteenth century. As the focus of Japanese culture for more than 1200 years, the site's cultural properties illustrate the development of Japanese wooden and religious architecture. Without parallel anywhere, this unique ensemble demonstrates the art of Japanese gardens, which has influenced landscape gardening the world over. The World Heritage Site consists of monuments in Kyoto, Uji and Otsu cities.

Kyoto's seventeen properties on the World Heritage List are but a small fraction of the city's 1800 shrines and temples.

Kyoto has the highest concentration of designated cultural properties in Japan, both in quantity and quality.

Among historic cities characterized by wooden architecture, Kyoto has functioned longer than any other (1200 years) as a cultural hub.

The seventeen properties (shrines, temples, palaces and a castle) consist of 198 nationally designated monuments and twelve designated gardens. Perhaps the best known of these are Kinkaku-ji, the Golden Pavilion, and Gingaku-ji, the Silver Pavilion. But each is important in its own right, reflecting the style of its era. Collectively they tell the story of Japanese architecture and gardens and have played a key role in influencing city development and religious culture. They are a precious archive of traditional construction techniques, and significant stylistic examples of their historic periods.

Flammable Wooden Structures in Earthquake Country
Over the centuries, Kyoto has been subjected to wars, fires and earthquakes which have destroyed portions of the heart of the city. Most of the surviving great temples are concentrated outside the core, at the edges of the wooded slopes that ring the basin in which the city sits. Many of them are uphill from dense clusters of homes separated only by narrow alleys – which fire engines could not get through – and are at great risk if fire were to break out below. Fire propagation models and studies, especially of major seismic events, illustrate the threat. Although Kyoto has a long history of preparedness and generations of trained and well-equipped citizens, the city fire department predicts that a magnitude 7.1–7.6 earthquake and the resulting fires would completely destroy 30,000 to 150,000 buildings and partially destroy more than 100,000 others. Despite the city's excellent management and disaster preparedness, the temples are in a precarious situation.

⊛ World Heritage Site inscribed 1994
http://whc.unesco.org/en/list/688

OPPOSITE PAGE: The glistening Kinkaku-ji or "Golden Pavilion" is Kyoto's most recognized temple. Built in 1397 as a country villa by Shogun Ashikaga Yoshimitsu, it was converted to a temple after his death. It has been painstakingly restored several times, most recently in 1987.

ABOVE RIGHT: The ancient timbers of the wooden framework on which Kiyomizu-dera sits are at risk of fire in this earthquake-prone region. There are three faults near Kyoto which could generate large tremors.

CONSTRAINTS

Many UNESCO World Heritage Sites are in danger from financial, political, technical or societal constraints, inhibiting their protection and conservation.

The most common challenge is financial. In many countries, where means are limited, heritage often has to take a back seat to more pressing social needs. When scarce funds are spent on preservation of monuments or animals, there can often be a backlash, as seen with the Taliban's destruction of the Buddhas of the Bamiyan site following an international offer for funding to support the monuments. In many cases, the cost of maintaining an abandoned city or monument, such as the Ruins of Kilwa Kisiwani and Songo Mnara in Tanzania, is simply not realistic for a developing nation. International assistance, from Non-Governmental Organizations to the United Nations, plays a crucial role in the survival of sites like these.

In some cases a lost art or skill leads to decay and collapse of historic structures. Technical expertise is sorely needed at many sites but is simply not available or too expensive to implement. The switch from traditional lime mortar to concrete for preservation work at numerous monuments during the twentieth century had devastating consequences. Stiffer concrete structures easily collapse in earthquakes – without expertise and knowledge mistakes are often made.

In places such as Baku, Azerbaijan, where rapid growth has followed disasters, political and technical constraints often limit the ability of governments to plan and guide development. The historic sixteenth-century city of Coro and its port, in Venezuela, for example, is located in a poor region, where lack of political support, money and expertise, combined with devastating rains, has led to the loss of important buildings.

An isolated or hard to reach location often compounds management challenges, as at the Minaret of Jam, in a remote valley in Afghanistan. The vast scale of some sites such as Salonga National Park in the Democratic Republic of the Congo, can present an enforcement challenge, from a lack of identified boundaries, to the physical challenge of patrolling enormous expanses. The shortage or absence of footpaths, signs and viewing platforms to provide safe access to some sites leads to the unwitting destruction by visitors of structures and important plants, insects and animals.

The weather is no respecter of protected sites. Rain, sun, salt-laden winds, frost and floods can all adversely affect unprotected areas, as can the lack of rain-water drainage. Damage from this erodes the bases of archaeological and cultural sites, monuments and buildings. Preventing the erosion of structures by natural causes is an ongoing battle in places where funds are limited and access restricted.

Other constraints include lack of management or conservation policies themselves, often resulting in dubious restoration efforts, with inappropriate materials being used, or worse, complete disrepair. Limited or non-existent funds result in ongoing conservation efforts and maintenance being severely compromised, and frequently no efforts are made to raise the quality of research, restoration, site management, visitor facilities and information. Lack of maintenance leads to encroaching vegetation and the fabric of ancient buildings can be destroyed by creeping roots and weeds. Likewise, the assessment and development of training programmes for staff, including guards, often have low priority, with inevitable consequences.

Political instability, invasion, or conflict can also constrain management of sites, as at Ashur in Iraq. Without a plan or supervision, the typical dangers of looting, poaching, illegal logging and destruction occur. These constraints are particularly frustrating, although many site employees brave dangerous conditions every day. Elsewhere, cultural differences mean that conservators are met with distrust and hostility from the local population.

To safeguard areas of cultural significance and protect those of outstanding natural beauty, UNESCO often assists in developing long-term "management" plans for the conservation and preservation of these sites. Plans of action to address the conservation issues are set up and committees formed to implement the measures. Some of the recommended initiatives include, as appropriate, protection from the elements for vulnerable buildings, realignment of encroaching roads, funds for the education and employment of local staff, resettlement of farmers, and discussion with local people to enable their traditional rights and practices to continue.

Manas Wildlife Sanctuary
India

IN DANGER

KEY THREATS Conflict | Theft | Development | Tourism | Pollution | Disasters | Constraints | Changing Uses | Invaders | Climate

On a gentle slope in the foothills of the Himalayas, where wooded hills give way to alluvial grasslands and tropical forests, sits the Manas Wildlife Sanctuary. Unique in being a tiger reserve, elephant reserve, national park and international biosphere reserve, as well as World Heritage Site, it is located in eastern India next to the Royal Manas Natural Park in Bhutan. Home to a great variety of wildlife, it shelters fifty-five mammals, of which fourteen are at high risk. Among these the World Conservation Union (IUCN) lists the pygmy hog, which is found nowhere else in the world, as critically endangered and the tiger, Asian one-horned rhinoceros and Indian elephant as endangered.

Manas once had the second-largest tiger population in India, as well as rare golden langurs, red pandas and the black panther, a beautiful leopard with a completely black coat. Black panthers were immortalized as Bagheera in Rudyard Kipling's children's classic The Jungle Book.

The site adjoins an even larger preserve across the Bhutanese border. Now that Bhutan has joined the 183 other signatory nations to the World Heritage Convention, it is hoped that protection can be enhanced and extended by creating a transfrontier site spanning the border.

More than 450 species of birds in the sanctuary include the largest surviving population of endangered Bengal floricans.

Other endangered mammals include the golden langur, capped langur, hoolock gibbon, particoloured flying squirrel, hispid hare, Ganges dolphin, Asiatic wild dog, hog deer and the last of the genetically pure Asiatic wild water buffalo. The IUCN species listed as vulnerable include the sloth bear, Asiatic black bear, gaur, clouded leopard, golden cat, fishing cat, marbled cat, swamp deer, Assamese macaque and smooth Indian otters. It also lists three species of amphibians, including the Assam roofed turtle, and fifty species of reptiles.

Years of Insurgency and a Park in Ruins

From 1988 to 2003 armed Bodo rebels occupied the park during their struggle to create a separate "Bodoland" in the state of Assam. The chaos led to the forced evacuation of park staff and, in the ensuing vacuum, to poaching, logging and illegal agriculture. The greater one-horned rhinoceros population was particularly devastated. No tiger census has been possible since 2000 (when only sixty-five were found), but the worst is feared as the most recent elephant count showed a 50 per cent decline in the three years from 2002 to 2005. The swamp deer is missing here, and may now be locally extinct. The park continues to suffer from a shortage of staff and from lack of funds dispersed to it, despite a Supreme Court ruling requiring their timely release. Tourism is still minimal in this poor and remote corner, although the infrastructure is gradually being rebuilt. The situation is finally improving, but after two decades with only limited management the species remain in critical danger.

⊚ World Heritage Site inscribed 1985
Inscription on the List of World Heritage in Danger: 1992
http://whc.unesco.org/en/list/338

OPPOSITE PAGE: One of the endangered mammals at Manas, the golden langur is an attractive leaf-eating monkey and, as its name suggests, its coat is a beautiful golden to creamy white. Golden langurs feed predominantly on leaves but will also eat fruit and seeds.

ABOVE RIGHT: The endangered Asian one-horned rhinoceros was particularly devastated during the years of rebel control of the park.

Minaret and Archaeological Remains of Jam
Afghanistan

IN DANGER

KEY THREATS Conflict | Theft | Development | Tourism | Pollution | Disasters | Constraints | Changing Uses | Invaders | Climate

Soaring 65 m (213 ft) into the sky, the graceful minaret of Jam is one of the oldest and most dramatic examples of Islamic architecture in Central Asia. A lonely sentinel, for more than 800 years it stands at the remote junction of two rivers in a deep narrow valley between towering mountains in western Afghanistan. It is covered in elaborate brickwork and is noted for the quality of its architecture and decoration. Representing the culmination of a regional architectural and artistic tradition, the minaret and its associated archaeological remains are an exceptional testimony to the power and quality of the Ghurid civilization who dominated the region in the twelfth and thirteenth centuries.

The minaret's origins remain shrouded in mystery – it may have been a victory tower of the Ghurids, the remnant of a mosque that has long since vanished or perhaps even a remnant of the legendary capital Firuzkoh, which was destroyed by Genghis Khan in the thirteenth century.

Forgotten in the West for centuries, the minaret was "rediscovered" in the 1930s. An expedition in 1957 finally reached the remote valley.

⊛ World Heritage Site inscribed 2002
Inscription on the List of World Heritage in Danger: 2002
http://whc.unesco.org/en/list/211

The innovative construction and ornamentation of the minaret played a significant role in the development of the arts and architecture of the Indian subcontinent and beyond. Decorated with elaborately patterned floral and geometric brickwork, the tower is unique in form – octagonal at the base, then circular and finally topped by a domed balcony supported by slender arches. Only a portion of the beautiful turquoise tiles that once graced the exterior remain. A surviving inscription in blue tiles near the top declares that it was completed in 1194 by Sultan Ghiyath ad-Din Muhammad. A double spiral stairway inside winds up to the balcony. The original entrance lies 3.9 m (13 ft) below the surface, buried in silt and sediment.

OPPOSITE PAGE: The minaret's scale and lean are clearly visible here. Protection has been installed around the base to prevent the river washing the foundation away.

ABOVE RIGHT: Although the minaret has seen increased protection in recent years, international attention also increases its vulnerability as traders in illegal antiquities are awoken to the importance of the remote, unexcavated site.

A Precarious Position

In a region which has been ravaged by war and lacking the resources to protect it properly, the Minaret of Jam is in a precarious position. During the years of conflict decorated blue tiles vanished, presumably lost to the international antiquities trade. Since the fall of the Taliban in 2001, US$1 million have been contributed to the restoration and stabilization of the Minarets of Jam and Herat. Local conservators have been trained and a proposed bridge, which could have subjected the tower to destructive vibration from traffic, has been rerouted. Although UNESCO and international donors have made important strides, stopping the minaret's lean from worsening and shoring up the eroding river bank on which it stands, much remains to be done to save the site.

BELOW LEFT: Hidden in its river valley, the minaret's remoteness adds to its problems – monitoring and guarding it are difficult.

BELOW RIGHT: The elaborate cut bricks are subject to erosion and are crumbling away rapidly.

OPPOSITE PAGE: Many of the beautiful blue tiles that decorated the minaret disappeared during the years of conflict.

Preservation in this remote valley remains a challenge – lacking adequate protection, the site has been subject to looting and illegal excavation. Without basic resources, adequate legal protection or an effective monument protection agency in a country that is in chaos, this great minaret is in extreme danger.

Ruins of Kilwa Kisiwani and Ruins of Songo Mnara
United Republic of Tanzania

IN DANGER · KEY THREATS Conflict | Theft | Development | Tourism | Pollution | Disasters | Constraints | Changing Uses | Invaders | Climate

Once the most powerful city on the East African coast, the port of Kilwa Kisiwani was a major trading hub on the Indian Ocean from the thirteenth to sixteenth centuries. Situated 280 km (175 miles) south of Zanzibar and just off the coast of southeast Tanzania, the islands of Kilwa Kisiwani and Songo Mnara contain the ruins of an extensive trading empire that thrived on the transshipment of gold, ivory, silver, iron, pearls, perfume, Arabian crockery, Persian earthenware, Chinese porcelain and slaves.

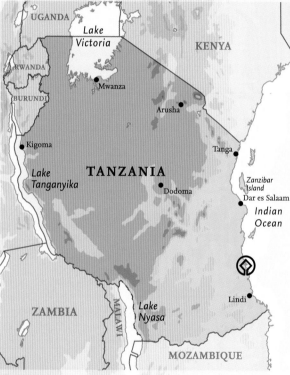

The great explorer, Ibn Battouta, who visited in 1331–1332, called Kilwa Kisiwani one of the most beautiful cities of the world.

Mentioned by John Milton in Paradise Lost, Kilwa (or "Quiloa" as its Portuguese conquerors called it) was legendary for its wealth.

◎ World Heritage Site inscribed 1981
Inscription on the List of World Heritage in Danger: 2004
http://whc.unesco.org/en/list/144

ABOVE RIGHT: Kilwa's architecture is notable for its use of domes, the earliest example of this practice on the East African coast.

Sold in the ninth century to an Arab trader from Shiraz, Kilwa Kisiwani became a small but powerful sultanate. It grew rich as the export point for gold mined near Great Zimbabwe and was the only place in sub-Saharan Africa to mint coins. At its peak during the thirteenth and fourteenth centuries it was said to be one of the world's most beautiful cities. Among the many ruins are those of a great mosque built of coral tiles in the twelfth century and expanded in the fifteenth, the Husuni Kubwa palace from the fourteenth century, the ruins of the sixteenth-century Portuguese Gereza fortress, the eighteenth-century Mukutani palace and the remains of an urban complex of numerous buildings, public spaces, burial grounds and mosques.

Abandoned and in Need of Assistance

Abandoned long ago, the site is facing rapid deterioration because of the elements, erosion and lack of maintenance. Rain comes in through the now roofless structures, washing away mortar and foundations, while trees and vegetation prise apart the masonry. Vandalism and a lack of understanding of the site contribute to its decay. The vast majority of the ancient city walls and portions of the Gereza fort, undercut by erosion, have collapsed into the sea. Some structures, such as the Husuni Kubwa palace, have been used as quarries, their coral stone burned to make lime for new building work. Although some repairs were undertaken in the 1960s, there were not the necessary resources to continue them. Tanzania has appealed for help, because without assistance these monuments will be lost forever.

Coro and its Port
Venezuela

With adobe and reinforced earthwork buildings unique to the Caribbean, brightly painted façades and cobbled streets, colonial Coro and the adjoining port of La Vela are the only remaining examples of their kind. Featuring a rich fusion of local urban tradition with Spanish Mudéjar and Dutch architectural techniques, more than 150 historic structures survive. Situated in northern present-day Venezuela, on the western side of the Gulf of Coro and Isthmus of Medanos, Coro was founded in 1527 and once served as capital of the region.

Although a number of Spanish colonial settlements on the South American coast, such as Maracaibo, once featured earthwork construction, Coro is the only one in which such structures have survived almost intact to the present day.

The site of the first bishopric in South America (1531), Coro was a hub for both Christianity and trade in the region. The cathedral, the first in the country, dates to 1583.

World Heritage Site inscribed 1993
Inscription on the List of World Heritage in Danger: 2005
http://whc.unesco.org/en/list/658

ABOVE RIGHT: Local, Dutch West Indian and Spanish traditions come together in Coro in a rich ensemble of historic structures.

Rain Plus Poor Maintenance Brings Collapse

More than a decade after being inscribed on the World Heritage List in 1993, the two cities of Coro and La Vela lack comprehensive management and conservation plans. Although some buildings are well cared for, lack of finance and expertise in this poorest of Venezuela's provinces puts the site's historic fabric in danger. Heavy rains in 2000 and between November 2004 and February 2005 damaged many structures, a situation exacerbated by the deteriorated condition of many of the historic structures. The construction and bad siting of fences and walls, made the flood damage worse. The lack of coherent management and conservation plans leads to decisions being taken on an ad hoc basis, causing further significant threat to the integrity of the site. Modern public works adjacent to the historic areas seem out of place and threaten to disrupt the relation of the city to the waterfront.

IN DANGER

KEY THREATS Conflict | Theft | Development | Tourism | Pollution | Disasters | Constraints | Changing Uses | Invaders | Climate

Ashur (Qal'at Sherqat)
Iraq

IN DANGER

KEY THREATS Conflict | Theft | Development | Tourism | Pollution | Disasters | Constraints | Changing Uses | Invaders | Climate

Founded almost 5000 years ago, the ancient town of Ashur would become the first capital of the Assyrian empire. Between the fourteenth and ninth centuries BC this city-state was a major religious, administrative and international trade hub. Even after the Assyrian capital moved to Nimrud, Ashur continued as the religious site, where the empire's kings were crowned and buried. The excavated remains of public and residential structures provide an outstanding record of the evolution of building practices for three millennia, from the Sumerian and Akkadian periods through the Assyrian to the city's brief revival in the Parthian period in the second century BC.

The city was the focus of worship of the god Ashur and goddess Ishtar (Inanna): the city and the Assyrian empire are his namesakes.

Protected by the river on two sides, and fortified by inner and outer walls, with several gateways, Ashur is shown in seventh-century BC records to have contained a large number of important religious buildings and several palaces.

◎ **World Heritage Site inscribed 2003**
Inscription on the List of World Heritage in Danger: 2003
http://whc.unesco.org/en/list/1130

OPPOSITE PAGE: Built of baked bricks, the ruins of the impressive Enlil Ziggurat (stepped pyramid) stand over the site.

ABOVE RIGHT: The site is largely intact because it has been unoccupied for most of the last 2000 years. Only a few of the structures have been excavated.

Located on a rocky bend along the Tigris in northern Iraq, Ashur sits at the boundary between areas where rain-fed and irrigation agriculture were practised. One of the oldest and best documented trading hubs of Mesopotamia, the city was destroyed twice and largely abandoned after the third century AD. The architectural and artistic record is accompanied by a large body of cuneiform texts which attest to the city's leading role in religion and scholarship, especially during the Middle and Neo-Assyrian periods.

Unguarded and Unmanaged but Spared from a Dam
Inscribed on the World Heritage List in 2003 following the fall of Saddam Hussein, the site was simultaneously placed on the List of World Heritage in Danger. Situated in a war zone, Ashur is at high risk from the instability brought on by the current conflict. Although Ashur has not been militarily targeted or damaged, because resources are limited the site lacks adequate protection and is at risk from looting. Research, which had resumed in the late 1980s after a forty-year hiatus, remains on hold. Ironically, the conflict has temporarily spared Ashur from perhaps its biggest threat – the Mak'houl dam, which was started under the administration of Saddam Hussein. Should this large dam have been completed downstream, the rising waters would have threatened to flood a portion of the site and saturate the banks and foundations of ancient structures. It is possible that the dam works may never be resumed.

IN DANGER

KEY THREATS Conflict | Theft | Development | Tourism | Pollution | Disasters | Constraints | Changing Uses | Invaders | Climate

Chan Chan Archaeological Zone
Peru

The largest pre-Columbian city in America, the vast and fragile mud-brick urban complex of Chan Chan covers roughly 20 sq km (8 sq miles). Located on the dry northern coast of Peru, not far from current day Trujillo, Chan Chan was the middle of an agricultural empire that stretched for some 1000 km (600 miles) along the Pacific coast. Chan Chan's extensive architectural ruins are noted for their high walls (as high as 11 m or 33 ft), wide streets, labyrinthine passages and intricate maritime motifs. The Chimú kingdom, with Chan Chan as its capital, reached its apogee in the fifteenth century, not long before falling to the Incas.

Estimates of the population at Chan Chan range from 30,000 to as many as 100,000 people.

The Chimú spoke a now extinct language called Yunca. There is no evidence of writing.

⊚ World Heritage Site inscribed 1986
Inscription on the List of World Heritage in Danger: 1986
http://whc.unesco.org/en/list/366

OPPOSITE PAGE: The vast adobe, or earthen, structures at Chan Chan are quickly damaged by natural erosion as they become exposed to air and rain. They require continuous conservation efforts and substantial ancillary measures.

ABOVE RIGHT: A view of Chan Chan's extensive Archaeological Zone and the encroaching farmland.

The planning of the city reflects a strict political and social strategy, marked by its division into "citadels" or "palaces" forming autonomous units. Over 500 years, a series of eleven of these large walled quadrangles were built in the 6-sq-km (2.3-sq-mile) urban core of the site. Also present are stepped pyramids and housing complexes for an estimated 12,000 artisans. The city's storerooms were found empty, but archaeological excavation shows evidence of an agricultural civilization skilled in metallurgy, woodworking and the large-scale production of ceramics, textiles and maize-beer. An extensive irrigation system and deep walk-in wells or sunken gardens are also visible.

Still in Danger After Twenty-One Years

With its vast ruins susceptible to rapid erosion from wind and rain and requiring continuous conservation efforts, Chan Chan was inscribed on the List of World Heritage in Danger in 1986 at the same time as it became a World Heritage Site. It is threatened today on numerous fronts, and because of its vast scale and the limited resources available to protect it, conservation is a great challenge. Once covered with wooden beams and terraces, the structures are now all exposed to the harsh coastal weather. The rapid growth of nearby Trujillo is threatening the site's integrity as fields march right up to the ruins, squatters have settled in the protected area and new developments rise across the landscape. Intensive irrigation is causing water levels to rise dangerously under the site – structures have collapsed and emergency drainage trenches are now being cut.

Pollution from agricultural runoff and dumping of refuse is also a concern, as are increasing numbers of tourists who wear away the fragile remains, walking and cycling across the site. Looting has been a problem ever since the Spanish conquest. Climate is an increasing worry: in 1998 the impact of El Niño, the abnormal advance of warm water to the eastern Pacific which affects climate world-wide, was unusually strong, leading to torrential rain and flooding. With assistance from the World Heritage Fund, emergency measures were taken to protect some of the most exposed ruins, and the site escaped with relatively minor damage. The World Heritage Committee has recommended that excavation work should be halted unless it is accompanied by appropriate conservation measures,

BELOW RIGHT: These carvings of warriors show signs of the erosion that is threatening the whole site.

BELOW LEFT: La Huaca Arco Iris (Rainbow Temple) is named after the rainbow friezes that adorn its walls.

OPPOSITE PAGE: Intricate patterns of fish and other sea creatures decorate the complex which runs along the Pacific coast.

and that all possible steps must be taken to control plundering of the site. Over the last two decades significant progress in management has been made with the development of plans and procedures and the training of personnel. But with limited funding and follow-up, and a vast area to protect, the site remains in danger.

Walled City of Baku/Shirvanshah's Palace/Maiden Tower
Azerbaijan

IN DANGER

KEY THREATS Conflict | Theft | Development | Tourism | Pollution | Disasters | Constraints | Changing Uses | Invaders | Climate

Built on a site inhabited since the Palaeolithic period, the Walled City of Baku reveals evidence of Zoroastrian, Sasanian, Arabic, Persian, Shirvani, Ottoman and Russian presences in its cultural continuity. Located on the Apsheron peninsula in present-day Azerbaijan on the Caspian Sea, Baku was part of the state of Shirvan from the ninth century until 1538 when it was annexed by Safavid Iran. In 1585, it was captured by the Ottomans, and was largely destroyed by fire in 1723 when occupied by the Russian General Matushkin. Noted for the Inner City's (Icheri Sheher) twelfth-century defensive walls and Maiden Tower (Giz Galasy), the fifteenth-century Shirvanshah's Palace is one of the pearls of Azerbaijani architecture.

⊛ World Heritage Site inscribed 2000
Inscription on the List of World Heritage in Danger: 2003
http://whc.unesco.org/en/list/958

OPPOSITE PAGE: This view from the Maiden Tower shows ancient buildings surrounded by more modern ones.

ABOVE RIGHT: The ruins of the Hamman (baths) at the Shirvanshah's Palace.

Built after Baku replaced Shamaha as the capital, the Shirvanshah's Palace survived until the eighteenth century when much of its upper floors were destroyed by a Russian naval bombardment. Its looted treasures, initially taken to Tabriz, were subsequently transferred to the Topkapi Palace in Istanbul.

The unique Maiden Tower is an astonishing eight-floor cylindrical structure 16.5 m (54 ft) in diameter. Its walls are 5 m (16.5 ft) thick at the base and 3.2–4 m (10.5–13 ft) at the top. The bottom three levels are thought to date from as early as the seventh or sixth centuries BC and to have been an astronomical observatory or fire temple.

There is a shaft still visible in niches at the back of the Maiden Tower. Extending 15 m (50 ft) below ground level, it appears to have been designed to channel natural gas to fuel an eternal flame at the top – making this a true fire temple.

The walls of the old town, which survive on the western and northern sides, were built by Menutsshochr Shah in the twelfth century and repaired in the nineteenth century. The narrow streets are congested with houses dating from the late-eighteenth century but also contain earlier monuments, mostly concentrated in the lower, seaward site of the town, including mosques, schools, baths, Zoroastrian fire temples and caravanserais.

Destructive Reconstructions Follow Earthquake

Struck by a massive, magnitude 6.7 earthquake in November 2000, Baku sustained significant loss, with more than 70 per cent of its structures damaged. Relatively intact up until the last preceding decades, in the wake of the earthquake, and with no conservation policies in place, the urban fabric quickly began to fray as damaged buildings were demolished and the sites released for new building projects. Dubious restorations and rapid urban development have subsequently dismantled much of the city's remaining historic form. Demand for office space, driven by an oil boom, has spurred construction. The medieval limit of two floors has quickly given way to three and four, and modern materials clash with traditional ones. With new buildings blocking views and encroaching on historic streets, and minimal resources to preserve public monuments, historic Baku is on the verge of disappearing.

Salonga National Park
Democratic Republic of the Congo

IN DANGER

KEY THREATS Conflict | Theft | Development | Tourism | Pollution | Disasters | Constraints | Changing Uses | Invaders | Climate

Spanning 36,000 sq km (13,900 sq miles), Salonga National Park encompasses the largest tract of protected tropical rainforest in the world. Situated at the heart of the Congo River basin in one of the most remote regions in central Africa, the park is extremely isolated and accessible only by water. Significant among the many endemic endangered species here is the little-known bonobo or dwarf chimpanzee, man's closest relative. This World Conservation Union (IUCN) red-listed species is not found in any other protected area on earth.

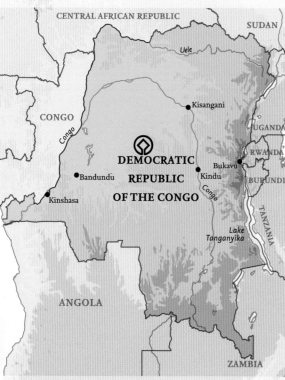

⊚ World Heritage Site inscribed 1984
Inscription on the List of World Heritage in Danger: 1999
http://whc.unesco.org/en/list/280

The bonobo (Pan paniscus) or pygmy chimpanzee was the last great ape species to be discovered, and could be the first to go extinct. More than 98 per cent (perhaps as much as 99.4 per cent) of this chimpanzee's DNA matches man's, a higher amount than we share with even gorillas.

Key birds include the endemic and vulnerable Congo peacock, crowned eagle, grey parrot, and African dwarf kingfisher.

The park is huge, encompassing an area bigger than the Democratic Republic of the Congo's former colonial power of Belgium.

The rivers in the park serve as both transport and communication routes because there are no roads.

OPPOSITE PAGE: A large female Bonobo (or dwarf chimpanzee) with her two-year-old-offspring. Bonobos are an endangered species, due to both habitat loss and hunting for bushmeat, the latter having increased dramatically at Salonga.

ABOVE RIGHT: The Goliath heron is one of the many species to be found in the Salonga National Park – Africa's largest tropical rainforest reserve.

Interlaced with water, and composed of two sectors of roughly equal size, the park ranges from low swamp-forested plateau to river terraces and high dry-forest. Systematic inventories of wildlife are needed, but other species known to be here include numerous primates, the endemic Congo peacock and the African and slender-snouted or "false" crocodile. Both subspecies of African elephant Loxodonta africana cyclotis and L. a. africana used to be very common in the park; only a few are thought to have survived years of savage poaching.

Under-funded, Under-equipped and Under-trained
Although less directly affected than the country's other four World Heritage Sites by the years of strife, Salonga has also suffered. For several decades it has received little or no domestic financial support, functioning as a park primarily on paper. With minimal resources and vast and difficult terrain, the under-funded, under-equipped and under-trained staff has been able to offer only limited resistance to widespread poaching of bonobos, forest elephants, grey parrots and other species. During the 1990s, the influx of automatic weapons and presence of armed rebel groups led to widespread poaching. Dedicated staff and international assistance have brought some progress in recent years, but a comprehensive management plan, sustainable funding and training are still badly needed. There is fear that without strong management when stability returns to the region, large-scale logging concessions, followed by roads, settlers, deforestation and renewed poaching, could undo the recent steps forward.

Historical Monuments of Thatta
Pakistan

AT RISK

KEY THREATS Conflict | Theft | Development | Tourism | Pollution | Disasters | Constraints | Changing Uses | Invaders | Climate

Situated some 100 km (60 miles) east of Karachi at the apex of the Indus delta near the coast of the Arabian Sea, Thatta was for 400 years a thriving capital. The seat of three successive dynasties (Samma, Arghun and Tarkhan), and later ruled by the Mughal emperors of Delhi, it was continually embellished from the fourteenth to the eighteenth centuries. Noted for its fusion of diverse influences into a unique architectural style – including its original concept of intricate carved stone and brick decoration – the remains of the city and its necropolis provide a unique view of civilization in Sind.

The mosque of Dagbir and numerous mausolea and tombs (including that of Diwan Shurfa Khan) feature colourful brickwork and glazed tiles.

Kings, queens, governors, saints, scholars, philosophers and soldiers are all buried here.

⊛ World Heritage Site inscribed 1981
http://whc.unesco.org/en/list/143

ABOVE RIGHT: The tomb of Prince Sultan Ibrahim bin Norza Mohammad Isa Tarkhan has stood here since the eleventh century.

The golden age of Thatta is still visible in the high quality brick- and stonework of the remaining monuments, including the tombs of Jam Nizamuddin (1461–1509) and Isa Khan Tarkhan the Younger and of his father Jan Baba. A number of monuments have vivid enamel tiles which were lavishly used for dadoes, panels and other decoration. The grand mosque of Shah Jahan (from 1644–1647), with its tiled complex of blue and white buildings capped by ninety-three domes, is unique. The nearby Makli Hills contain over 500,000 tombs and graves spread over an area of 10 sq km (4 sq miles), making this the largest Muslim necropolis in the world.

A Race Against the Elements
The city fell into neglect after 1739 when it was ceded to the Shah of Iran and has been in a steady decline ever since. Located on a ridge and exposed for eight months of the year to harsh and saline southwesterly winds off the Arabian Sea, the detailed brickwork is gradually disappearing. Rains, topsoil erosion and a shifting riverbed are adding to the decay. Subject to looting and disasters such as earthquakes, the site is on tenuous ground. Caring for a funerary complex of this scale would be a challenge anywhere, but with limited resources and other significant sites such as Moenjodaro to also care for, Pakistan has warned it is losing the battle against the elements. Inscribed on the World Heritage List in 1981 and on the World Monument Fund's 2006 List of Most Endangered Sites, Thatta is in urgent need of assistance.

Um er-Rasas (Kastrom Mefa'a)
Jordan

Located in central Jordan 60 km (35 miles) south of Amman and 35 km (25 miles) east of the Dead Sea on the fertile plateau of Madaba, the largely unexcavated site of Um er-Rasas offers a valuable, well-preserved archaeological record of the life of a small frontier town from the third to ninth centuries AD. Its most visible remains include a tall stone "stylite" tower, the only known remnant of an ascetic monastic movement once common in this part of the world, and a Byzantine mosaic with an incredible depiction of towns in Palestine, Jordan and Egypt, including their names.

AT RISK

KEY THREATS Conflict | Theft | Development | Tourism | Pollution | Disasters | Constraints | Changing Uses | Invaders | Climate

⦿ World Heritage Site inscribed 2004
http://whc.unesco.org/en/list/1093

ABOVE RIGHT: The site's richly decorated mosaic floors are at risk from both salt damage and looting.

The limes, or border, of the Roman Empire stretched in a series of towers, walls and fortified camps from Britain, through Europe to the Black Sea, and from there to the Red Sea and across North Africa to the Atlantic coast. It is marked in Germany and the United Kingdom by the "Frontiers of the Roman Empire" World Heritage Site, which includes Hadrian's Wall.

The fortress of Kastron Mefaa, built in around AD 300, has a 2-m (6.5-ft) thick solid perimeter wall, reinforced by corner towers and two main gates, one in the north, and another in the south. The massive mortar-less walls are made of large undressed blocks of stone wedged with smaller stones.

Um er-Rasas is surrounded by, and dotted with, remains of ancient farming, from reservoirs to terracing, water channels, dams and cisterns.

Mentioned in the Bible and Roman and Arabic sources, Kastrom Mefa'a, as it was once called, began as a Roman cavalry camp. At the edge of the desert and possibly on a branch of the incense route, its roughly 150-m (400-ft) square fortified castrum (still largely unexcavated) formed part of the empire's border. By the end of the fifth century, the site was a town and a number of Byzantine churches were built in an open area north of the castrum and the 13-m (42-ft) high, square stairless tower used by followers of St Simeon Stylites to sit in isolation. Deserted and unoccupied after the Umayyad period, the city has survived relatively undisturbed for the last 1200 years.

Still Neglected After 1200 Years

Um er-Rasas managed to survive in the arid climate through isolation. Archaeological work, which began in 1986, and World Heritage status, have brought attention to it. Today it suffers from a lack of management capacity and financial and personnel resources. Without clear boundaries or a fenced perimeter, the site is at risk from urban encroachment and illegal excavations. In the last few years the number of exposed and dangerous open pits and trenches has grown as looters have pockmarked the site. With no paths or signs here, visitors walk and climb upon the fragile remains. Poor reconstructions are ongoing, while fragile important mosaics have been left exposed to the elements – the mosaics in St Stephen's Church are showing signs of saline efflorescence damage. Tourist development of the site, especially in the current condition, would be especially damaging.

Rock-Hewn Churches of Lalibela
Ethiopia

GUARDED | KEY THREATS Conflict | Theft | Development | Tourism | Pollution | Disasters | Constraints | Changing Uses | Invaders | Climate

Hewn from solid rock, the expertly carved medieval churches of Lalibela have been a sacred place of pilgrimage and devotion for Ethiopian Christians for centuries. Hidden away in the volcanic hills in the north of the country, these eleven unique monolithic cave churches are recessed below the ground level and linked by an extensive system of trenches and tunnels. Everything from doors, windows and detailing, to the elaborately decorated interiors, was cut out of the bedrock. The site's placement in the landscape next to a traditional village with circular stone dwellings makes it of unique aesthetic value.

Cut from soft, red volcanic tuff, the structures sit on an underlying dark basalt.

Discoveries made during restoration work in the twentieth century suggest that some of the churches may have been used originally as fortifications and royal residences.

◎ World Heritage Site inscribed 1978
http://whc.unesco.org/en/list/18

OPPOSITE PAGE: The walls of the churches are prone to damage from water both inside and out.

ABOVE RIGHT: The churches were carved straight into the volcanic tuff below ground level.

Attributed to King Lalibela (late twelfth–early thirteenth century) of the Zagwe Dynasty, this "New Jerusalem" may have been built as a pilgrimage site after Jerusalem fell under Muslim rule. Tended by Coptic priests, the churches still attract thousands of pilgrims on major holy days.

Worn Down by Centuries of Wind and Rain

The rock-hewn churches of Lalibela are in danger of wearing away. These large monolithic stone structures are suffering from chemical and physical weathering, as rain, wind, salts and mechanical erosion degrade the rock. In a seismically active region, cracks have allowed water to penetrate, threatening the sculptures and murals inside. Photographs reveal serious decay in the paintings over the last thirty years and some sculpted elements are no longer recognizable. Critical structural problems are also a threat: experts warn Biet Amanuel is in danger of imminent collapse. Although Biet Aba Libanos and Biet Mercurios are now presumed to be stable, in the past they have suffered from slippage and structural failures. The traditional village, which is integral to the site and its upkeep, is in turn at risk from urban development and serious sanitation problems.

Restorations in the 1950s and 1960s stabilized some areas but affected others. With major new support from the European Union, the government of Norway and the World Monuments Fund, the site is receiving much-needed assistance. With UNESCO's help, a lightweight temporary protective shelter is being deployed to replace the tin roof, while research continues and long-term solutions are sought.

CHANGING USES

At the opposite end of the spectrum from development, some of our richest heritage is threatened not by new infrastructure but by shifting populations in a modern world and the resulting changing patterns of usage. From outright abandonment and the decay that comes with it, to encroaching agriculture and grazing in once virgin lands, changing uses are placing a growing amount of our heritage in danger.

As communities adjust to a shifting social and economic climate, inhabitants may abandon traditional housing for more modern accommodation with all its conveniences. Although places like the Pueblo de Taos in the American southwest have survived for centuries by ingeniously adjusting to the external world and adopting what they needed, the greatly accelerated pace of change today leaves little time to adapt. Communal living give way to individual housing, and traditional building methods and materials are replaced by automated processes and mass-produced components, leading to visually incompatible structures. Sometimes in the rush to adopt modern methods, the centuries-old rationale for traditional construction is forgotten or lost, from the raised houses of the Philippine Rice Terraces which kept vermin and moisture from grain, to the thick adobe walls of the Pueblos that once helped regulate temperature without the need for costly air conditioning. Change is complex and often hard to judge from the outside — who is to say that just to preserve a tradition a community should not have the modern conveniences everyone else has?

The lure of the modern world means that younger generations are abandoning traditional family life for employment in larger towns and cities, giving up low-paid work for higher-paid jobs outside the family. The traditional way of life is dying out and only the older generations remain to work their fields or small businesses; the economic circumstances of all but the most affluent do not permit them to hire additional workers, with the result that eventually land and historic buildings are abandoned or left in disrepair. With tourism increasingly the last viable source of income, a growing number of sites are at a difficult crossroads, left to choose between losing their tradition altogether, or performing staged ceremonies every hour on the hour for the cameras.

Elsewhere, the closing down of industrial areas has led to abandonment, and ghost towns such as the historic sites of the Humberstone and Santa Laura Saltpeter Works in Chile, are left to decay, at risk from structural collapse and prey to the elements and looters. A last vestige of a bygone era, these industrial company towns were once key to the growth of industrialized agriculture but are today more valuable to looters for the timbers holding the buildings up than for the ore in the ground or the heritage preserved in the vacant structures.

Incoming industry and agriculture provide work, but also degradation, with overgrazing, land clearance, pollution by pesticides and fertilizers, and other environmental risks. Forced irrigation and land reclamation causes water tables to rise, weakening the structure of the soil and damaging underground sites of interest.

Action to limit the negative effect of changing use in World Heritage Sites takes many forms. Water tables are lowered by means of drainage ditches and pipes, inside and around archaeological areas, and efficient systems for monitoring water levels are established. Protection zones to control urban development and conserve archaeological reserves are created, while regulations aim to avoid development that does not harmonize with ancient buildings and sites. These might include a policy of ensuring that all repair and reconstruction work is carried out using traditional materials and techniques, and ensuring that discordant elements, such as inappropriate doors, are repaired or replaced using harmonious designs and materials.

Rice Terraces of the Philippine Cordilleras
Philippines

IN DANGER

KEY THREATS Conflict | Theft | Development | Tourism | Pollution | Disasters | Constraints | Changing Uses | Invaders | Climate

For 2000 years, the high rice fields of the Ifugao have followed the contours of the mountains. The fruit of knowledge handed down from one generation to the next, and the expression of sacred traditions and a delicate social balance, today they are part of a landscape of great beauty that expresses the harmony between humankind and the environment. On the island of Luzon in the Philippines, these remote mountain terraces have been called "Stairways to Heaven."

⊗ World Heritage Site inscribed 1995
Inscribed on the List of World Heritage in Danger: 2001
http://whc.unesco.org/en/list/722

The terraces span 200 sq km (77 sq miles) and if laid end to end would stretch half-way around the Earth. They average 2–3 m (6.5–10 ft) in height, although some can reach up to 6 or 7 m (20 or 23 ft).

The Ifugao live in stilt houses reached by a ladder. Rice is stored in the attic under steeply pitched thatched roofs, while smoke from the fire in the one-room dwelling below helps to keep mice away. A centrally located ritual rice field is the first parcel to be planted and harvested. Near villages is a ritual hill, usually marked by a grove of sacred betel trees where holy men (mumbaki) carry out traditional rites.

The forty epic tales ("Hudhud") traditionally chanted during planting and harvest have been inscribed as Masterpieces of the Oral and Intangible Heritages of Humanity by UNESCO.

High in the Philippine Cordilleras, the fields climb like giant steps from the base of the mountains to the peaks, up slopes as steep as 70 degrees. They are irrigated by mountain streams and springs that have been diverted into ancient canals and through bamboo pipes, bringing water down terrace by terrace from holding pools by gravity alone.

The terraced fields of the Cordilleras are said to be unique in both their extent and their altitude – at up to 1500 m (5000 ft). The site includes five major groups of terraces: Banaue – home to the Ifugao carvers and the Ikat weavers – is the most famous; Batad features spectacular tiered, amphitheater-shaped terraces; Mayoyao is known for its organic red and white Tinawon rice; Hapao has stone-walled terraces dating to AD 650 and Kiangan is the site of the vast and stunning Nagacadan and Julungan terraces. Long beyond the reach of foreign influence, the Ifugao, or "people of the hills" have managed to preserve their ancestral way of life and animistic traditions. For centuries, the orally transferred techniques in use here have remained virtually unchanged, with a near-total absence of chemicals or other modern interventions.

OPPOSITE PAGE: Built by the Igorot over 2000 years ago with only primitive tools, the terraces are a national treasure in the Philippines.

ABOVE RIGHT: Traditional stilt houses allow villagers to live among the rice fields and be protected from rodents and the damp.

A Vanishing Culture

For 2000 years the rice terraces have existed in harmony with the native people of the Cordilleras, passed from father to eldest son. Yet today they are at risk of being lost as younger generations leave for the cities and the lure of a modern life. Able to earn far more in industry, farming flat valley fields with tractors or as tourguides, others have sold up or moved on. Deforestation, damming of rivers for hydroelectricity and unregulated development compound the problem. Rats and giant worms have invaded fields, causing leaks and crop loss. A major earthquake in 1990 altered the flow of mountain streams and disrupted ancient water courses, causing erosion and terrace failure. With one third of the ancient fields abandoned and collapsing, the site and its culture are in grave danger.

Yet there is hope. UNESCO and the Philippines launched a major effort with the former governor of Ifugao to find solutions and non-governmental organizations such as "RICE" have begun marketing the organically grown and delicately aromatic rice in international markets, helping to bring financial benefit to this extremely poor region. Old traditions are being revived; twelve annual Ifugao rituals associated with rice production that had not been performed for decades have recently been resurrected.

Abu Mena
Egypt

IN DANGER

KEY THREATS Conflict | Theft | Development | Tourism | Pollution | Disasters | Constraints | Changing Uses | Invaders | Climate

Once Egypt's most important pilgrimage destination, the early Christian settlement of Abu Mena reached its peak at the end of the fifth or early in the sixth century. The church, baptistry, basilicas, streets, monasteries, houses and workshops were built around the tomb of the martyr Menas of Alexandria, who died in AD 296. Located in Egypt's Mariut Desert, 75 km (47 miles) southwest of Alexandria, the "Marble City" of Abu Mena grew up around a natural oasis. Menas, an officer in Diocletian's army, refused to kill Christians who had been defeated by his troops. Martyred after declaring his Christianity, he was buried on the way back from Phrygia, where it is said the camel carrying his body refused to walk any further.

Mediterranean Sea

ISRAEL
WEST BANK
GAZA
Alexandria
JORDAN
Giza • Cairo
SAUDI ARABIA
Nile
LIBYA
EGYPT
Luxor
Aswan
Red Sea
Lake Nasser
SUDAN

World Heritage Site inscribed 1979
Inscribed on the List of World Heritage in Danger: 2001
http://whc.unesco.org/en/list/90

Constructed in the fifth century to accommodate the increasing number of Christian pilgrims, the thermal basilica stored the medicinal waters that were used for the heated baths and pools. Pilgrims would fill tiny flasks with water from it, and these, stamped with the seal of St Menas, showing the martyr standing between two kneeling camels, have been found widely distributed in the Roman world. During the fifth and sixth centuries, many buildings were erected around the thermal basilica, including a monastery on its north side.

Abu Mena was described in awestruck language by the eleventh-century geographer Al-Bakri and other medieval visitors: it was said to have been built of marble and was decorated with magnificent mosaics and statues.

OPPOSITE PAGE: Excavations, which began in the early twentieth century, have to date gradually unearthed ten major buildings and an entire town.

ABOVE RIGHT: The holy city of Abu Mena grew up around an oasis. Ironically, it is on the List of World Heritage in Danger due to its vulnerability to groundwater erosion.

Menas' crypt was soon found to have miraculous powers and the small oasis grew rapidly. By AD 600, it had become a pilgrimage city, focused on a great thermal basilica complex.

Underwater in a Desert!

As the surrounding parched desert has been reclaimed for agriculture, Abu Mena has been literally flooded and is collapsing into the ground. Since irrigation started in the 1960s, the water table has been rising. A land-reclamation scheme, funded by the World Bank, has accelerated the problem in the last decade. The water table, which until 1988 had stood approximately 35 m (115 ft) below ground, has now risen to within just 10 cm (4 inches) of the surface in some places. The local clay soil, although hard when dry, becomes semi-liquid when wet and loses its ability to support structures. Buried cisterns have collapsed and huge cavities have opened in the ground. Salt is efflorescing on exposed stonework. Further threats come from looters who continue to raid the inadequately guarded site.

In a desperate attempt to save the remaining buildings, the bases of some, including the crypt of Abu Mena, have been closed and filled with sand. A large banked road had to be constructed to allow movement within the waterlogged site. Egypt's heritage body, the Supreme Council of Antiquities, has worked to enlarge the listed area. Yet the damage continues despite efforts to ring the site with deep trenches in order to drain excess water away. The lack of adequate resources and personnel for the huge task have added to the challenge.

Humberstone and Santa Laura Saltpeter Works
Chile

IN DANGER

KEY THREATS Conflict | Theft | Development | Tourism | Pollution | Disasters | Constraints | Changing Uses | Invaders | Climate

The ghost towns of Humberstone and Santa Laura in the northern Chilean Altiplano (high plains) were established in 1872 to process the world's largest saltpeter (saltpetre) deposit. For more than eighty years people here refined the caliche ore to produce sodium nitrate. Used in explosives before World War I, sodium nitrate went on to become the fertilizer that transformed vast agricultural tracts in North and South America and Europe and to produce great wealth for Chile.

Following the synthesis of ammonia by Haber and Bosch, the fertilizer industry changed and the economic value of saltpeter began a long decline.

The saltpeter mines and their associated company towns developed into an extensive and very distinctive urban community with their own language, organization, customs and creative expressions, as well as technical entrepreneurship.

Characterized by lovely buildings in the English style, the adjacent towns were founded by James Thomas Humberstone and Guillermo Wendell in 1872.

World Heritage Site inscribed 2005
Inscription on the List of World Heritage in Danger: 2005
http://whc.unesco.org/en/list/1178

OPPOSITE PAGE: When the mines and processing works were closed in the 1960s, the buildings were left to rot, creating a ghostly landscape of rusting metal.

ABOVE RIGHT: Now that much of the metal has been looted, the Douglas fir timbers, which are preserved by the dry climate, are at risk of theft.

Situated in the remote pampa near one of the driest spots on Earth, the Atacama Desert, this is where thousands of pampinos lived and worked until the mines were closed in 1960. The now abandoned company towns, in one of the most hostile environments imaginable, contain more than 200 former saltpeter works where Chileans, Peruvians and Bolivians lived together and forged a distinctive communal pampino culture. That culture was manifest in their rich language, creativity and solidarity and, above all, in their pioneering struggle for social justice, which had a profound impact on social history.

A Ghost Town Stripped of its Past

With the closure of the mines in 1960, the towns were soon abandoned. Although a foresighted Chilean, Isidoro Andia, bought the land to preserve the great structures, they soon succumbed to looting. An ancient locomotive from the site has found its way back to England and in recent years structures such as the leaching plant have been stripped of their timber. Looters first targeted the site for its metal, but today it is the old-growth Douglas fir used in its construction that is the prime target. Designed to be easy to move as mining operations shifted, the lightweight structures have suffered from almost half a century without maintenance and are collapsing even in this arid climate. Several buildings, such as the leaching house, will collapse without repair. Unless action is taken soon, this remarkable reminder of the industrial age will soon disappear.

Historic Town of Zabid
Yemen

IN DANGER

KEY THREATS Conflict | Theft | Development | Tourism | Pollution | Disasters | Constraints | Changing Uses | Invaders | Climate

Zabid's domestic and military architecture and its urban plan make it an outstanding archaeological and historical site. Besides being the capital of Yemen from the thirteenth century to the fifteenth, the city played an important role in the Arab and Muslim world for many centuries because of its Islamic university.

Zabid's glistening white traditional buildings were made from stucco-covered baked brick and richly embellished with geometric patterns and calligraphy.

Residential areas still follow ancient street patterns and include mud-brick houses with thatched roofs built around courtyards.

◎ World Heritage Site inscribed 1993
Inscription on the List of World Heritage in Danger: 2000
http://whc.unesco.org/en/list/611

OPPOSITE PAGE: Even the minaret of the Great Mosque was covered in stucco decoration.

ABOVE RIGHT: Owner-maintained structures show the past magnificence of Zabid's traditional architecture.

The city is situated on the eastern edge of Yemen's Tihamal coastal plain, a short distance from the Red Sea. It became a major hub and capital under the Abbasid Ibn Ziyad in AD 820, the same year that its Great Mosque was founded. This capital of large areas of southwestern Arabia had thick circular fortifications to protect it, but suffered destruction twice over the next few centuries, because of attacks by the Najahids and Mahdids. It was rebuilt and at its height featured canals, fountains, plazas and some 240 mosques. After the end of the Tahrid dynasty in the sixteenth century, it fell into a long period of decline. Today it is a fraction of its former size.

Decline and Destruction

Zabid is in rapid decline and in a very poor state of conservation. Experts estimate that in recent years more than 50 per cent of the city's historic houses have been replaced by modern concrete block structures. The rest, together with the ancient souk, are deteriorating, with historic buildings abandoned and collapsing and termites rampant. There is extensive unplanned and illegal construction, disrupting the historic fabric and invading public spaces and courtyards. Unsightly water towers and masts, as well as twenty-five new high-rise buildings invade the skyline. Elaborate ancient wooden doors have been replaced with sheet metal. A lack of care is apparent – although it has now been cleared, the souk was until recently knee deep in litter and detritus. The Yemeni government has sought international assistance and asked for Zabid to be inscribed on the List of World Heritage in Danger in order to help to save it.

Simien National Park
Ethiopia

IN DANGER

KEY THREATS Conflict | Theft | Development | Tourism | Pollution | Disasters | Constraints | Changing Uses | Invaders | Climate

Massive erosion over millennia on the high Ethiopian plateau has created one of the most spectacular landscapes in the world, with jagged mountain peaks, deep valleys and sharp precipices dropping some 1500 m (5000 ft). One of the first World Heritage Sites, inscribed in 1978, the park is home to the critically endangered walia ibex, a mountain goat found nowhere else on the planet, and the endangered Simien fox (also known as the Ethiopian wolf), the rarest canid in the world.

This rugged 75-million-year-old landscape of igneous basalts is pierced by soaring pinnacles, the last remnants of volcanic plugs whose surroundings have eroded away.

⊚ World Heritage Site inscribed 1978
Inscription on the List of World Heritage in Danger: 1996
http://whc.unesco.org/en/list/9

OPPOSITE PAGE: The Gishe Abbai is considered by many to be the sacred source of the Blue Nile. The high plateau of the mountains is deeply cut by gorges and waterfalls.

ABOVE RIGHT: Once almost extinct, the gelada baboon is making a comeback here. Unable to climb trees, it was easy prey. Feeding on alpine grasses, the gentle creature still faces long-term threats from encroaching farmland and climate change.

Fewer than 500 Simien foxes (Canis simensis) survive in isolated high mountain pockets in Ethiopia. It is almost gone from the park, and survives primarily in the south of the country. Numbers collapsed in the early 1990s because of rabies, until a massive vaccination programme of 40,000 domestic dogs – the source of the infection – reduced the losses. However, with its territory shrinking, the species population has fallen by 25 per cent in the last three years. A specialized carnivore, it is a close relative of grey wolves and coyotes and lives in large family packs with an intricate social structure.

The critically endangered walia ibex is now confined to roughly 25 km (15 miles) of the northern escarpment of the Simien mountains. Strikingly coloured, with a chestnut-brown coat, white belly and magnificent arching horns, it is an unforgettable sight as it roams the jagged cliffs. Once hunted to near extinction for its horns and meat, with fewer than 200 remaining in the world by 1963, the species may now number 500 individuals, but its extremely limited natural habitat means that it remains at extreme risk.

Ras Dejen, the highest point in Ethiopia, and fifth highest in Africa at 4533 m (14,872 ft), overlooks the park – work is in progress to extend the protected area to include it. The region is much cooler than the surrounding African lowlands, experiencing temperature drops occasionally as low as –18 °C (0 °F). Twenty-one mammals, including seven endemic species, are found here. In addition to the ibex and wolf, are gelada, hamadryas and anubis baboons, black-and-white vervet, colobus monkey, serval, leopard, caracal, wild cat, spotted hyena, golden jackal and several large herbivores, including bushbuck, bush duiker and klipspringer. Sixty-three bird species, including twenty-five raptors, can be found, including the rare lammergeier.

Teetering on the Brink

Although the walia ibex is an expert at balancing on the precarious slopes, it and the Simien fox are teetering on the edge of extinction as their habitats shrink. Ethiopia's highlands are among the most densely populated in the world and with the human population inside the park growing by 2 per cent a year, encroachment by grazing, roads and villages is a serious problem. A quarter of the protected area was under cultivation in 2000, and 60 per cent of the grasslands overgrazed, with only 15 per cent in their natural state. Strife in this region near the Eritrean border has compounded the management challenges – in the 1980s most facilities were destroyed and renewed conflict in the last decade has made enforcement of order difficult.

Historic Areas of Istanbul
Turkey

AT RISK

KEY THREATS Conflict | Theft | Development | Tourism | Pollution | Disasters | Constraints | Changing Uses | Invaders | Climate

At a strategic location on the Bosphorus peninsula between the Balkans (in Europe) and Anatolia (in Asia) and separating the Black Sea and the Mediterranean, Istanbul has been associated with major political, religious and artistic events for more than 2000 years. Spanning East and West and Christianity and Islam, it has been a bridge between civilizations and capital of the Eastern Roman Empire (AD 330–395), Byzantine Empire (395–1204 and 1261–1453), Latin Empire (1204–1261) and Ottoman Empire (1453–1922). The site includes four zones: the Archaeological Park at the tip of the peninsula, the Süleymaniye quarter, the Zeyrek quarter and the zone of the ramparts.

⊚ World Heritage Site inscribed 1985
http://whc.unesco.org/en/list/356

OPPOSITE PAGE: The Church of the Holy Wisdom, known as Hagia Sophia in Greek and Aya Sofya in Turkish, is a former Byzantine church and former Ottoman mosque. Now a museum, Hagia Sophia is universally acknowledged as one of the great buildings of the world.

ABOVE RIGHT: Designed by the Ottoman Empire's greatest architect, Sinan, the Mosque of Suleyman (Süleymaniye) dominates the city's Third Hill, just north of Istanbul University, overlooking the Golden Horn.

The fortified walls, stretching from the Golden Horn to the Sea of Marmara, span Roman, Byzantine and Crusader architecture and are considered to be some of the most remarkable standing fortifications. They have been in disrepair since they were damaged by an earthquake in 1894, and either abandoned or appropriated into houses and other structures.

Istanbul's history goes back 5000 years. The Greek city of Byzantion was established on the earlier Thracian Lygos in 667 BC. Roman Emperor Constantine proclaimed it the site of his new capital Constantinople in AD 330. Later it was variously called Stamboul and Tsarigrad before Istanbul was adopted as the official name shortly after the founding of modern Turkey.

The fourth-century Hagia Irene is the oldest standing Byzantine church in the city. Its interior mosaics were removed during the iconoclastic period and replaced with simple crosses.

During the Fourth Crusade in 1204 the city was sacked and many of the great treasures were taken back to Venice, including the Statue of the Tetrarchs and the four bronze horses of the Hippodrome which later graced the façade of St Mark's in Venice.

Istanbul's masterpieces include the ancient Hippodrome of Constantine, the sixth-century Hagia Sophia (Aya Sofya) and the sixteenth-century Süleymaniye Mosque, all now under threat from the pressures of population, industrial pollution and uncontrolled urbanization.

The four protected areas illustrate the major successive phases in the city's history. The ancient city and capital of the Eastern Roman Empire is represented in the Hippodrome of Constantine (AD 324), the aqueduct of Valens (378), and the extensive ramparts (begun in 413 by order of Theodosius II) with their fifty-five gates. The Byzantine capital is highlighted by the churches of Hagia Sophia and Hagia Irene (Aya Irini) from the period of Justinian (527–565), the former Church of the Pantocrator (now the mosque of Zeyrek Camii) in the Zeyrek quarter (founded by Empress Irene in the twelfth century), the old Church of the Holy Saviour in Chora (now the Kariye Museum) with its fourteenth- and fifteenth-century mosaics, and the seventh-to-twelfth-century modifications of the Constantinian walls. The Ottoman capital is illustrated in the great Topkapi Palace (Topkapi Sarayi) and Blue Mosque (Sultanahment Camii), the sixteenth-century Sehzade and Süleymaniye mosques by the great architect Mimar Sinan and the vernacular vestiges of the settlement including more than 500 protected wooden houses.

Caught Between Present and Past

Squeezed within a huge metropolis, the Historic Areas of Istanbul are under threat from modernization and a burgeoning population and Istanbul's heritage is

jeopardized by development, pollution and uncontrolled urbanization. In particular, the vernacular wooden houses in Istanbul are at risk from abandonment and shifting uses, as people have moved on. Although the city has been rebuilt many times following earthquakes, fires and invasions, the current pace of change presents new challenges. From the launch by UNESCO of an international safeguarding campaign in 1983 to current assistance from the European Union in preserving the timber structures of Zeyrek, and the efforts of the World Monuments Fund to focus attention on the derelict walls, the global community has been active in helping to preserve Istanbul's past. Yet the challenges remain great in a city of this size – without action the history of the "Queen of Cities" will continue to disappear.

BELOW LEFT: The Sultanahmet District and the imposing Hagia Sophia at sunrise.

BELOW RIGHT: Once thriving areas of the city are at risk from dereliction and abandonment as people move out.

OPPOSITE PAGE: The Suleymaniye complex consists of caravanserai, imaret and madrassa around a magnificent mosque. Like other historic buildings it is under threat from pollution and disasters.

"If the Earth was a single state, Istanbul would be its capital."
NAPOLEON BONAPARTE

Old Towns of Djenné
Mali

AT RISK

KEY THREATS Conflict | Theft | Development | Tourism | Pollution | Disasters | Constraints | Changing Uses | Invaders | Climate

In the inland Niger delta in western Africa, the ancient town of Djenné is home to the world's largest adobe building, the iconic spired mud-brick Great Mosque. Inhabited since 250 BC, Djenné became a market town and an important link in the trans-Saharan gold trade in the thirteenth century, challenging even Timbuktu. In the fifteenth and sixteenth centuries, it was an important location for the propagation of Islam. The entire town sits on a knoll which becomes a temporary island during seasonal flooding of the Bani river. The town's traditional houses, of which nearly 2000 have survived, are built on hillocks (toguere) to protect them from the waters.

Djenné thrived on the river transportation of alluvial gold and traded in leather crafts and rock salt.

In the past decade, international assistance has helped to restore 130 historic houses.

Buildings are made from sun-dried mud-bricks called ferey. The mud is mixed with rice husks and straw and allowed to ferment to make a thick, tough and rain-resistant plaster.

The town was originally located upstream at Djenné-Djenno (Zoboro) but was later moved to its present site.

⊛ World Heritage Site inscribed 1988
http://whc.unesco.org/en/list/116

OPPOSITE PAGE: Bundles of palm wood protrude from the Great Mosque's walls, serving as platforms for seasonal patching after the rains.

ABOVE RIGHT: The Great Mosque of Djenné is said to be the largest adobe brick building in the world. A masterpiece of the Sudano-Sahelian architectural style, it also merges Islamic influences.

The Great Mosque at the hub of the city is Djenné's tallest building. Originally built in the thirteenth century as a palace, it was converted to a mosque by Koi Kunburo, the city-state's first Muslim ruler. By 1834 it was considered too lavish and was destroyed and replaced by a simpler structure. This, too, was torn down and in 1906 work began on the current structure. At the crossroads of cultures, and successively captured by Moroccans, Peulhs, Toucouleurs and French colonial troops, it is a cosmopolitan city.

History Washed Away

The mud-brick architecture of Djenné is disappearing. With limited resources and extreme pressure from development, many people are abandoning traditional buildings for more modern conveniences. Even the new municipal water fountains are problematic because they are discharging excess water into the streets, which adds to erosion. Cement, fired bricks and metal window frames and doors are replacing traditional materials, and old buildings are plundered for their cultural goods. Without constant maintenance, mud-brick structures quickly erode in the seasonal rains. The site lacks a proper management plan, boundaries and much-needed planning regulations. In addition, with a changing climate, some fear that increasing rain may cause flooding and erosion of the raised hillocks upon which the structures sit. With limited resources and extreme pressure from development, the situation has been termed dire, as the historic urban fabric of this once great city is in danger of being washed away.

Pueblo de Taos
United States of America

AT RISK

KEY THREATS Conflict | Theft | Development | Tourism | Pollution | Disasters | Constraints | Changing Uses | Invaders | Climate

Located in the fertile valley plateau of a small tributary of the Rio Grande, the Pueblo de Taos sits at 2130 m (7000 ft) in the shadow of the Sangre de Cristo mountains. A walled adobe town on many levels, this ancient agricultural settlement in the southwestern United States has been a focus of Native American culture since the seventeenth century. The largest and best preserved continuously-occupied pueblo north of the Mexican border, Taos's five-tiered North House surpasses in height and size all other present-day pueblo dwellings. It dates to roughly 1400, while the ruins of the adjacent Cornfield Taos have been traced to 1325–1350.

⊛ World Heritage Site inscribed 1992
http://whc.unesco.org/en/list/492

OPPOSITE PAGE: The Church of San Geronimo was built in the nineteenth century on the site of an earlier church of the same name.

ABOVE RIGHT: The insertion of doorways and windows has made the buildings easier to access, but there are few other modern conveniences here.

Although the stone pueblos of Oraibi and Acoma can lay claim to greater antiquity, neither presents a clearer, more striking picture than Taos of what most view as the archetypal multi-tiered Peublo style.

The first written record of the pueblo comes from one of Francisco Vasquez de Coronado's captains, Hernando de Alvarez in 1540–1542, who said, "It must have twenty districts, and is well worth seeing. The houses have three storeys of mud wall and three others of wood or small timbers. On the three storeys of mud there are three terraces on the outside. We thought this pueblo must have had up to 15,000 people."

The settlement has two main structures, the North and South Houses, which sit on either side of a large ceremonial plaza with a stream. Once they were entered via ladders and through rooftop openings, but more peaceful times mean that windows and doors have been inserted. Near the outer wall are seven underground kivas or large ceremonial halls. Other notable features include several middens (large ash piles), ruins of an earlier site, the nineteenth-century Church of San Geronimo, the remains of an earlier mission station and an ancient foot-race track.

The End of Tradition?

Taos has survived and adapted to the pressures of the outside world for centuries, adopting selected customs and architectural features such as windows and doors. Although many in Taos are deeply conscious of their heritage, they face a difficult decision in the twenty-first century. In an effort to maintain authenticity and preserve the structures, traditional materials and maintenance techniques are enforced. But without modern conveniences, the traditional homes are less popular – the pueblo has largely become a seasonal site reserved for ceremonial uses, with most people now living permanently in modern "summer" residences beyond the enclosure. Increasingly assuming the role of tourist attraction, the community is held in a bubble. With changes in laws to allow Native American gaming, many traditional lands have become sites for casinos rather than refuges for ancient culture and customs. The challenge here is how to remain a vital, living community and not go the way of the pueblos of Mesa Verde, Chaco Canyon or Paquimé.

Ichkeul National Park
Tunisia

Located on the coast in the northeast of Tunisia, Ichkeul National Park's lake and marshes are the most productive wetland for wildfowl in North Africa and form one of the most important sites in the entire Mediterranean region for wintering of Palaearctic (European and north Asian) birds. The last remaining example of a chain of shallow freshwater lakes which once extended all along the north African seaboard, Ichkeul is a vital habitat for hundreds of thousands of migrant birds, from ducks including wigeons and pochards to coots, greylag geese, storks and pink flamingoes.

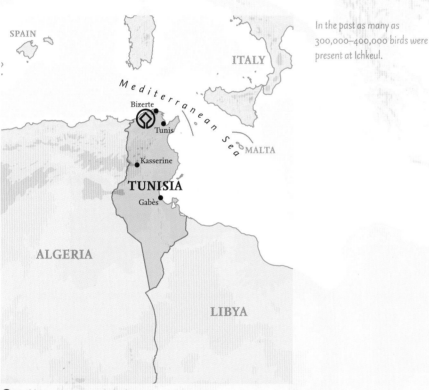

In the past as many as 300,000–400,000 birds were present at Ichkeul.

⊚ World Heritage Site inscribed 1980
http://whc.unesco.org/en/list/8

OPPOSITE PAGE: Lake Ichkeul's ability to support hundreds of thousands of birds depends on a fragile balance between fresh and salt water.

ABOVE RIGHT: Ichkeul is a vital habitat for migrant birds, including pink flamingoes.

The shallow, brackish lake is fed by six main rivers and connected to the sea by a canal. In summer, the rivers dry out, the lake level falls and inflowing sea water causes the salinity to rise. This has led to the growth of massive beds of pondweed in the lake and bulrush in the marshes. These serve as habitat for birds; 226 species, including thirty-four breeding residents, have been recorded.

A Struggle for Water

By the end of the twentieth century, dams on the rivers had cut off almost all of the fresh water. This, coupled with a drought from 1999–2002, caused the salinity of the lake to rise to twice that of the sea. Salt-loving plants replaced freshwater species, reducing the available habitat for migrants, reed-dependent birds disappeared and the site was placed on the List of World Heritage in Danger. Conservationists and the government worked to develop a management plan, increase the supply of fresh water and restore habitat. The end of the drought and concerted efforts resulted in improved conditions for four years. Although no longer in imminent danger, the site remains at risk from the continued demands for water, potential droughts and climate change, farms, grazing cattle and agricultural pollutants. Although the site is slowly recovering, talk of further dams on the rivers indicates that its future is far from secure.

Because of the increase in salinity, by 2000, wintering wildfowl numbers had decreased from 200,000 to 50,000. By 2007 improving conditions had had a positive impact on the wetland vegetation, resulting in wintering migrant numbers climbing again to more than 120,000.

The Sassi and the Park of the Rupestrian Churches of Matera
Italy

Located in the southern Italian region of Basilicata, Matera's rock-hewn dwellings (the sassi) and churches are the most outstanding, intact example of a troglodyte settlement in the Mediterranean region. Dating back to the Palaeolithic period, this unique city illustrates a number of significant stages in human history. Homes for 50,000 people were carved out of the belt of soft calcareous "tufa" stone on the slopes of this canyon over the centuries. More than 120 rupestrian (rock-hewn) churches shelter Byzantine murals from the eighth to the eighteenth centuries. The city is perfectly adapted to the harsh terrain and ecosystem, beautifully integrating life and land.

Matera claims to be the only place in the world where people are still living in the same houses as their ancestors of 9000 years ago.

During the period of Greek expansion, from the eighth century BC on, the sassi (literally "stones") housed exiles from Metapontum and Heraclea, which led to the city's name, "Met" and "Hera".

Although well-managed the site is in guarded condition as large portions remain vacant.

⊚ World Heritage Site inscribed: 1993
http://whc.unesco.org/en/list/670

OPPOSITE PAGE: The porous tufa from which the sassi were carved is soft and prone to erosion, so the penetration of the rock by water has caused many of the sassi to crumble.

ABOVE RIGHT: The sassi were built into one side of the ravine known as La Gravina.

Making full use of limited resources in a difficult environment, the dwellings were a model of efficiency. Channels harvested the limited rainfall and brought it down the hill, level by level through the homes, into cisterns. Material excavated from the cliffs was used for façades and the roof of each layer supported roads and gardens for the one above. As the city grew during the twentieth century, overcrowding, limited water and lack of conveniences, sewage and hygiene became a problem. Exposing the misery of peasant life in southern Italy Carlo Levi's depiction of the grotto-dwellers in his 1945 novel, Christ stopped at Eboli, embarrassed the nation so much that by 1952 the government had forcibly relocated the remaining 15,000–20,000 inhabitants to new homes on the plain above. Abandoned, the porous dwellings quickly fell into disrepair.

The Death and Life of a Great Italian City

The sassi have been "rediscovered" in recent years, and new regulations have slowly allowed shops, restaurants and families to return. But there have been numerous problems, from the use of incompatible construction materials to the high natural humidity of the spaces.

Because of the way the caves interlink and the water travels through the slope, disruption of the ancient water system continues to present problems for the renovated sassi, as does the continuing decay of the abandoned ones. Because they were built up level by level, a failure low down can have ramifications for sassi far above. The 150 remaining churches, too, are threatened because without active use they are slowly deteriorating.

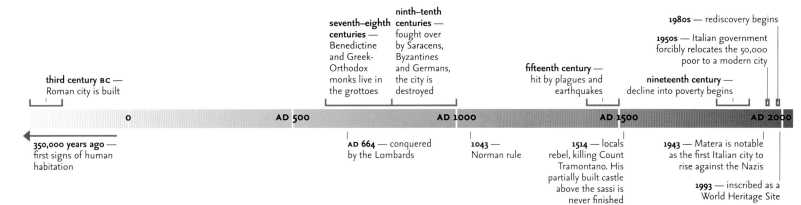

ninth–tenth centuries — fought over by Saracens, Byzantines and Germans, the city is destroyed

seventh–eighth centuries — Benedictine and Greek-Orthodox monks live in the grottoes

third century BC — Roman city is built

fifteenth century — hit by plagues and earthquakes

1980s — rediscovery begins

1950s — Italian government forcibly relocates the 50,000 poor to a modern city

nineteenth century — decline into poverty begins

| 0 | AD 500 | AD 1000 | AD 1500 | AD 2000 |

350,000 years ago — first signs of human habitation

AD 664 — conquered by the Lombards

1043 — Norman rule

1514 — locals rebel, killing Count Tramontano. His partially built castle above the sassi is never finished

1943 — Matera is notable as the first Italian city to rise against the Nazis

1993 — inscribed as a World Heritage Site

INVADERS

Our heritage is also under threat from "foreign" invaders – introduced species that do not belong. Although man himself is often the ultimate "invader", our introduction of non-native plants and animals, be it accidental or intentional, continues to have a devastating impact on heritage even today. Sites at high risk range from a coral atoll, to a biodiversity hot spot, Pacific islands, a wetland bird sanctuary, and even prehistoric cave art.

In many areas, the introduction of alien species such as plants and trees has a rapid and devastating effect. Deliberate planting or accidental release, through seed dispersal by insects and wind and subsequent pollination by birds and mammals, can introduce fast-growing non-native plants and trees, which can threaten the genetic purity of native species and take a heavy toll on the landscape. In the Cape Floral Protected Area in South Africa, for example, where fire is part of the natural cycle of flora regeneration, the introduction of resinous fast-burning trees such as pines, acacias and eucalypti has notably increased the intensity of fire, which has led to erosion and soil loss.

Invaders in the form of feral animals, especially rapid breeders such as rabbits, cats and goats, are a cause for concern since they compete with wildlife for valuable forage and can cause damage to seedlings and roots. Rabbits, in particular, can rapidly breed and destroy the stability of the soil, inducing landslides and destroying bird habitats, while foraging pigs uproot bulbs and shoots, and eat the eggs of ground-nesting birds. Deliberate introduction, as with the cane toad in Australia's Wet Tropics of Queensland more than a half century ago in an attempt to control a beetle, can often spiral out of control (the cane toad is now threatening additional World Heritage Sites such as Kakadu National Park, 1450 km (900 miles) to the north-west. Whether accidentally or deliberately introduced, these invaders can also become hunters, further putting local fauna at risk. Additionally, they bring their parasites with them.

One of the worst marine invaders is water weed, an invasive and destructive plant that starves the water of oxygen, killing fish and other aquatic life and threatening the ecosystem. It can also increase the habitat for disease-bearing snails and mosquitoes and forms a substrate for other invasive weeds. Often, invasive species are aided by other actions of man, such as in Djoudj National Bird Sanctuary in Senegal where changes in water flows have contributed to the explosion in weeds. At sites such as the Galápagos Islands in Ecuador and Cocos Island in Costa Rica, concerted efforts have finally brought progress against invaders such as pigs and goats, only to be replaced by invasions from new human-borne contaminants. The growth in tourism and settlement to support the visitors has inevitably led to introductions of rodents, blackberry bushes (presumably from seeds cast aside after a lunch), ants and micro-organisms. Although visible attackers can potentially be removed with enough time and effort, the smaller the species, the greater the challenge.

Tourism entails the construction of hotels, restaurants, and other leisure facilities, while the related boats, buses, and other vehicles necessitate access. At even well-run sites, visitors to locations such as poorly ventilated caves can cause damage just through the moisture in their breath, while introduced light, air, microorganisms and damp, with its ensuing algae and mould, can all have a harmful effect.

Although many sites have long ago succumbed to invasive species, islands and other isolated spots still have a chance to be saved. UNESCO, governments and numerous international Non-Governmental Organizations are working together at places from the Galápagos to Keoladeo in India to eradicate pests, repair past damage, and institute better monitoring regimes and visitor controls. But the challenges are huge. Unless we are all willing to take the extra precautions needed, some sites might be better off locked away than left accessible to careless visitors.

Galápagos Islands
Ecuador

IN DANGER · KEY THREATS Conflict | Theft | Development | Tourism | Pollution | Disasters | Constraints | Changing Uses | Invaders | Climate

Straddling the equator in the Pacific Ocean some 1000 km (620 miles) west of Ecuador, these nineteen major and nearly 100 minor islands and surrounding waters have been called a "living museum and showcase of evolution." This active volcanic archipelago springing from the ocean floor is still relatively young. At the confluence of three major ocean currents (bringing cold, warm and nutrient-rich waters together), the Galápagos are a melting pot of marine species, from sharks to penguins, marine mammals and corals. On land, the extreme isolation and harsh volcanic landscape led to the development of unique animal life – such as the land iguana, the giant tortoise and the many types of Darwin's finches.

COLOMBIA

Esmeraldas

Quito

ECUADOR

Guayaquil

Machala

Galápagos Islands

Pacific Ocean

PERU

ⓌWorld Heritage Site inscribed: 1978, expanded 2001
Inscribed on the List of World Heritage in Danger: 2007
http://www.unesco.org/en/list/1

Among the first group of properties to be inscribed on the World Heritage List in 1978, the site was further expanded in 2001 with the addition of 133,000 sq km (51,340 sq miles) of protected marine habitat.

The Galápagos sit at the intersection of three major geological plates – the Pacific, Nazca and Cocos.

The term "Darwin's finches" was not coined until the 1930s.

The islands range in age from 700,000 years to 2.4–3 million for the oldest.

Additional threats include pollution from the growing population, overfishing and poaching in the protected waters (300,000 sharks are taken illegally every year to feed the Asian shark fin soup market), and an overall lack of capacity to deal with the challenges.

OPPOSITE: The giant tortoise is synonymous with the Galápagos Islands. With a saddle-back shell reminiscent of a type of riding saddle, they were in fact dubbed "galápago" by early Spaniards.

ABOVE RIGHT: According to Darwin land iguanas "… are ugly animals, of a yellowish orange beneath, and of a brownish-red colour above: from their low facial angle they have a singularly stupid appearance."

Combining sub-Antarctic and tropical biota, the Galápagos are the "largest, most diverse, almost pristine archipelago remaining in the world." Approximately 5500–6000 species have been identified here, out of a probable 7000–9000. A third of the vascular land plants are endemic, as are nearly all the reptiles, half of the breeding land birds, and almost 30 per cent of the marine species. Of roughly 100 species of birds found in the Galápagos, thirteen species and subspecies occur nowhere else and either have populations of fewer than 1500 individuals or are restricted to a single island. The islands are home to some of the most beautiful birds on earth: flightless cormorants, blue- and red-footed boobies and Darwin's finches, the latter inspiring his theory of evolution following his visit in 1835.

Illegal Immigrants from Man to Microbes

Because of their remote location and harsh conditions, the Galápagos Islands had until recently escaped intense human colonization and their original rich biological make-up had been left relatively intact. However, since the establishment of permanent human settlements here, about 5 per cent of the species are estimated to have become extinct and the World Conservation Union (IUCN) lists 25 per cent of the endemic plant species as either on the brink of extinction or in serious decline.

Over 100,000 tourists a year now come to the islands, and in their wake a vast service industry has grown up to support them. Today, 30,000 people live in this once barely inhabited archipelago, bringing infrastructure issues from roads and water to waste management.

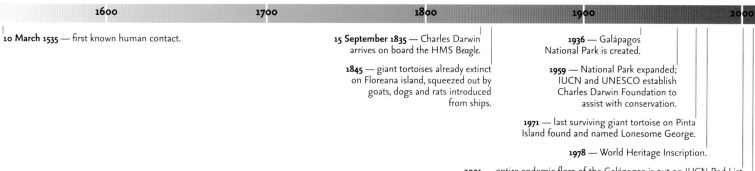

1600	1700	1800	1900	2000

10 March 1535 — first known human contact.

15 September 1835 — Charles Darwin arrives on board the HMS Beagle.

1845 — giant tortoises already extinct on Floreana island, squeezed out by goats, dogs and rats introduced from ships.

1936 — Galápagos National Park is created.

1959 — National Park expanded; IUCN and UNESCO establish Charles Darwin Foundation to assist with conservation.

1971 — last surviving giant tortoise on Pinta Island found and named Lonesome George.

1978 — World Heritage Inscription.

2001 — entire endemic flora of the Galápagos is put on IUCN Red List of Endangered and Threatened Species; the World Heritage Site is extended to protect 133,000 sq km (51,1340 sq miles) of marine habitat.

2007 — placed on the List of World Heritage in Danger.

The growing population on the islands and increasing movement of goods from the mainland and between islands has led to a rapid rate of introduction of non-native species, which is the greatest threat to Galápagos biodiversity.

Inspection regimes have been instituted but cannot realistically keep pace with the flow of people and goods. However, pigs have been cleared from Santiago, cats from Baltra, and Project Isabela – the largest habitat restoration project in the world – successfully eradicated 150,000 feral goats from northern Isabela.

Despite the progress, new threats loom large. Tilapia, a highly invasive freshwater fish, was found in 2006, and experts fear that the West Nile virus could arrive by 2008 and devastate the long-isolated bird population.

BELOW: Animals and humans seem oblivious to each other on Floreana.

OPPOSITE PAGE: Although immigration to the islands is in theory restricted, booming tourism requires people and infrastructure. Here, beyond the view of tourists, a sand and gravel pit scars the landscape to provide construction materials for the 30,000 person-strong service industry's roads and buildings.

The "differences between the inhabitants of the different islands [and how] perfectly adapted to their environment [they are] strikes me with wonder."

CHARLES DARWIN (1809–1882), WHO LAID THE FOUNDATIONS OF THE THEORY OF EVOLUTION IN HIS LOG OF THE HMS Beagle's EXPEDITION

Mosi-oa-Tunya / Victoria Falls
Zambia and Zimbabwe

AT RISK

KEY THREATS Conflict | Theft | Development | Tourism | Pollution | Disasters | Constraints | Changing Uses | Invaders | Climate

Forming the boundary between Zambia and Zimbabwe, these are among the most spectacular waterfalls in the world. The seemingly tranquil Zambezi River, which is more than 2 km (1.2 miles) wide at this point, suddenly plunges noisily down a series of zigzagging basalt gorges and raises an iridescent mist that can be seen for more than 30 km (19 miles). The Kololo tribe who were living here in the 1800s gave them the name Mosi-oa-Tunya – the smoke that thunders. At 1708 m (5604 ft) wide, the falls form the largest curtain of water in the world. They drop from as high as 107 m (351 ft) into the Zambezi Gorge, gushing an average of 550 million litres (145 million gallons) of water per minute in peak months.

⊛ World Heritage Site inscribed 1989
http://whc.unesco.org/en/list/509

"Creeping with awe to the verge, I peered down into a large rent which had been made from bank to bank of the broad Zambezi, and saw that a stream of a thousand yards broad leaped down a hundred feet and then became suddenly compressed into a space of fifteen to twenty yards … the most wonderful sight I had witnessed in Africa."

DR DAVID LIVINGSTONE DESCRIBING HIS FIRST ENOUNTER WITH THE FALLS IN 1855

The Zambezi is slowly cutting through the basalt rock uplifted two million years ago. Seven previous waterfalls occupied the gorges below the present-day spectacle. The site is home to large numbers of animals from hippopotamuses and crocodiles upstream to monkeys, baboons, zebra, wildebeest, buffalo, warthogs and lions.

Unrest, Tourism and an Invasive Weed

Most people used to stay on the Zimbabwean side, but after land seizures authorized by President Mugabe, the facilities have fallen into decay and tourist revenues have plunged by more than 70 per cent. More than half of Zimbabwe's wildlife has reportedly been destroyed. Most visitors now approach the falls from the Zambian side, where a massive, chaotic boom is taking place. Overseas arrivals doubled between 2003 and 2005 and hotels and golf courses are springing up with no controls, threatening access, views and the water itself with untreated waste. The towns of Livingstone (Maramba) and Victoria Falls have swelled with incomers and refugees. Settlers have encroached within the site boundaries, grazing cattle and planting maize and sorghum. The unique and fragile riverine "rainforest" that thrives within the moist and humid spray zone is now threatened by invasive species, including the shrubby weed *Lantana camara*, which is taking over. Because of a lack of plans, controls or management resources, the biodiversity of this globally important ecosystem is under threat.

OPPOSITE PAGE: The unique vegetation that lives in the area, soaked by the spray from the falls, is in danger from invasive species.

ABOVE RIGHT: The landscape and fauna are at risk on both sides of the border: in Zimbabwe because of the chaos following the land seizures and in Zambia because of uncontrolled, rapid development and tourism.

Keoladeo National Park
India

AT RISK

KEY THREATS Conflict | Theft | Development | Tourism | Pollution | Disasters | Constraints | Changing Uses | Invaders | Climate

An avian paradise, this former duck-hunting reserve of the maharajas is a major wintering area for vast numbers of migrant birds from Afghanistan to China, and Europe to western Siberia. Set in the arid state of Rajasthan in northwest India, this walled sanctuary's unique mosaic of habitats (wetlands, woodlands, scrub forests and grasslands) supports an amazing diversity of both plant and animal species. It is justly considered to be one of the world's finest bird reserves: 364 species, including the rare and critically endangered Siberian crane, have been recorded here.

⊛ World Heritage Site inscribed: 1985
http://whc.unesco.org/en/list/340

OPPOSITE PAGE: The park supports a wide variety of bird species. With the onset of winter, migratory birds from all over, including pelicans come here. They arrive by August and leave in February.

ABOVE RIGHT: As wetlands around the world disappear because of development, sanctuaries like Keoladeo become even more crucial to the tens of thousands of birds which visit every year.

Created in 1901 through flooding a natural depression to create a royal hunting reserve, the park was soon teeming with birds. In its heyday it hosted grand shoots. It was declared a bird sanctuary in 1956 and royal hunting ceased in 1972.

The western population of the critically endangered Siberian crane once wintered here. Numbers in the park declined steadily from 200 in 1964–1965 to 41 in 1984–1985 and none by 1993–1994. Although two were seen in 2000, it is now considered locally extinct.

Grazing was banned here in 1982, leading to violent clashes between police and farmers in which eight people were killed. Some suggest bringing livestock back might help to keep invasive plants at bay.

"Before, the skies were so full of birds it was a wonder they didn't collide into each other. Now nothing is there."
MAHENDRA VYAS, A LAWYER WHO ADVISES INDIA'S SUPREME COURT ON CONSERVATION ISSUES

For more than 100 years, with the first showers of the season, the park is filled with noise, from the trumpeting of Sarus cranes to the hoots of dusky eagle owls and the babble of parakeets. Thousands of herons, cormorants, egrets, darters, harriers, kingfishers, ibises, spoonbills, storks, geese, pelicans, flamingos, ducks, coots, larks, chats, buntings, kites, eagles and vultures are to be found, many of them roosting in an estimated 50,000 trees.

Covering one third of the park's 29 sq km (18 sq miles), the wetlands host the most spectacular heronry of the region with fifteen species courting, mating and nesting here from July to September. In addition, twenty-seven mammals, thirteen reptiles, seven amphibians, forty-three fish and many macro invertebrates can be found.

Choked out by Weeds

In India, wetlands are among the most threatened of all ecosystems, making the few surviving areas all the more vital. Suffering from the effects of both invasive species and a lack of water, the birds appear to be leaving here. The monsoons have failed for several years, drying the once glistening oasis into muddy puddles. Non-native water hyacinth and vine-like ipomea threaten to choke the remaining waterways and Prosopis juliflora the land, while larvae of the Asian aquatic moth (Parapoynx diminutalis) devour native vegetation. Pollutants, from sedimentation to pesticides, heavy metals and even drugs cause concern. In 2006, the government banned the use of the anti-inflammatory diclofenac (commonly administered to livestock), after it was incriminated in the decline of the white-backed vulture in Keoladeo.

Cape Floral Region Protected Areas
South Africa

AT RISK

KEY THREATS Conflict | Theft | Development | Tourism | Pollution | Disasters | Constraints | Changing Uses | Invaders | Climate

Called the world's "hottest" biodiversity hot spot, the Cape Floral Region is one of the richest centres of plant life on Earth. Although it occupies less than 0.38 per cent of the area of Africa it is home to nearly 20 per cent of the continent's flora. Made up of eight separate protected areas in Cape Province, South Africa, and home to one of the planet's six floral kingdoms, the site covers 5530 sq km (2135 sq miles). The site is important for the study of the ecological and biological processes associated with fynbos vegetation, which is unique to the region.

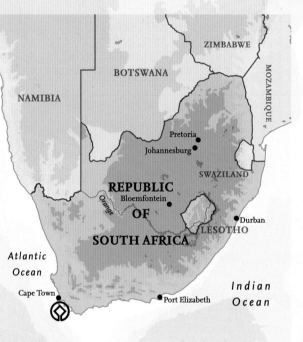

⊛ World Heritage Site inscribed 2004
http://whc.unesco.org/en/list/1007

OPPOSITE PAGE: Fynbos (Afrikaans for "fine bush") is the natural, primarily evergreen, shrubland vegetation of the Cape Floral Region. Some 1700 plant species in the region are threatened by invasive species and development.

ABOVE RIGHT: Sun setting over Table Mountain and Devil's Peak above Cape Town. Increasing development in the Cape Province is putting pressure on the unique ecosystem of the protected areas.

Since the late Stone Age, the San hunter-gatherer people have lived in the region, making use of controlled burning of plants to encourage fresh growth for food.

Adaptations to fire here include geophytes which sprout from underground and store seed both underground and in the canopy. Some species require fire for germination.

One of South Africa's best known landmarks, Table Mountain, is within the site.

The plants here have developed unique reproductive strategies, adaptive responses to fire and patterns of seed dispersal by ants and termites. Methods of pollination, nutrient cycling, levels of endemism and adaptive spreading are also distinctive to the region. The outstanding diversity (close to 9000 plant species), density (with nine species per genus and fifty-two per family) and endemism (at 31.9 per cent) of the flora here are among the highest worldwide. Five of the twelve indigenous plant families of the continent are to be found here.

Fire among the Fynbos

The survival of the fynbos ecosystem is, however, under threat. Alien plants have invaded large areas of the site, particularly in the coastal habitats. With farming and forestry, they have already affected a quarter of the site. Although fire is part of the natural cycle in the region, non-native, fast-burning pine, eucalyptus and acacia have affected its role in this ecosystem. The frequency of fires has altered and they have been allowed to spread farther, so changing the risks they pose. In 2000, one fire burned 40 per cent of Cape Peninsula National Park.

Although considerable efforts have gone into trying to manage invasive species, the size and splintered nature of the site make this a challenge. Climate change adds to the threat, as native plants are more susceptible to higher temperatures and reduced rainfall than five of the main invaders. Predictions for the site show that the foreseen doubling of atmospheric CO_2 by 2050 would cause the loss of 10–40 per cent of the plant species.

Macquarie Island
Australia

AT RISK

KEY THREATS Conflict | Theft | Development | Tourism | Pollution | Disasters | Constraints | Changing Uses | Invaders | Climate

The only land on Earth composed entirely of oceanic crust and rocks from the mantle deep below the sea floor, Macquarie is home to albatrosses, fur and elephant seals and hundreds of thousands of penguins. In the Tasman Sea, it lies 1,500 km (930 miles) southeast of Tasmania, roughly halfway between the Australian and Antarctic continents. Inscribed on the World Heritage List in 1997 for its geological importance, this island provides evidence of plate tectonics and is a unique record of sea-floor spreading. The exposed crest of the undersea ridge where the Pacific and Indo-Australian plates meet, Macquarie has active faults and excellent examples of pillow basalts and other extrusive rocks.

The island was struck on 23 December 2004 by a magnitude 8.1 earthquake. As there are no large structures on the island, damage was negligible.

More than 80,000 elephant seals, which can grow to over 4.5 m (15 ft) in length and to a weight of 3.5 tonnes (2200 lbs), breed here.

Macquarie's existence began as a spreading ridge beneath the sea some 11–30 million years ago. This movement later reversed, squeezing rocks upwards from deep within the earth. The island reached the surface 600,000 years ago, and is still actively forming, undeformed and uncontaminated by other rock and soil. Without glaciers to carve it, the island has been eroded only by wind, waves and rain.

The cost of eradicating the rabbits has been estimated at more than US$20 million. A new seven-year plan to eradicate all of the rats and 95 per cent of the rabbits was put in place in June 2007.

Ⓦ **World Heritage Site inscribed: 1997**
http://whc.unesco.org/en/list/629

OPPOSITE PAGE: Rabbits are stripping the island of vegetation and endangering both the landscape and vital bird habitat, as can be seen in this comparison of a tussock pictured in 1990 and 2005.

ABOVE RIGHT: The grey-headed albatross is one of the four species of albatross that breed on Macquarie Island. Their nesting sites are in danger because of the damage caused by rabbits.

Slaughtered in their hundreds of thousands for oil in the nineteenth and early twentieth centuries, penguins have made a dramatic recovery here. Home to one of the greatest concentrations of seabirds on the planet, the island has more than 850,000 breeding pairs of royal penguins, as well as over 500,000 rockhopper, 400,000 king and 5000 gentoo penguin pairs. Dotted with lakes, pools and peat beds, this windswept landscape of tall and short tussock grasslands, bog and feldmark is home to seventy-two bird species including four albatrosses, four species of fur seal and the southern elephant seal.

Rabbits, Rats and Mice

Rabbits, introduced in the nineteenth century by seal hunters for food, have taken over, causing erosion, loss of nesting colonies and landscape degradation. Invasive species led to the extinction of the banded rail and red-fronted parakeet here more than 100 years ago – today albatrosses and many others are at risk from rabbits, rats escaped from ships and house mice. In the 1980s, the government rounded up the feral cats and introduced myxomatosis to eliminate the 10,000 rabbits. The rabbits became immune to the virus and, with no predators, the population exploded and stands at more than 100,000.

The nesting habitat of three albatross species is under threat. At the only breeding site on the island of the grey-headed albatross, the entire slope has been cleared of vegetation, triggering landslides. In September 2006, a slide buried an unknown number of king penguins. It is a chilling example of what can happen to a pristine ecosystem if invasive species are left unchecked.

Djoudj National Bird Sanctuary
Senegal

AT RISK

KEY THREATS Conflict | Theft | Development | Tourism | Pollution | Disasters | Constraints | Changing Uses | Invaders | Climate

One of the world's most important bird sanctuaries, this wetland forms a vibrant but fragile reserve for three million migrant birds including white pelican, purple heron, African spoonbill, great egret and cormorant. Located in the Sénégal river delta not far from St-Louis on the western coast of Africa, this World Heritage Site protects 160 sq km (62 sq miles) of habitat comprising of seasonally flooded lakes, ponds and marshy areas, surrounded by streams and backwaters.

⊚ World Heritage Site inscribed 1981
http://whc.unesco.org/en/list/25

OPPOSITE PAGE: An adult, non-breeding black tern (Guifette noir; Chlidonias niger) about to launch an attack. Over the years there have been huge migrations of black terns along the coast of Senegal.

ABOVE RIGHT: A crocodile weaves his way through the dense freshwater weeds found at Djoudj.

Giant salvinia (Salvinia molesta) was first spotted in the sanctuary in 1999. Within a year this free-floating, buoyant aquatic fern had inundated the area. Covering the water's surface, the weed quickly chokes out all sunlight and oxygen, killing off aquatic life. Mechanical removal and biocontrol with a tiny weevil were used to eradicate it, but accidental reintroduction cannot be ruled out, so vigilance is maintained.

The site was recently discovered to be one of the most important wintering grounds for Eastern Europe's threatened Aquatic warbler.

A welcome wintering ground for millions of ducks and other aquatic birds after the long voyage across the Sahara, the sanctuary hosts 366 different bird species. Some 500,000 members of the duck family, 250,000 waders and 20,000 greater flamingoes, as well as lesser flamingoes and European spoonbills, owe their winter survival to this vital environment.

A Brazilian Invasion

On the List of World Heritage in Danger from 1984 to 1988 because of changes in water levels through drought and the construction of dams, and again from 2000 to 2006 because of an infestation of the highly destructive south Brazilian water weed *Salvinia molesta*, the site is recovering, but is still at risk. It is subject to seasonal flooding, but a barrage downstream to block salt water and a series of dams upstream have disrupted the natural balance of wet and dry, and fresh- and salt-water cycles.

The amount of rainfall has also dropped in recent years, perhaps from a changing climate. These factors have come together to create ideal conditions for invasive freshwater weeds including reed mace (which forms very dense barriers), water lettuce and *Salvinia molesta*, which can double its area every four days and whose floating mat chokes out all other life.

A costly campaign has finally brought salvinia under control, but the site remains under threat as water continues to be diverted for irrigation and drinking, management is limited and the growing human population around the sanctuary grazes increasing numbers of cattle at the boundaries .

Wet Tropics of Queensland
Australia

Of exceptional beauty, the wet tropics' sweeping landscapes range from white sandy beaches and rugged peaks to dramatic gorges and Australia's tallest waterfall. Covering 8944 sq km (3450 sq miles), this vast area of largely tropical rainforest harbours one of the most complete and diverse living records in the evolution of land plants, as well as of the history of marsupials and songbirds. Stretching 450 km (280 miles) along Australia's northeast coast, it parallels the Great Barrier Reef. With the highest diversity of animals in Australia (62 per cent of the butterflies, 60 per cent of the bats and 30 per cent of the marsupials), this biotope provides the only habitat for many rare and threatened species of plants and animals.

◎ World Heritage Site inscribed: 1988
http://whc.unesco.org/en/list/486

In what is arguably one of Australia's worst environmental disasters, the Central American cane toad has in the seventy years since its introduction been steadily eating its way across the continent. Spread over Queensland, it has appeared as far south as Sydney and now threatens the Kakadu World Heritage Site in the Northern Territory as well. The cane toad, with poison glands behind the eyes, is lethal to most animals which try to eat it, from mammals to birds and crocodiles.

Aboriginal occupation here is thought to date back at least 40,000 years and represents the first wave of aboriginals to come to the continent. With the oldest rainforest culture in the world, the traditions of these Barrinean people are markedly different from other Australian aboriginal tribes.

The wet tropics have a history of species dating back 415 million years, beginning with the Pangaean landmass to when they were part of the ancient supercontinent Gondwana, and more recently from a mixing of species during their collision with Asia 15 million years ago.

OPPOSITE PAGE: The coastal mangroves are important because they prevent erosion and provide food supplies for snails and small crustaceans, habitat for juvenile fish, including commercially fished species, shelter for bats, mud for crabs and shrimp to burrow in and tidal waters for bivalves.

ABOVE RIGHT: Comprising forty-one national parks, forty-three state forests, fifteen timber reserves and one aboriginal and islander reserve, the wet tropics protect a large area yet remain vulnerable to logging, development and encroachment, because diverse owners have differing goals.

Although relatively small in comparison to the world's other rainforests, the wet tropics are unique in being home to a large number of primitive plants and animals dating back to the supercontinent Gondwana, with the greatest number of the living relics from that time which remain on Earth. One of the most significant regional ecosystems, this diverse forested landscape supports 3000 plant species, 500 of which are found only here. It has the highest diversity of animal species in Australia with 370 birds, 217 land snails, 200 butterflies, 170 reptiles, 78 freshwater fish and 53 frogs among others.

The Cane Toad Eating its Way Across Australia

The greatest threat to the wet tropics comes from invasive species – this ancient ecosystem has not fared well at the hands of alien invaders. Feral pigs, cats, dogs, cane toads and, most recently, feral deer are threatening to eat and trample away the flora and fauna. Alien root rot fungus has caused dieback of the rainforest and native frogs, whose numbers have been in decline, are suffering from a skin fungus. Many exotic plants, significantly the pond apple (a small densely growing tree which invades wetlands), also threaten to choke out the native environment if left uncontrolled. A changing climate and increasing numbers of weather-related disasters also pose a threat, from wildfires during drier seasons to cyclones. Category 5 cyclone Larry caused extensive damage in 2006, cutting a 200-km (120-mile) wide swathe through the site, some of which was still recovering from a storm twenty years before.

Prehistoric Sites and Decorated Caves of the Vézère Valley
France

AT RISK

KEY THREATS Conflict | Theft | Development | Tourism | Pollution | Disasters | Constraints | Changing Uses | Invaders | Climate

Home to the "Sistine Chapel of Prehistory", this site in southwestern France is best known for the 600 paintings and 1500 engravings in the cave at Lascaux in Montignac which have been dated to about 17,000 years ago, but also contains the "Venus de Laussel" at Marquay and the horse frieze of Cap-Blanc. The Vézère Valley contains 147 prehistoric sites dating from the Palaeolithic period, and 25 decorated caves. It is particularly interesting from ethnological, anthropological and aesthetic points of view because of its cave paintings, especially those of Lascaux, the discovery of which in 1940 was of great importance for the understanding of prehistoric art.

⊚ World Heritage Site inscribed 1979
http://whc.unesco.org/en/list/85

OPPOSITE PAGE: The level of skill displayed by the people who created these drawings is astonishing – such techniques were not rediscovered until the early Renaissance.

ABOVE RIGHT: The cave paintings are being attacked by a fungus. Black spots are appearing on the cave ceilings as can be seen above the bull's head.

Called the birthplace of animation, the caves have hunts drawn on the wall as in a comic strip, with a series of images from left to right until the prey is captured.

Although there is one human image, most of Lascaux' paintings depict animals found in the surrounding landscape, from horses to bison, mammoth, ibex, aurochs, deer, cats, birds, bears and rhinoceroses. There are ninety paintings of stags, although curiously none of reindeer, which are believed to have been a primary food source.

Roughly 500,000 visitors a year come to see a replica of the main chamber near the entrance of the actual cave.

"We have invented nothing."
PABLO PICASSO UPON EMERGING FROM THE CAVE IN 1940, IMPRESSED BY MODERNISM OF THE IMAGES

Lascaux has almost 2000 figures, although many are deteriorated or are too faint to discern. Some 600 are known animals, more than half of these are horses.

Minute Invaders and a Cave in Crisis

Since its discovery in 1940, Lascaux's celebrity has been tied to the challenges of its preservation. After years of crowding, followed by outbreaks of algae and calcite crystals, the cave was closed to the public in 1963. Despite this, in the summer of 2001 an agricultural pest, a Fusarium fungus, took hold and rapidly engulfed the space, sending fibrous roots through the pigment and stone. After vast quantities of quicklime and disinfectants failed to stop it, a bacterium, Pseudomonas fluorescens, was also found. Antibiotic patches, vacuuming and even tweezers eventually stemmed the plague, but not before damage was done. The once sparkling white calcite canvas is now grey and experts say that 150 paintings and hundreds of etchings and sketches are lost – in part because of methods meant to preserve them. Although officials claim that the fungus is now contained, Time magazine and Non-Governmental Organizations report that serious problems continue – the air-conditioning at the heart of the outbreak has yet to be removed and Lascaux must be checked daily by scientists.

The caves remain at risk. As Lascaux's curator has noted, its challenges should be a warning to those caring for ancient environments everywhere. Freezing and thawing, light, air circulation, rainwater, micro-organisms and even bureaucracy can all quickly and catastrophically disrupt the delicate balance in these prehistoric spaces.

1950s — with the interior temperature rising to the point where some are fainting, the entry is widened to accommodate 1,000 visitors a day.

| 1950 | 1960 | 1970 | 1980 | 1990 | 2000 |

1948 — after the war, daily tours were given and crowds flocked to see the paintings.

December 1940 — the caves are designated a heritage site in record time.

September 1940 — Lascaux is discovered by four boys who come across a small opening in the woods.

1955 — the first signs of deterioration are spotted and are thought to be caused by the carbon dioxide exhaled by the countless visitors.

1958 — the first air-conditioning system is installed, damaging archaeological evidence on the cave floor.

20 April 1963 — after the discovery of a "green leprosy" (an algae) growing on the walls and later a "white disease" (calcite crystals), the Minister of Culture closes the cave to the general public, restricting access to a limited number of researchers. The cooling system is blamed and the attack fought with antibiotics. From now on the few who are allowed to enter will have to walk through a formaldehyde bath.

1983 — Lascaux II, a 40-m (130-ft) long replica of the main chamber is created nearby to allow visitors a chance to gain some of the experience.

April 2001 — a new air-conditioning system is installed to replace the ageing 1968 unit, but the messy installation during a storm and complexity of the unit brings instant trouble.

Summer 2001 — "a pernicious white fungus" appears on the floor and quickly engulfs the cave in a blanket of fuzzy wool.

2003 — the cave is declared out of danger as disaster is averted after a long battle against the fungus using quicklime, fungicides and even antibiotics. But small outbreaks apparently continue and the cave remains closed to researchers and independent experts (including UNESCO). Currently — outbreaks are regularly checked for and painstakingly removed, apparently now with tweezers.

Cocos Island National Park
Costa Rica

AT RISK

KEY THREATS Conflict | Theft | Development | Tourism | Pollution | Disasters | Constraints | Changing Uses | Invaders | Climate

Cocos Island National Park, located 550 km (330 miles) off the Pacific coast of Costa Rica, is the only island in the tropical eastern Pacific with a tropical rainforest. Its position as the first point of contact with the north equatorial counter current, and the interactions between the island and the surrounding marine ecosystem, make the area an ideal laboratory for the study of biological processes. The underwater world of the national park has become famous because of the attraction it holds for divers, who rate it as one of the best places in the world to view large species that live in the upper waters of the open ocean, such as sharks, rays, tuna and dolphins.

After habitat destruction, invasive alien species are considered the second leading cause of biodiversity loss throughout the world.

Known since at least the mid-sixteenth century, stories of buried treasure on Cocos have persisted for years. Thought to be the inspiration behind Robert Louis Stevenson's Treasure Island, Cocos may also be the inspiration for the Isla Nublar in Michael Crichton's Jurassic Park.

Cocos Island is the only one of the five island groups in the tropical eastern Pacific (including the Galápagos) not to be dry.

⊗ World Heritage Site inscribed 1997, extended 2002
http://whc.unesco.org/en/list/820

ABOVE RIGHT: The fish species of the waters around Cocos are vulnerable to over-fishing while the coral reefs around which many of them make their home are at risk from warming seas.

An Island Overrun

Cocos, like many island sites, has suffered from new species introduced by man. Coffee and guava trees, have replaced much of the understorey on this 24-sq-km (9-sq-mile) volcanic island, while feral pigs, cats, two species of rat and white-tailed deer have trampled and eaten their way through vulnerable native species. Pigs have badly scarred the landscape causing erosion, which in turn pollutes surrounding waters, harming coral and marine life already under threat from climate change.

Although not as ecologically diverse as the nearby Galápagos Islands, but with a dense canopy and steep slopes, Cocos is nonetheless similarly threatened. Having only a limited budget the Costa Rican government faces a real challenge in tackling the problem before the ecosystem is completely overtaken. What few resources there are, are needed to patrol a vast marine protected area spanning 1997 sq km (771 sq miles). In addition to the invasive species, the park is at risk from the effects of illegal- and over-fishing (especially of sharks) and accidental catching of sea turtles, rays, seabirds, sharks and cetaceans among others. Finally, pollution (from oil spills to noise and sedimentary runoff) presents a threat, while the changing climate is also cause for concern – for example many coral species were severely damaged by the El Niño events of the early 1990s.

Aldabra Atoll
Seychelles

Located off the eastern coast of Africa, approximately 400 km (250 miles) northwest of Madagascar, Aldabra is the largest raised coral atoll in the world, with coral dating back 125,000 years. Built up from the seabed this classic atoll comprises four large coral islands which enclose a shallow 140-sq-km (54-sq-mile) lagoon; the whole system is itself ringed by a coral reef. Remote, far from major seafaring routes and long protected from human influence, Aldabra is one of the few places on earth where reptiles dominate.

⊚ World Heritage Site inscribed 1982
http://whc.unesco.org/en/list/185

ABOVE RIGHT: A satellite image of Aldabra Atoll, with Assumption Island to the left. The pale blue lagoon in the Atoll takes its colour from shallow sand deposits, the dark blue intrusion being a deep channel.

"Aldabra, wonder of nature given to humanity by the people of the Republic of Seychelles."
PLAQUE ON THE ATOLL

Although the giant tortoise is associated in most people's minds with the Galápagos, ten times as many individuals live on Aldabra. Charles Darwin was in fact one of Aldabra's early supporters, championing conservation efforts.

Giant turtles have incredible longevity. Adwaita, captured on the atoll in the eighteenth century by British seafarers, became a pet of the British general, Robert Clive, before being donated to the Alipore Zoo in Calcutta in 1875. Believed to have been born in approximately 1750, he lived until 23 March 2006, giving him a presumed age of roughly 250 years.

Aldabra is a refuge for several endangered species, including one of the largest concentrations of nesting green turtles in the Indian Ocean, the world's second largest breeding population of great and lesser frigatebirds, and the last flightless bird species in the Indian Ocean – the white-throated (or Cuvier's) rail.

The majority of the land surface is now 8 m (25 ft) above sea level. Mangrove swamp grows around the lagoon and inshore waters support sea-grass meadows. There are 178 indigenous flowering plants, of which about 20 per cent are thought to be endemic and many of which are under threat. In addition to the rail, the island is home to several birds including the potentially extinct Aldabra warbler. It is the main breeding site in the Indian Ocean for the red-tailed tropicbird and red-footed booby, as well as hosting white-tailed tropicbirds, masked and Abbott's boobies and thousands of nesting terns.

Rats versus Cats

The island is relatively pristine, but it has not been spared introductions which threaten native animals and habitats – the giant tortoise population has fallen from 152,000 in 1982 to 100,000 today. Accidentally introduced mealy bugs caused significant damage to native vegetation before being tackled with biological control methods, and there are large populations of rats, cats and goats. Two UNESCO-supported campaigns in the late 1980s reduced, but did not get rid of, the feral animals. The Seychelles Islands Foundation is currently raising funds for a campaign against goats and cats. Regulations are in force to protect the ecosystem from new introductions.

GUARDED

KEY THREATS Conflict | Theft | Development | Tourism | Pollution | Disasters | Constraints | Changing Uses | Invaders | Climate

CLIMATE CHANGE

The impact of a changing climate is affecting many natural and cultural World Heritage Sites, and is likely to affect many more in the years to come. The newest threat to heritage, climate change, has emerged in the twenty-first century as a significant and looming challenge to sites across the globe. Although glacial areas are most commonly thought of when climate change is brought up, the threat is much greater, ranging from deserts to reefs and coastal cities to high mountain villages. Among the natural sites under stress are the Great Barrier Reef in Australia and Kilimanjaro National Park in Tanzania, while cultural sites threatened include Venice in Italy and ancient trading posts in Mauritania. In this chapter we look at just some of the most at risk sites from among the many inscribed on the World Heritage List.

The world's climate has always been variable, but today there is a growing concern as the magnitude of the change seems unprecedented and, more importantly, there is strong evidence to suggest that humanity may be directly responsible. Effects of climate change include increasingly severe seasonal and unseasonal rainfall, extended droughts, heightened humidity, rising water-tables, shifting sands, melting glaciers and permafrost,

and higher air temperatures. Longer summers, increased wildfires, and even worsened allergies are all part of the picture.

Prime among the dangers are rising sea levels, brought about by thermal expansion of warmer sea water, higher temperatures and the melting of ice over land. Two-thirds of the world's population occupies a coastal strip just 400-km (248-miles) wide around the oceans. If all the world's ice caps thawed completely, the sea level would rise enough to inundate half of the world's cities.

The accelerated melting of glaciers and ice caps around the world not only contributes to the rising global sea-level, but also adds freshwater to the ocean, with potential impacts on ocean circulation, regional climate and marine life. Glacial melting threatens species with destruction of, or change to, their habitats—avalanches, mudslides, and outbursts from swollen glacial lakes have already inundated mountain villages and ecosystems. Additionally, it can put whole cultures at risk, such as the indigenous peoples of the Arctic who rely on sea ice for traditional hunting and fishing.

Rising sea levels and flooding due to climate change could have a devastating effect on both the buildings and social fabric of historic cities and settlements. Record floods in the last few years have inundated historic cities on some of Europe's great rivers, while Venice's squares are under water more and more frequently. The increase in soil moisture after flooding can lead to a rise in salt deposits on the exterior of buildings, which is particularly damaging to decorated surfaces. Increased humidity can also lead to ground heave and subsidence. Wetlands are threatened as a result of salt intrusion, while tree plantations in tropical areas, a critical buffer for people and ecosystems against the often devastating tropical storms, disappear under rising seas or are killed off by salinity.

Many marine World Heritage Sites are tropical coral reefs, which play a crucial role in the ocean ecosystem, providing food and habitat for thousands of species. Corals are very sensitive to increases in sea surface temperature – as coral gets too warm, its nutrient provider, the algae, departs. Known as bleaching, the loss of the colourful algae leaves coral almost pure white instead of its normal vivid hues. If the algae do not return, the coral will die. Rising sea temperatures also reduce phytoplankton supplies, with a ripple effect across the marine food chain.

Inland, global warming and droughts can reduce soil moisture over large areas of semi-arid grasslands and thus increase the extent of desertified lands – that is, land whose biological potential is degraded, which can lead ultimately to desert-like conditions. In large desert areas, sand dunes, helped by the wind, can encroach on human habitats, as is happening in Mauritania, threatening to engulf World Heritage Sites.

In 2005 The World Heritage Committee launched an initiative to assess the impact of global climate change on World Heritage Sites. Its remit was to review the nature and scale of the risks posed to World Heritage properties arising specifically from climate change, and to assist local authorities to implement appropriate strategies.

In 2006 Mr Koichiro Matsuura, the Director-General of UNESCO said: "Climate changes are impacting on all aspects of the human and natural systems, including both cultural and natural World Heritage properties. Protecting and ensuring the sustainable management of these sites has therefore become an intergovernmental priority of the highest order."

Kilimanjaro National Park
United Republic of Tanzania

AT RISK

KEY THREATS Conflict | Theft | Development | Tourism | Pollution | Disasters | Constraints | Changing Uses | Invaders | Climate

At 5895 m (19,340 feet), Kilimanjaro is the highest point in Africa and the world's tallest "free-standing" mountain, towering roughly 4600 m (15,000 feet) above the surrounding arid lowland plains. Located in northeastern Tanzania, near the Kenyan border, Kilimanjaro is the largest of an east–west belt of about twenty volcanoes near the southern end of the East African Rift Valley. Covering an area of 3885 sq km (1500 sq miles) it is one of the world's most massive volcanoes – its summit crater alone measures an amazing 2.4 km (1.5 miles) across. This volcanic massif stands in splendid isolation, with its symmetrical snow-capped cone looming over the savanna.

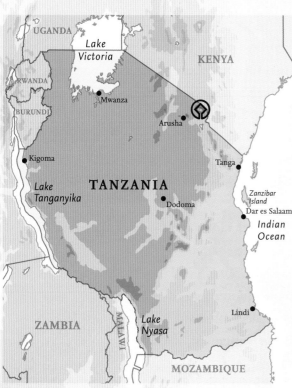

Composed of three distinct volcanoes, this giant dormant stratovolcano's highest peak, Kibo, grew up from the raised shoulders of its older siblings, Mawenzi (5150 m [16,896 ft]) and Shira (3962 m [13,000 ft]).

First ascended by westerners in 1889, the "Roof of Africa" was dubbed Kaiser-Wilhelm-Spitze by its German-Austrian climbers. Although the origins of the name Kilimanjaro are uncertain, kilima translates from Swahili as "little mountain" and njaro as white or shining (the similar jaro could also mean caravan in Kichagga).

Visited by Ernest Hemingway in the 1930s, the symbolic mountain serves as the backdrop for his classic short story The Snows of Kilimanjaro (1936).

Because of its great height, the mountain creates its own weather. As moisture-laden winds from over the Indian Ocean hit its slopes they shower snow, rain and mist, replenishing this equatorial ice cap and watering the lush rainforests below. There are several eco-climatic zones on the mountain, ranging from scrublands teeming with wildlife at the base to a belt of tropical rainforest, grassy moorlands, alpine bogs, a high-altitude desert and eventually a barren lunar landscape of rock and ice above 4600 m (15,000 feet). There is a rich array of flora, from giant groundsel (senecio) at upper elevations to heath and scrub plants and then forests of camphor and ferns on the south and olive and cedar on the north. Numerous animals, including several species of primates, lions, tree hyraxes, Abbott's duikers and red-fronted parrots, among others, live in the park. It is (or was) home to a number of threatened or endangered species, including elephant, leopard and black rhinoceros.

World Heritage Site inscribed 1987
http://whc.unesco.org/en/list/403

OPPOSITE PAGE: In 1974, the snow-covered crater on top of Kibo peak is 2.4 km (1.5 miles) across. Although there is magma just below the surface of the peak, the chief fear is that it might collapse, causing an eruption like that of Mt St Helens in 1980.

ABOVE RIGHT: The world's tallest free-standing mountain towers over the lowland plains of this national park.

The Disappearing "Snows of Kilimanjaro"

Known as the "shining mountain", Kilimanjaro may soon glisten no more as the ice fields on its peak are rapidly retreating, with great implications for the surrounding ecosystem, wildlife and people. Scientists predict that it will be gone between 2015 and 2040.

Meanwhile, near the park's edges, efficient traditional farming methods of the native Chagga are giving way to large-scale clearing for coffee, corn and other fertilized crops. Illegal poaching and logging (particularly of old growth camphor and cedar) continue, despite dedicated rangers. Under-funded, they are often less well-equipped than the tour guides.

As more and more of the forest canopy disappears, the mountain's ability to capture vital wind-borne moisture

BELOW: These three satellite images of Kilimanjaro taken (from left to right) in 1993, 2000 and 2002 show the great mountain with progressively less and less snow on the cap. Formed over 11,700 years ago, the ice cap has shrunk by more than 80 per cent in the last century – from 12,058 sq m (129,800 sq ft) in 1912 to 3,305 sq m (35,760 sq ft) in 1989.

OPPOSITE PAGE: Again this photograph, taken in 2005, shows the rapidly retreating ice-cap. The snows of Kilimanjaro will soon exist as only a memory and a book title.

is decreased, accelerating the climatic changes around it and causing even greater loss of habitat. With less moisture, fires are an increasing risk – in recent years major blazes have been set off by poachers and careless tourists (whose numbers have doubled in the last decade). Finally, while the mountain's volcano appears dormant or inactive, Kilimanjaro is in a volcanically active area. Magma sits just 400m (1300 feet) below the summit crater and there is some concern that the volcanic cone may collapse (as happened in the past on the western flank), leading to a catastrophic eruption.

Ancient Ksour of Ouadane, Chinguetti, Tichitt and Oualata
Mauritania

AT RISK

KEY THREATS Conflict | Theft | Development | Tourism | Pollution | Disasters | Constraints | Changing Uses | Invaders | Climate

Founded in the eleventh and twelfth centuries to serve the caravans crossing the Sahara, these four trading and religious sites became focal points of Islamic culture. They have managed to preserve an urban fabric that developed between the twelfth and sixteenth centuries and illustrate a traditional way of life based on the nomadic culture of the people of the western Sahara. Typically, houses with patios crowd along narrow streets around a mosque with a square minaret.

Ⓦ World Heritage Site inscribed 1996
http://whc.unesco.org/en/list/750

Regarded as the seventh holy city of Islam, Chinguetti was a religious and intellectual seat, and is famous for its many Koranic schools.

The houses of Oualata are ornately decorated by the women, with white gypsum contrasting against the mud walls. They have walls of stone and roofs of split palm trunks, overlain with palm-frond matting and mud.

OPPOSITE PAGE: Although the mosque and ancient street structure is relatively intact, weather and time have taken their toll on the old stone structures of Chinguetti. Held together with a clay mortar, without renewal the stone walls eventually give way.

ABOVE RIGHT: Like other parts of Chinguetti, the cemetery, photographed in 1998, is at risk of being buried by the encroaching desert.

Ringing the edge of the Sahara in present-day Mauritania, the mud-plastered stone structures of these towns have largely survived the passage of time. Chinguetti's Koranic school is still active, and its ancient libraries still house hundreds of centuries-old Islamic manuscripts.

Buried in a Sea of Sand

Desertification is eating away at Africa: in the recent past it has reduced by 25 per cent the vegetative productivity of more than 7 million sq km (2.7 million sq miles), or one quarter of the continent's land area. Triggered by extended droughts, and perhaps also by longer term climate change, encroaching sands threaten to engulf several World Heritage Sites including legendary Timbuktu. Here in Mauritania, Chinguetti is particularly at risk: its ancient quarters are already largely buried under the dunes. As residents move to newer homes outside the historic site, or even away all together, the old structures become even more vulnerable. Seasonal rains are also playing a role – increasingly severe in recent years, they now flood the city's most important buildings including the mosque. Although this building is stable at the moment, without conservation it may not survive for future generations. Tourism is slowly growing and the remote area's isolation is being bridged by new roads and increasing air traffic. But growth has also brought problems, ranging from careless refuse disposal to the abandonment of traditional building methods.

Kluane / Wrangell-St Elias / Glacier Bay / Tatshenshini-Alsek
Canada and the United States of America

This wilderness of glacier-draped mountains, forest and thundering rivers covers 98,000 sq km (38,000 sq miles) and is the largest internationally protected area. Spanning four parks in the Yukon Territory, British Columbia and Alaska, it was the first trans-frontier World Heritage Site. The region's tremendous snowfall feeds the world's largest non-polar icefield and North America's greatest field of glaciers. These include some of the world's largest and fastest moving with over 350 valley glaciers and an estimated thirty-one surge glaciers. The spectacular landscape is home to grizzly bears, the huge Kenai moose, Glacier Bay wolf spider, caribou, mountain goat and the world's largest concentration of Dall sheep.

In 1794 the ice that filled Glacier Bay was more than 1200 m (4000 feet) thick, up to 32 km (20 miles) or more wide, and extended more than 160 km (100 miles) to the St Elias Mountain Range. Today the remaining pieces have receded more than 105 km (65 miles). Such rapid glacial retreat is known nowhere else.

While half of the landscape is permanently covered in snow and ice, the rest nurtures lush spruce forests and tundra rich with wildlife.

Some 10 per cent of our world is under ice today, equivalent to the amount of land being farmed.

If the ice caps thawed completely, sea level would rise enough to inundate half of the world's cities.

⊚ World Heritage Site inscribed 1979, extended 1992 and 1994
http://whc.unesco.org/en/list/72

OPPOSITE PAGE: In 1941 (above) Muir Glacier filled its valley, but by 2004 (below) ocean water filled the new bay as it retreated back more than 12 km (7 miles) and thinned by more than 800 m (2620 feet). Trees and shrubs fill the foreground where glacial ice had once scoured the rocks bare.

ABOVE RIGHT: Tatshenshini River is sustained by meltwater from the glaciers of the Fairweather Range on the border of Canada and Alaska.

This mountain kingdom of North America has the continent's biggest collection of peaks above 4800 m (16,000 ft), including the 5959-m (19,550-foot) Mount Logan (Canada's highest summit), 5488-m (18,008-foot) Mount St Elias (the second highest in the United States), and 4663-m (15,298-ft) Mount Fairweather (the highest in British Columbia). The only river drainage system in North America that is completely safeguarded, the Tatshenshini and Alsek rivers carve a rugged 300-km (186-mile) corridor from alpine tundra to the coast through deep canyons, broad alluvial valleys and boreal forests. Species such as the grizzly bear, grey wolf, wolverine, bald eagle, trumpeter swan, Arctic grayling, Kokanee salmon and peregrine falcon, which are extinct, rare, threatened or endangered elsewhere, are found here in stable, self-regulating populations. The park is the last home of the "glacier bear", the extremely rare blue-grey phase of the black bear.

Almost 200 bird species (from bald and golden eagles to gyrfalcons, plovers, jaegers, ptarmigan, eiders, hummingbirds and harlequin ducks, as well as songbirds) are found here — the trumpeter swan breeding areas are the largest in Alaska and one of only three remaining in North America.

Retreating Glaciers

The greatest threat to this vast expanse of pristine wilderness is a changing climate. Summer air temperature here has been steadily increasing since 1940 when records began, endangering the many glaciers throughout the protected area. Most mountain glaciers and small ice caps have been in general retreat since the end of the Little Ice Age (estimated to be roughly 250 years ago). Yet the recent increase in the rate of melting cannot be explained by natural climate variability, pointing to a human factor. Glacial melting, in addition to the obvious aesthetic consequences, threatens species with changing habitat and sudden floods as glacial lakes collapse.

Glacier Bay, at this site's coastal edge, is one of the best-studied examples of glacial change. Two centuries ago, the bay was not even visible as it was completely filled by the Grand Pacific Glacier. The bay was first mapped by George Vancouver in 1794, and by the time the famed naturalist and explorer John Muir came here in 1879 the ice had already retreated more than 50 km (30 miles) from the mouth of the bay. As it receded, twenty separate smaller glaciers were left in its wake. Although not all of the glaciers here are receding, the non-tidewater glaciers provide excellent indications of regional climate and climate change. In the last 200 years, many of the large glaciers have retreated up to 80 km (50 miles).

Venice and its Lagoon
Italy

AT RISK

KEY THREATS Conflict | Theft | Development | Tourism | Pollution | Disasters | Constraints | Changing Uses | Invaders | Climate

One of the most enduring mercantile sea powers in history, for more than a thousand years Venice, the "Queen of the Seas", has symbolized the victorious struggle of mankind against the elements. Spread over 118 small islands linked by canals and bridges, this great city sits in the middle of the marshy Laguna Venetta, 3 km (1.9 miles) from the Italian mainland on the northwestern Adriatic coast. Its beauty has inspired countless painters from Canaletto to Guardi, Turner and others. The city links east and west and Islam and Christianity, and it was from here that Marco Polo (1254–1324) set out in search of the Far East. The city has one of the highest concentrations of architectural masterpieces in the world.

Ⓤ World Heritage Site inscribed 1987
http://whc.unesco.org/en/list/394

OPPOSITE PAGE: With canals instead of streets, and boats instead of cars, Venice's waterways are its lifeblood. The largest, the Grand Canal, carves a giant inverted "S" through the heart of the red-tiled roofs.

ABOVE RIGHT: A detail of St Mark's Church in Piazza San Marco (St Mark's Square). The Byzantine Church was built in the twelfth century.

The iconic campanile – bell tower – on Piazza San Marco was rebuilt in the early twentieth century after the previous tower collapsed on 14 July 1902.

The Basilica of St Mark (San Marco) is known for the pala d'oro, one of the richest altar screens in the world. It is covered with more than 3000 precious stones and enamelled icons inlaid in gold.

The arrival from Alexandria of the smuggled relics of St Mark in 828 AD raised the city's power and prestige and gave it its patron saint.

Venice is an extraordinary ensemble in which even the smallest building contains works by some of the period's greatest artists, from Bellini and Giorgione, to Titian, Tintoretto, Veronese, and Tiepolo.

Founded by Roman refugees from successive waves of barbarian invasions, by the fifth century AD the settlement on sandy islands of the lagoon was home to a growing city. In the sheltered waters, and at the western boundaries of the Byzantine Empire, the city thrived with a wide degree of independence, developing into an autonomous city state overseen by an elected duke or "doge". One of four Italian maritime republics, by the tenth century Venice was a growing naval power and controlled the Dalmatian coast. In 1204, Venice allied with the Crusaders to capture Constantinople, bringing back many of the great treasures of Byzantium and extending its sphere of influence from the Brenner Pass in the Alps across the entire eastern Mediterranean to the Levant. By the late thirteenth century it was the most prosperous city in all of Europe, with 36,000 sailors operating 3300 ships. As trade shifted to the Atlantic several centuries later, and the Turks retook Byzantium, Venice slowly faded. In 1797 Napoleon's troops sacked the city, marking the twilight of the "Serenissima" (the Most Serene Republic).

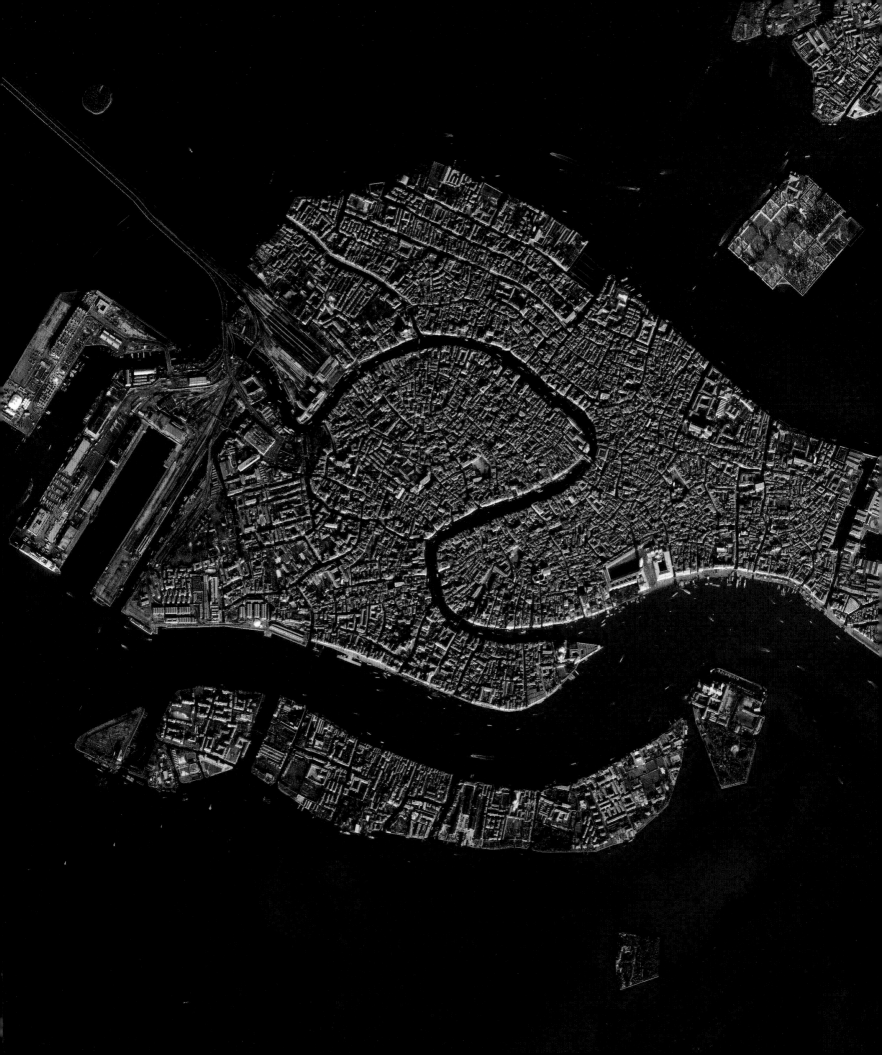

Sinking into the Sea

Since its foundation Venice has been fighting a losing
battle with the sea. Erected on wooden pilings, it
is slowly sinking into the soft mud of its lagoon.
Archaeological records show a rate of about 10 cm
(4 inches) per century in the past, but in the last century
it lost an extra 10 to 13 cm (4 to 5.5 inches) as industrial
pumping of water from deep aquifers increased the
subsidence. Lower levels of many buildings are now
under water. After devastating floods on 4 November
1966, an International Safeguarding Campaign was
launched by UNESCO and the global community.
Corrective measures were taken, water extraction was
stopped and new breakwaters were built.

Although Venice has successfully coped with the Acqua
Alta (or high tide) for more than 1000 years, climate
change puts the fragile balance at risk. The frequency
of high tides has greatly increased in recent times, with
eight out of the ten highest floods of the last 100 years
occurring since 1960. The melting of glaciers and thermal
expansion of warmer seas are causing the oceans to rise –
the UN Intergovernmental Panel on Climate Change
predicts an additional 9–88 cm (3.5–35-inch) rise from
1990 to 2100. The multi-billion US dollar Moses Project, a
series of giant mobile sluice gates, which should rise
from the seabed by 2010, will help to protect the city from
high tides, but cannot permanently keep the water out.
With Venice already at the brink, natural subsidence and
rising seas threaten to sink its heritage.

Ilulissat Icefjord
Greenland (Denmark)

AT RISK

KEY THREATS Conflict | Theft | Development | Tourism | Pollution | Disasters | Constraints | Changing Uses | Invaders | Climate

Located 250 km (180 miles) north of the Arctic Circle on the west coast of Greenland, the Ilulissat Icefjord encompasses 402 sq km (155 sq miles) of wild and scenic rock, ice and sea. It forms the mouth of Sermeq Kujalleq, one of the world's fastest flowing and most active glaciers. The combination of this huge ice sheet and the dramatic sounds of the fast-moving glacial ice stream calving into the ice-choked fjord constitutes a dramatic and awe-inspiring natural spectacle.

Ilulissat offers both scientists and visitors alike easy access for close view of the 80-m (260-ft) high calving glacier front as it cascades down from the moving ice sheet into the ice-choked waters of the fjord. The mean ice thickness in the fjord is over 700 m (2300 ft).

Here, 250km (180 miles) north of the Arctic Circle, the climate is characterized by sunless winters and nightless summers.

With recordings going back 150 years, ongoing scientific research has made the site one of the best observed ice streams in the world.

The glacier has been the object of scientific attention for more than 250 years and, because of its relative ease of access, has significantly added to our understanding of ice-cap glaciology, climate change and related geomorphic processes. Moving at the extraordinary rate of 19 m (60 ft) per day 7 km (4.5 miles) per year, the glacier is one of the few points through which Greenland's ice cap reaches the sea. It produces over 35 cubic km (8 cubic miles) of ice per year (10 per cent of all Greenland's calf ice and more than any other glacier outside Antarctica).

An outstanding example of the last ice age of the Quaternary Period, Illulissat Icefjord is particularly important for the information retrieved from the 3-km (2-mile) long ice cores taken from it, revealing temperature, precipitation trends and atmospheric conditions (in trapped air bubbles) through almost 250,000 years. No other glacier in the northern hemisphere provides such a long and continuous record of our past.

⊚ World Heritage Site inscribed 2004
http://whc.unesco.org/en/list/1149

OPPOSITE PAGE: The fjord links the Greenland ice cap with the sea, draining some 6 per cent of the island's ice sheet area.

ABOVE RIGHT: The increased amount of ice calving from the edge of the glacier is evident from the growing number of icebergs in the bay.

Rising Temperatures and Melting Ice

The fjord is threatened by climate change, as the rate of increase in atmospheric temperature is highest in the polar regions. According to the recent Arctic Climate Impact Assessment, local warming over Greenland could be between one and three times more than the average rate of global warming. The ice expanded and receded through the last ice age, which ended some 11,550 years ago, and during the "Little Ice Age" (from c. AD 1500 to 1900). Its size is believed to have peaked more than 100 years ago. From 1851 to 1950 the fjord's ice front retreated 26 km (16 miles) inland. The dramatic increase in the last few decades in melting across the whole Greenland ice sheet has become particularly worrying.

BELOW: The loss of ice in the polar regions will add to the rate of average global warming as the land and oceans will absorb heat that is currently reflected back to space by the ice. The glacier itself is thinning rapidly, losing up to 15 m (49 ft) of ice each year since 1997.

OPPOSITE PAGE: Although there are more bergs in the fjord, the ice tongue between the glacier and the sea underwent rapid melting from 2000 and by 2003 had almost completely disappeared. The loss of this ice appears to have helped to speed up the flow of the glacier itself.

Seasonal surface melt extent on the Greenland Ice Sheet has been observed by satellite since 1979 and shows an increasing trend. The melt zone, where summer warmth turns snow and ice around the edges of the ice sheet into slush and ponds of meltwater, has been expanding inland and to record high elevations in recent years. When the meltwater seeps down through cracks in the ice sheet, it may accelerate melting and, in some areas, allow the ice to slide more easily over the bedrock below, speeding its movement to the sea. In addition to contributing to global sea-level rise, this process adds fresh water to the ocean, with potential impacts on ocean circulation and thus regional climate.

The Sundarbans & Sundarbans National Park
Bangladesh & India

AT RISK | KEY THREATS Conflict | Theft | Development | Tourism | Pollution | Disasters | Constraints | Changing Uses | Invaders | Climate

The world's largest remaining mangrove forest, the Sundarbans stretch over 10,000 sq km (6200 sq miles) of land and water across the border of India and southwest Bangladesh. An intricate tapestry of tidal waterways, mudflats and small islands, this green oasis at the mouth of the Earth's largest delta forms the confluence of the Ganges, Brahmaputra and Meghna rivers on the Bay of Bengal. Named for the sundari mangrove (Heritiera fomes), or "elegant" tree, the Sundarbans are a transition from marine to freshwater and terrestrial systems. They provide a significant example of ongoing ecological processes, including monsoon rains, flooding, delta formation, tidal influence and plant colonization.

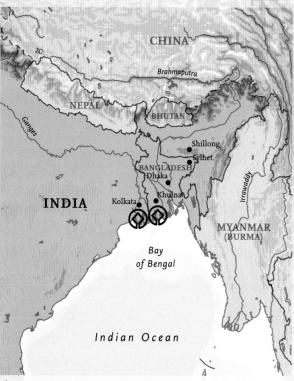

⊕ World Heritage Site inscribed 1987 (India) & 1997 (Bangladesh)
http://whc.unesco.org/en/list/798
http://whc.unesco.org/en/list/452

OPPOSITE PAGE: A beautiful tapestry stretching 265 km (165 miles) along the coast and up to 130 km (80 miles) inland, the remnants of the mangrove forests (deep green) are being encroached upon by eroding fields (light green) and settlements (tan).

ABOVE RIGHT: The Indo-Pacific's largest predator, the Bengal tiger lives among the mangroves and stalks scarce prey such as chital and barking deer, wild pigs and even macaques. Able to consume up to about 18 kg (40 lbs) of meat at a time, they can then go for days without eating.

Since the seventeenth century, the Sundarbans have been notorious for their man-eating Bengal tigers. Over the last fifty years, tigers have killed on average twenty-two people a year, although the toll has been much worse in some years (sixty-five in 1988 for example).

In 2002 there were estimated to be only 300 Bengal Tigers remaining in Bangladesh. A decade earlier the number had been put at 600. Hunting and poaching remain problems.

Among the many interesting inhabitants of the mangroves are mudskippers, gobioid fish with specially adapted gills which climb out of the water onto mudflats and even up trees.

Growing numbers of ponds for shrimp aquaculture, especially in Bangladesh, sit right at the edge of the protected area, creating an added problem for water quality and biodiversity.

The two adjoining World Heritage Sites in India and Bangladesh (inscribed in 1987 and 1997) protect 1330 and 5950 sq km (506 and 2297 sq miles) respectively. Known for their wide range of fauna, the Sundarbans are home to numerous endangered species, including the world's largest remaining population of wild Bengal tigers (Panthera tigris), as well as swamp deer, Ganges river dolphin, greater adjutant bird, river terrapin, estuarine crocodile, and loggerhead, green, and olive ridley turtles. Varied and unique birdlife includes a total of 315 recorded species, including 12 birds of prey such as osprey, white-bellied sea eagle and grey-headed fish eagle. Wild boar, spotted deer, rhesus macaque, several species of otter and wild cat, sharks, water monitors, hump-backed dolphin and Indian python are also to be found.

Sadly, the endangered water buffalo and Javan rhinoceros have not been seen here for more than 150 years, while the endangered Indian muntjac has disappeared from the area in the last 30 years.

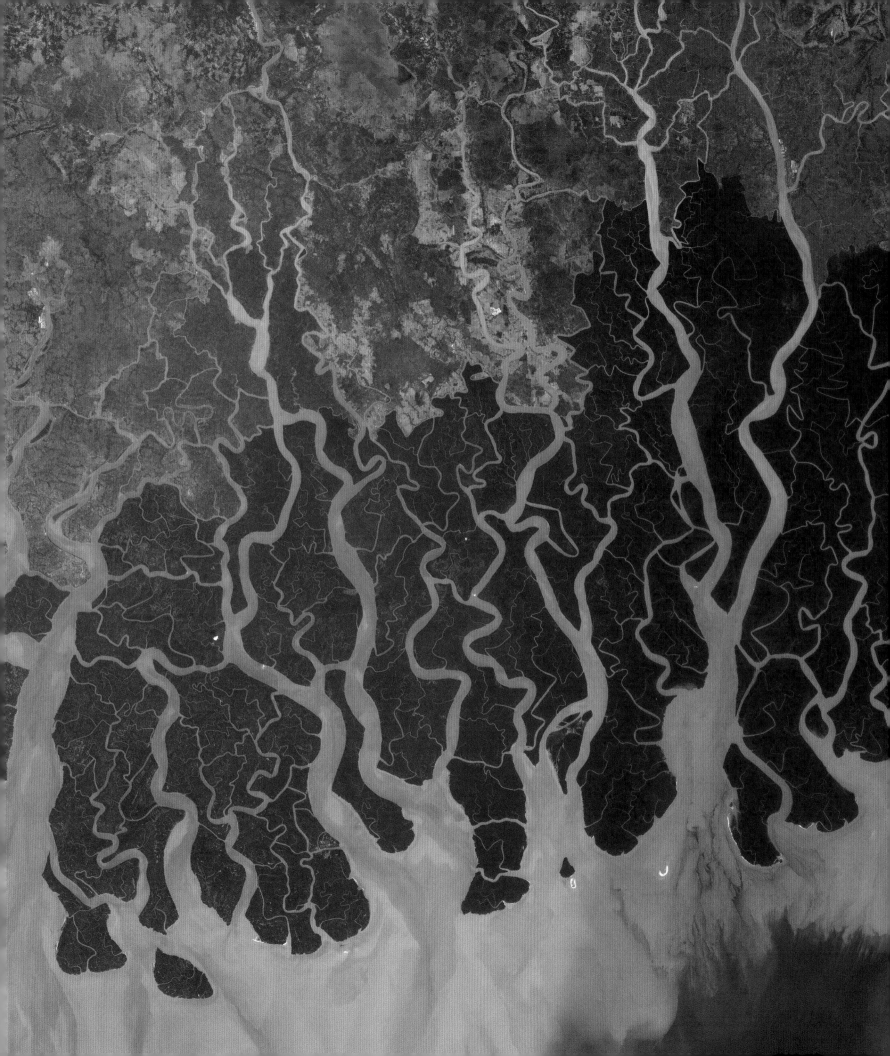

A River's End

The Sundarbans are at severe risk from rising seas. As land-based ice melts around the globe, ocean volume increases and waters rise. In the Sundarbans, the natural subsidence of the Bengal Basin is accelerating the effect, causing seas to rise by 3.1 mm (0.12 inches) per year relative to the land, almost one and a half times faster than in the rest of the world. Four islands have already disappeared, displacing populations and putting greater stress on the protected region. A predicted 1-m (3-foot) rise in the next fifty years would inundate 1000 sq km (400 sq miles) with much of this loss in the last protected areas at the tip of the delta.

Since the first settlements in 1770, the population in the Indian portion has risen to more than 4.3 million.

Diversion of the Ganges for human use has caused a 40 per cent reduction in its flow. Together with more rapid evapotranspiration, this has increased the salinity of the water, further threatening the natural balance. If the mangroves were lost, the results for nature and the region's population would be catastrophic. The mangroves form a critical buffer for people and ecosystems against the often devastating tropical storms (a cyclone in 1991 claimed 139,000 lives) which lash this region every year. They help to reduce the impact of the annual surges in one of the world's most densely populated regions. The UN estimate that close to 40 million people will be living in nearby Dhaka and Kolkata by 2015, and the possible effects of the loss of this "sea wall" would be profound.

Chavin (Archaeological Site) / Huascarán National Park
Peru

AT RISK

KEY THREATS Conflict | Theft | Development | Tourism | Pollution | Disasters | Constraints | Changing Uses | Invaders | Climate

Two World Heritage Sites sit near each other in the heights of the northern Peruvian Andes: Huascarán National Park and, in a high valley on the eastern flank, the Archaeological Site of Chavin.

The tallest of twenty-seven snow-capped peaks, Mount Huascarán rises 6768 m (22,205 feet) above sea level. Crowning the rugged Cordillera Blanco – the world's highest tropical mountain range – the national park is a site of spectacular beauty with glacier lakes, deep ravines watered by numerous torrents and a wide range of vegetation. Its 3400 sq km (1300 sq miles) are home to rare species such as the spectacled bear and Andean condor.

Huascarán National Park has some 663 glaciers, 296 lakes and 41 rivers. About 2 million people rely on water originating in the glaciers of Huascarán and the demand is increasing.

It is home to close to 800 species of high Andean plants, 112 species of birds and endangered mammals including the colocolo, Andean cat, spectacled bear, Peruvian gemal, and vicuña.

Although decades of archaeological research at Chavin have helped to clear the passages of the Old Temple and shed light on the structure and meaning of the site, many questions remain. Numerous items, from anthropomorphically carved mortars and pestles to conch-shell trumpets, bone and metal tubes and spatulas and tapestries and rich burials have added to our understanding.

⊚ World Heritage Sites inscribed 1985
http://whc.unesco.org/en/list/330, http://whc.unesco.org/en/list/333

OPPOSITE PAGE: The glacier-fed lakes above the site pose a real threat. Increasing amounts of meltwater could break the moraine walls and send vast floods or mud slides down the valleys below.

ABOVE RIGHT: One of the many guardian deities of Chavín, this feline head represents a creator god with earthly power.

In a high valley below, at the confluence of the Mosna and Wacheqsa rivers, lie the impressive stone temple ruins of Chavin de Huantar. One of the earliest and best known pre-Columbian archaeological sites, Chavin is the namesake of the culture that developed here between 1500 and 300 BC. This place of worship is striking, with a complex of terraces and squares surrounded by structures of dressed stone and primarily zoomorphic ornamentation of jaguars, caymans and other forms. Major features include the Circular Plaza, Old Temple and New Temple. The so-called Old Temple is lined with an intricate network of water channels, air or sound ducts, internal passageways and chambers, culminating in the Lanzón Gallery. It features a 4.5-m (15-foot) high, 2-tonne white granite monolith of the Lanzón, the presumed supreme deity of the place. The towering stele is carved with a smiling anthropomorphic figure with a feline head and human body. It has clawed hands and feet, a fanged mouth, circular ear pendants, bracelets and snakes writhing from its head.

A Threat of Sudden Glacial Outbursts

Climate change appears to be taking a toll on the region: it is estimated that 22 per cent of the volume of glacial ice in the Cordillera Blanca has disappeared since the late 1960s. The 2 million people and important archaeological remains downhill are under severe threat of slope instability and glacial lake outbursts, especially given the active seismology of the region. In 1945 a massive debris flow rushed down Chavin's river valley, burying the site with tons of mud in an instant. In 1962 another mudslide hit the town of Huaraz, killing 5000 people. And on 31 May 1970 the Ancash earthquake triggered a substantial part of Huascarán to collapse, sending a 2-km (1-mile) long mass of debris rushing downhill. Within five minutes it had flowed 18 km

BELOW LEFT: A new road was recently bulldozed through the narrow Chavin valley, destroying important archaeological evidence of life beyond the temple plaza, despite urgent rescue efforts by archaeologists seen here.

BELOW RIGHT: Regarded as the birthplace of indigenous Peruvian culture, Chavín and its iconic Lanzon stele have smiled for more than two millennia. But the growing risk to the valley from climate change has experts worried.

OPPOSITE PAGE: Inundated by a mudslide in 1945, and later damaged by a truck, the 12-m (39-foot) high main temple has been partially rebuilt, but is in need of further assistance.

(11 miles) to Yungay, smothering the entire town and 23,000 residents under tons of debris. With climate models predicting an increased rate of glacial melt in the future, catastrophic rock avalanches triggered by melting glacier headwalls are sadly more likely.

NO TREPAR
DONT CLIMB

Great Barrier Reef
Australia

A vast marine expanse of remarkable richness and beauty, the Great Barrier Reef is the world's largest coral reef ecosystem. Visible from space, it stretches 2300 km (1430 miles) along Australia's northeast coast from Cape York to near Fraser Island and encompasses 350,000 sq km (135,000 sq miles) of protected area. It contains the world's biggest collection of coral reefs (2900) and is built from more than 360 species of hard coral. Of great scientific interest, it is also the breeding area for humpback and other whale species, as well as the threatened dugong ("sea cow") and green turtle.

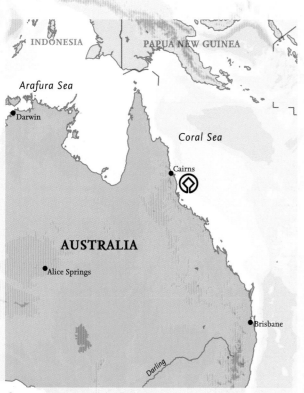

⊚ World Heritage Site inscribed 1981
http://whc.unesco.org/en/list/154

OPPOSITE PAGE: From the air the vast reef's coral-ringed islands glimmer like aquamarine pearls.

ABOVE RIGHT: Corals live in a symbiotic partnership with algae which give them their vivid brown, yellow, green blue and pink.

Highly dependent on climate, reefs generally only occur where temperatures remain above 18° C (64° F) most of the time. But they are also susceptible to too high a temperature and an increase of just 1–2 ° C (2–4 °F) above normal summertime maxima is enough to cause harm and even death. With the average global temperature having already risen 0.6–0.8 °C (1.08–1.44 °F) in the last 100 years, there is real cause for concern.

As levels of carbon dioxide increase in the atmosphere, more becomes dissolved in the oceans. This process is raising acidity levels in sea water, which slows coral growth rates and weakens their calcium frames.

Culturally important to both Aboriginal and Torres Strait Islander people, it is a major tourist destination, receiving several million visitors a year and contributing billions of dollars to the Australian economy.

With arguably the highest biodiversity of any World Heritage Site, the reef's variety and the interconnectedness of species and habitats are amazing. In addition to the coral, it has:

- more than 2000 sq km (770 sq miles) of mangroves, including 54 per cent of the world's mangrove diversity
- more than 3000 sq km (1160 sq miles) of sea grasses and 500 species of seaweed
- some 2000 fish, 5000 mollusc, 1500 sponge and 800 echinoderm (eg starfish) species
- six of the world's seven turtle species, including the largest green turtle breeding area on earth
- one of the world's largest dugong populations
- 2200 species of native plants (25 per cent of Queensland's total)
- 175 bird species

An Ecosystem in Hot Water

Coral plays a crucial role in the marine ecosystem providing food and habitat for thousands of species. Many corals live close to their upper thermal tolerance levels so just a small change in sea-surface temperature can be a threat and cause bleaching and death. Raised temperatures also harm other lifeforms: phytoplankton production is reduced, reducing fish supplies and starving birds. Tourism and coastal development in turn further threaten the reef with runoff and sediments despite stringent controls. Some have linked destructive crown of thorns starfish outbreaks to human pollution weakening the ecosystem. Shipping also poses risks: in November 2000 a container ship grounded on the reef.

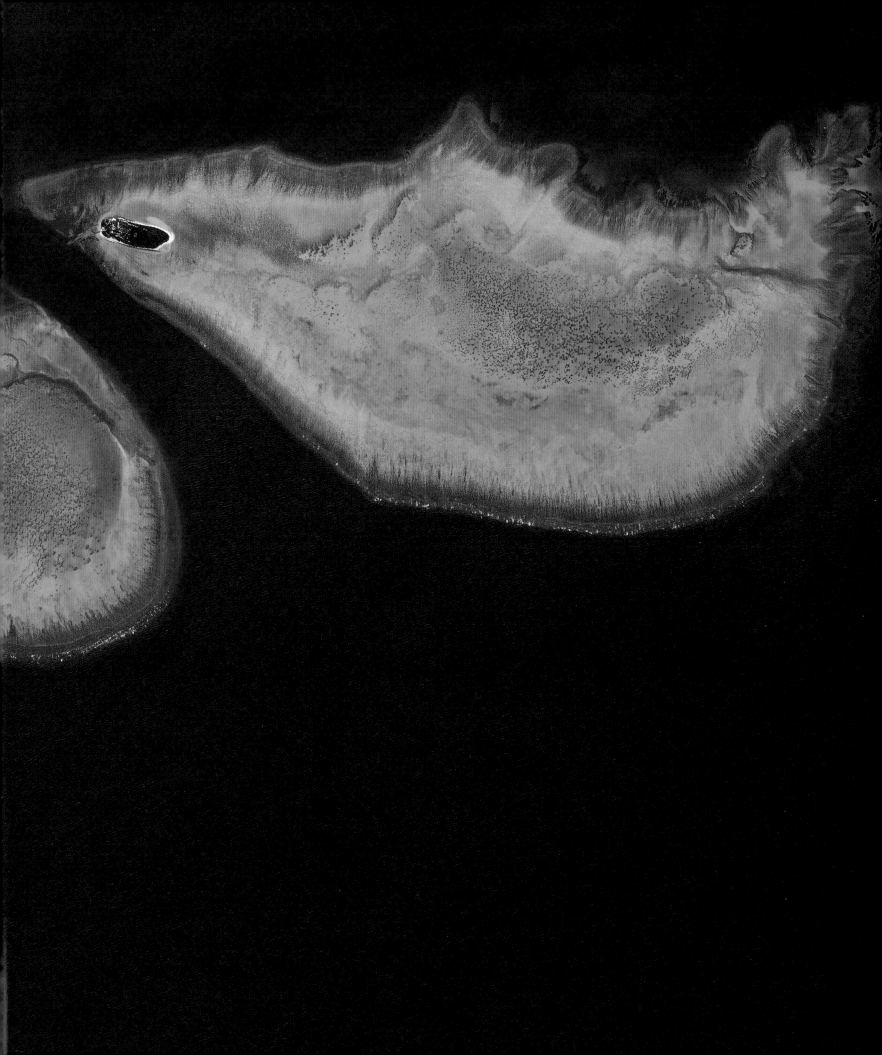

Fortunately damage was controlled, but fishing and bottom trawling also pose risks.

Although the best practices in heritage management are employed, the reef is at risk from climate changes far beyond local control. It experienced major bleaching events in 1998 and 2002, affecting 60–95 per cent of reefs. While the effects of bleaching were widespread, the reef has escaped extensive mortality to date. However, scientists predict that rising global temperatures present a major threat to coral reefs over the next thirty years. The UN Intergovernmental Panel on Climate Change estimates that coral cover in reefs around the world will decrease to less than 5 per cent by 2050.

BELOW LEFT: One of the wonders of the natural world, the Great Barrier Reef is the biggest structure on Earth made by living organisms.

BELOW RIGHT: Some of the 2900 individual reefs, 600 inshore islands and passages are visible in this satellite image of a 380-km (240-mile) swathe in the middle of the reef.

OPPOSITE PAGE: Global climate change threatens coral reefs, which provide food and habitat for thousands of species. As the water gets too warm, the algae depart, leaving the coral almost pure white. This loss of colour is called bleaching. If the algae do not return within a few months, the coral will die.

"Twenty per cent of the earth's coral reefs, arguably the richest of all marine ecosystems, have been effectively destroyed today."
CARL GUSTAF LUNDIN, HEAD OF THE IUCN MARINE ENVIRONMENT PROGRAMME

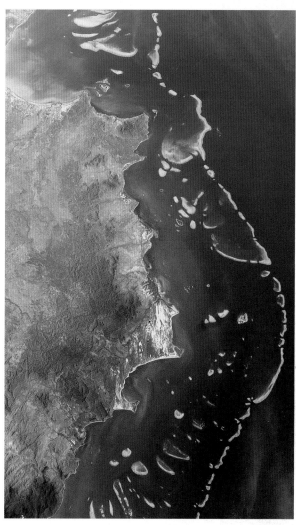

World Heritage and UNESCO's World Heritage Mission

Heritage is our legacy from the past, what we live with today, and what we pass on to future generations. Our cultural and natural heritage are both irreplaceable sources of life and inspiration. Places as unique and diverse as the wilds of East Africa's Serengeti, the Pyramids of Egypt, the Great Barrier Reef in Australia and the Baroque cathedrals of Latin America make up our world's heritage.

The United Nations Educational, Scientific and Cultural Organization (UNESCO) seeks to encourage the identification, protection and preservation of cultural and natural heritage around the world of outstanding universal value to humanity. This is embodied in a unique international "treaty", the *Convention Concerning the Protection of the World Cultural and Natural Heritage* (see http://whc.unesco.org/en/conventiontext), adopted by UNESCO in 1972.

One of the world's most successful conservation instruments, the World Heritage Convention is exceptional in that it links together in a single document the concepts of nature conservation and the preservation of cultural properties. It is also significant in its universal application – World Heritage Sites belong to all the peoples of the world, irrespective of the territory on which they are located. By regarding heritage as both cultural and natural, the Convention recognizes the ways in which people interact with nature, and of the fundamental need to preserve the balance between the two.

UNESCO's World Heritage mission is to:

- encourage countries to sign the World Heritage Convention and to ensure the protection of their natural and cultural heritage;

- encourage States Parties to the Convention to nominate sites within their national territory for inclusion on the World Heritage List;

- encourage States Parties to establish management plans and set up reporting systems on the state of conservation of their World Heritage Sites;

- help States Parties safeguard World Heritage properties by providing technical assistance and professional training;

- provide emergency assistance for World Heritage Sites in immediate danger;

- support States Parties' public awareness-building activities for World Heritage conservation;

- encourage participation of the local population in the preservation of their cultural and natural heritage;

- encourage international cooperation in the conservation of our world's cultural and natural heritage.

THE CRITERIA FOR SELECTION

The World Heritage Convention stipulates the creation of a World Heritage List. In a detailed process, potential properties are inscribed by a twenty-one member elected Committee, only after a detailed preselection, nomination, and review process. Two leading international Non-Governmental Organizations, the World Conservation Union (IUCN) and the International Council on Monuments and Sites (ICOMOS), review and advise on the natural and cultural nominations respectively. To be included, sites must be of outstanding universal value and meet at least one out of ten selection criteria:

i.   to represent a masterpiece of human creative genius;

ii.   to exhibit an important interchange of human values, over a span of time or within a cultural area of the world, on developments in architecture or technology, monumental arts, town-planning or landscape design;

iii.   to bear a unique or at least exceptional testimony to a cultural tradition or to a civilization which is living or which has disappeared;

iv.   to be an outstanding example of a type of building, architectural or technological ensemble or landscape which illustrates (a) significant stage(s) in human history;

v.   to be an outstanding example of a traditional human settlement, land-use, or sea-use which is representative of a culture (or cultures), or human interaction with the environment especially when it has become vulnerable under the impact of irreversible change;

vi.   to be directly or tangibly associated with events or living traditions, with ideas, or with beliefs, with artistic and literary works of outstanding universal significance. (The Committee considers that this criterion should preferably be used in conjunction with other criteria);

vii.   to contain superlative natural phenomena or areas of exceptional natural beauty and aesthetic importance;

viii.   to be outstanding examples representing major stages of earth's history, including the record of life, significant on-going geological processes in the development of landforms, or significant geomorphic or physiographic features;

ix.   to be outstanding examples representing significant on-going ecological and biological processes in the evolution and development of terrestrial, fresh water, coastal and marine ecosystems and communities of plants and animals;

x.   to contain the most important and significant natural habitats for in-situ conservation of biological diversity, including those containing threatened species of outstanding universal value from the point of view of science or conservation.

The protection, management, authenticity and integrity of properties are also important considerations. The process is further detailed in the *Operational Guidelines for the Implementation of the World Heritage Convention* which, along with the actual text of the Convention, is the main working tool on World Heritage.

UNESCO World Heritage List with Dates of Inscription

The World Heritage List includes 851 properties forming part of the cultural and natural heritage which the World Heritage Committee considers as having outstanding universal value. These include 660 cultural, 166 natural and 25 mixed properties in 141 States Parties. Thirty properties are included on the List of World Heritage in Danger in accordance with Article 11(4) of the World Heritage Convention. As of October 2006, 184 States Parties had ratified the World Heritage Convention.

The list, and links to full details on each site, can be found at http://whc.unesco.org/en/list

Afghanistan: Minaret and Archaeological Remains of Jam (2002); Cultural Landscape and Archaeological Remains of the Bamiyan Valley (2003)

Albania: Butrint (1992, 1999); Museum-City of Gjirokastra (2005)

Algeria: Al Qal'a of Beni Hammad (1980); Djémila (1982); M'Zab Valley (1982); Tassili n'Ajjer (1982); Timgad (1982); Tipasa (1982); Kasbah of Algiers (1992)

Andorra: Madriu-Perafita-Claror Valley (2004, 2006)

Argentina: Los Glaciares (1981); Jesuit Missions of the Guaranis: San Ignacio Mini, Santa Ana, Nuestra Señora de Loreto and Santa Maria Mayor (Argentina), Ruins of Sao Miguel das Missoes (Brazil) (1983, 1984); Iguazu National Park (1984); Cueva de las Manos, Río Pinturas (1999); Península Valdés (1999); Ischigualasto / Talampaya Natural Parks (2000); Jesuit Block and Estancias of Córdoba (2000); Quebrada de Humahuaca (2003)

Armenia: Monasteries of Haghpat and Sanahin (1996, 2000); Cathedral and Churches of Echmiatsin and the Archaeological Site of Zvartnots (2000); Monastery of Geghard and the Upper Azat Valley (2000)

Australia: Great Barrier Reef (1981); Kakadu National Park (1981, 1987, 1992); Willandra Lakes Region (1981); Lord Howe Island Group (1982); Tasmanian Wilderness (1982, 1989); Central Eastern Rainforests Reserves (Australia) (1986, 1994); Uluru-Kata Tjuṯa National Park (1987, 1994); Wet Tropics of Queensland (1988); Shark Bay, Western Australia (1991); Fraser Island (1992); Australian Fossil Mammal Sites (Riversleigh / Naracoorte) (1994); Heard and McDonald Islands (1997); Macquarie Island (1997); Greater Blue Mountains Area (2000); Purnululu National Park (2003); Royal Exhibition Building and Carlton Gardens (2004); Sydney Opera House (2007)

Austria: Historic Centre of the City of Salzburg (1996); Palace and Gardens of Schönbrunn (1996); Hallstatt-Dachstein Salzkammergut Cultural Landscape (1997); Semmering Railway (1998); City of Graz Historic Centre (1999); Wachau Cultural Landscape (2000); Fertő / Neusiedlersee Cultural Landscape (2001); Historic Centre of Vienna (2001)

Azerbaijan: Walled City of Baku with the Shirvanshah's Palace and Maiden Tower (2000); Gobustan Rock Art Cultural Landscape (2007)

Bahrain: Qal'at al-Bahrain – Ancient Harbour and Capital of Dilmun (2005)

Bangladesh: Historic Mosque City of Bagerhat (1985); Ruins of the Buddhist Vihara at Paharpur (1985); The Sundarbans (1997)

Belarus: Belovezhskaya Pushcha / Białowieża Forest (1979, 1992); Mir Castle Complex (2000); Architectural, Residential and Cultural Complex of the Radziwill Family at Nesvizh (2005); Struve Geodetic Arc (2005)

Belgium: Flemish Béguinages (1998); La Grand-Place, Brussels (1998); The Four Lifts on the Canal du Centre and their Environs, La Louvière and Le Roeulx (Hainault) (1998); Belfries of Belgium and France (1999, 2005); Historic Centre of Brugge (2000); Major Town Houses of the Architect Victor Horta (Brussels) (2000); Neolithic Flint Mines at Spiennes (Mons) (2000); Notre-Dame Cathedral in Tournai (2000); Plantin-Moretus House–Workshops–Museum Complex (2005)

Belize: Belize Barrier Reef Reserve System (1996)

Benin: Royal Palaces of Abomey (1985)

Bolivia: City of Potosí (1987); Jesuit Missions of the Chiquitos (1990); Historic City of Sucre (1991); Fuerte de Samaipata (1998); Noel Kempff Mercado National Park (2000); Tiwanaku: Spiritual and Political Centre of the Tiwanaku Culture (2000)

Bosnia and Herzegovina: Old Bridge Area of the Old City of Mostar (2005); Mehmed Paša Sokolović Bridge in Višegrad (2007)

Botswana: Tsodilo (2001)

Brazil: Historic Town of Ouro Preto (1980); Historic Centre of the Town of Olinda (1982); Jesuit Missions of the Guaranis: San Ignacio Mini, Santa Ana, Nuestra Señora de Loreto and Santa Maria Mayor (Argentina), Ruins of São Miguel das Missões (Brazil) (1983, 1984); Historic Centre of Salvador de Bahia (1985); Sanctuary of Bom Jesus do Congonhas (1985); Iguaçu National Park (1986); Brasilia (1987); Serra da Capivara National Park (1991); Historic Centre of São Luís (1997); Atlantic Forest South-East Reserves (1999); Discovery Coast Atlantic Forest Reserves (1999); Historic Centre of the Town of Diamantina (1999); Central Amazon Conservation Complex (2000, 2003); Pantanal Conservation Area (2000); Brazilian Atlantic Islands: Fernando de Noronha and Atol das Rocas Reserves (2001); Cerrado Protected

Areas: Chapada dos Veadeiros and Emas National Parks (2001); Historic Centre of the Town of Goiás (2001)

Bulgaria: Boyana Church (1979); Madara Rider (1979); Rock-Hewn Churches of Ivanovo (1979); Thracian Tomb of Kazanlak (1979); Ancient City of Nessebar (1983); Pirin National Park (1983); Rila Monastery (1983); Srebarna Nature Reserve (1983); Thracian Tomb of Sveshtari (1985)

Cambodia: Angkor (1992)

Cameroon: Dja Faunal Reserve (1987)

Canada: L'Anse aux Meadows National Historic Site (1978); Nahanni National Park (1978); Dinosaur Provincial Park (1979); Kluane / Wrangell-St Elias / Glacier Bay / Tatshenshini-Alsek (1979, 1992, 1994); Head-Smashed-In Buffalo Jump (1981); SGang Gwaay (1981); Wood Buffalo National Park (1983); Canadian Rocky Mountain Parks (1984, 1990); Historic District of Old Québec (1985); Gros Morne National Park (1987); Old Town Lunenburg (1995); Waterton Glacier International Peace Park (1995); Miguasha National Park (1999); Rideau Canal (2007)

Central African Republic: Manovo-Gounda St Floris National Park (1988)

Chile: Rapa Nui National Park (1995); Churches of Chiloé (2000); Historic Quarter of the Seaport City of Valparaíso (2003); Humberstone and Santa Laura Saltpeter Works (2005); Sewell Mining Town (2006)

China: Imperial Palaces of the Ming and Qing Dynasties in Beijing and Shenyang (1987, 2004); Mausoleum of the First Qin Emperor (1987); Mogao Caves (1987); Mount Taishan (1987); Peking Man Site at Zhoukoudian (1987); The Great Wall (1987); Mount Huangshan (1990); Huanglong Scenic and Historic Interest Area (1992); Jiuzhaigou Valley Scenic and Historic Interest Area (1992); Wulingyuan Scenic and Historic Interest Area (1992); Ancient Building Complex in the Wudang Mountains (1994); Historic Ensemble of the Potala Palace, Lhasa (1994, 2000, 2001); Mountain Resort and its Outlying Temples, Chengde (1994); Temple and Cemetery of Confucius and the Kong Family Mansion in Qufu (1994); Lushan National Park (1996); Mount Emei Scenic Area, including Leshan Giant Buddha Scenic Area (1996); Ancient City of Ping Yao (1997); Classical Gardens of Suzhou (1997, 2000); Old Town of Lijiang (1997); Summer Palace, an Imperial Garden in Beijing (1998); Temple of Heaven: an Imperial Sacrificial Altar in Beijing (1998); Dazu Rock Carvings (1999); Mount Wuyi (1999); Ancient Villages in Southern Anhui –

Xidi and Hongcun (2000); Imperial Tombs of the Ming and Qing Dynasties (2000, 2003, 2004); Longmen Grottoes (2000); Mount Qingcheng and the Dujiangyan Irrigation System (2000); Yungang Grottoes (2001); Three Parallel Rivers of Yunnan Protected Areas (2003); Capital Cities and Tombs of the Ancient Koguryo Kingdom (2004); Historic Centre of Macao (2005); Sichuan Giant Panda Sanctuaries (2006); Yin Xu (2006); Kaiping Diaolou and Villages (2007); South China Karst (2007)

Colombia: Port, Fortresses and Group of Monuments, Cartagena (1984); Los Katíos National Park (1994); Historic Centre of Santa Cruz de Mompox (1995); National Archaeological Park of Tierradentro (1995); San Agustín Archaeological Park (1995); Malpelo Fauna and Flora Sanctuary (2006)

Congo (Democratic Republic of the Congo): Virunga National Park (1979); Garamba National Park (1980); Kahuzi-Biega National Park (1980); Salonga National Park (1984); Okapi Wildlife Reserve (1996)

Costa Rica: Talamanca Range–La Amistad Reserves / La Amistad National Park (1983, 1990); Cocos Island National Park (1997, 2002); Area de Conservación Guanacaste (1999, 2004)

Côte d'Ivoire: Mount Nimba Strict Nature Reserve (1981, 1982); Taï National Park (1982); Comoé National Park (1983)

Croatia: Historical Complex of Split with the Palace of Diocletian (1979); Old City of Dubrovnik (1979, 1994); Plitvice Lakes National Park (1979, 2000); Episcopal Complex of the Euphrasian Basilica in the Historic Centre of Poreč (1997); Historic City of Trogir (1997); The Cathedral of St James in Šibenik (2000)

Cuba: Old Havana and its Fortifications (1982); Trinidad and the Valley de los Ingenios (1988); San Pedro de la Roca Castle, Santiago de Cuba (1997); Desembarco del Granma National Park (1999); Viñales Valley (1999); Archaeological Landscape of the First Coffee Plantations in the South-East of Cuba (2000); Alejandro de Humboldt National Park (2001); Urban Historic Centre of Cienfuegos (2005)

Cyprus: Paphos (1980); Painted Churches in the Troodos Region (1985, 2001); Choirokoitia (1998)

Czech Republic: Historic Centre of Český Krumlov (1992); Historic Centre of Prague (1992); Historic Centre of Telč (1992); Pilgrimage Church of St John of Nepomuk at Zelená Hora (1994); Kutná Hora: Historical

Town Centre with the Church of St Barbara and the Cathedral of Our Lady at Sedlec (1995); Lednice-Valtice Cultural Landscape (1996); Gardens and Castle at Kroměříž (1998); Holašovice Historical Village Reservation (1998); Litomyšl Castle (1999); Holy Trinity Column in Olomouc (2000); Tugendhat Villa in Brno (2001); Jewish Quarter and St Procopius' Basilica in Třebíč (2003)

Denmark: Jelling Mounds, Runic Stones and Church (1994); Roskilde Cathedral (1995); Kronborg Castle (2000); Ilulissat Icefjord (2004)

Dominica: Morne Trois Pitons National Park (1997)

Dominican Republic: Colonial City of Santo Domingo (1990)

Ecuador: City of Quito (1978); Galápagos Islands (1978, 2001); Sangay National Park (1983); Historic Centre of Santa Ana de los Ríos de Cuenca (1999)

Egypt: Abu Mena (1979); Ancient Thebes with its Necropolis (1979); Historic Cairo (1979); Memphis and its Necropolis – the Pyramid Fields from Giza to Dahshur (1979); Nubian Monuments from Abu Simbel to Philae (1979); Saint Catherine Area (2002); Wadi Al-Hitan (Whale Valley) (2005)

El Salvador: Joya de Ceren Archaeological Site (1993)

Estonia: Historic Centre (Old Town) of Tallinn (1997); Struve Geodetic Arc (2005)

Ethiopia: Rock-Hewn Churches, Lalibela (1978); Simien National Park (1978); Fasil Ghebbi, Gondar Region (1979); Aksum (1980); Lower Valley of the Awash (1980); Lower Valley of the Omo (1980); Tiya (1980); Harar Jugol, the Fortified Historic Town (2006)

Finland: Fortress of Suomenlinna (1991); Old Rauma (1991); Petäjävesi Old Church (1994); Verla Groundwood and Board Mill (1996); Bronze Age Burial Site of Sammallahdenmäki (1999); Kvarken Archipelago / High Coast (2000, 2006); Struve Geodetic Arc (2005)

France: Chartres Cathedral (1979); Mont-Saint-Michel and its Bay (1979); Palace and Park of Versailles (1979); Prehistoric Sites and Decorated Caves of the Vézère Valley (1979); Vézelay, Church and Hill (1979); Amiens Cathedral (1981); Arles, Roman and Romanesque Monuments (1981); Cistercian Abbey of Fontenay (1981); Palace and Park of Fontainebleau (1981); Roman Theatre and its Surroundings and the "Triumphal Arch" of Orange (1981); Royal Saltworks of Arc-et-

Senans (1982); Abbey Church of Saint-Savin sur Gartempe (1983); Gulf of Porto: Calanche of Piana, Gulf of Girolata, Scandola Reserve (1983); Place Stanislas, Place de la Carrière and Place d'Alliance in Nancy (1983); Pont du Gard (Roman Aqueduct) (1985); Strasbourg – Grande île (1988); Cathedral of Notre-Dame, Former Abbey of Saint-Remi and Palace of Tau, Reims (1991); Paris, Banks of the Seine (1991); Bourges Cathedral (1992); Historic Centre of Avignon: Papal Palace, Episcopal Ensemble and Avignon Bridge (1995); Canal du Midi (1996); Historic Fortified City of Carcassonne (1997); Pyrénées – Mont Perdu (1997, 1999); Historic Site of Lyons (1998); Routes of Santiago de Compostela in France (1998); Belfries of Belgium and France (1999, 2005); Jurisdiction of Saint-Emilion (1999); The Loire Valley between Sully-sur-Loire and Chalonnes (2000); Provins, Town of Medieval Fairs (2001); Le Havre, the City Rebuilt by Auguste Perret (2005); Bordeaux, Port of the Moon (2007)

Gabon: Ecosystem and Relict Cultural Landscape of Lopé-Okanda (2007)

Gambia: James Island and Related Sites (2003); Stone Circles of Senegambia (2006)

Georgia: Bagrati Cathedral and Gelati Monastery (1994); Historical Monuments of Mtskheta (1994); Upper Svaneti (1996)

Germany: Aachen Cathedral (1978); Speyer Cathedral (1981); Würzburg Residence with the Court Gardens and Residence Square (1981); Pilgrimage Church of Wies (1983); Castles of Augustusburg and Falkenlust at Brühl (1984); St Mary's Cathedral and St Michael's Church at Hildesheim (1985); Roman Monuments, Cathedral of St Peter and Church of Our Lady in Trier (1986); Frontiers of the Roman Empire (1987, 2005); Hanseatic City of Lübeck (1987); Palaces and Parks of Potsdam and Berlin (1990, 1992, 1999); Abbey and Altenmünster of Lorsch (1991); Mines of Rammelsberg and Historic Town of Goslar (1992); Maulbronn Monastery Complex (1993); Town of Bamberg (1993); Collegiate Church, Castle, and Old Town of Quedlinburg (1994); Völklingen Ironworks (1994); Messel Pit Fossil Site (1995); Bauhaus and its Sites in Weimar and Dessau (1996); Cologne Cathedral (1996); Luther Memorials in Eisleben and Wittenberg (1996); Classical Weimar (1998); Museumsinsel (Museum Island), Berlin (1999); Wartburg Castle (1999); Garden Kingdom of Dessau-Wörlitz (2000); Monastic Island of Reichenau (2000); Zollverein Coal Mine Industrial Complex in Essen (2001); Historic Centres of Stralsund and Wismar (2002); Upper Middle Rhine Valley (2002); Dresden Elbe Valley (2004); Muskauer Park / Park Muzakowski (2004); Town Hall and Roland on the Marketplace of Bremen (2004); Old town of Regensburg with Stadtamhof (2006)

Ghana: Forts and Castles, Volta, Greater Accra, Central and Western Regions (1979); Asante Traditional Buildings (1980)

Greece: Temple of Apollo Epicurius at Bassae (1986); Acropolis, Athens (1987); Archaeological Site of Delphi (1987); Medieval City of Rhodes (1988); Meteora (1988); Mount Athos (1988); Paleochristian and Byzantine Monuments of Thessalonika (1988); Sanctuary of Asklepios at Epidaurus (1988); Archaeological Site of Mystras (1989); Archaeological Site of Olympia (1989); Delos (1990); Monasteries of Daphni, Hosios Loukas and Nea Moni of Chios (1990); Pythagoreion and Heraion of Samos (1992); Archaeological Site of Aigai (modern name Vergina) (1996); Archaeological Sites of Mycenae and Tiryns (1999); Historic Centre (Chorá) with the Monastery of Saint John "the Theologian" and the Cave of the Apocalypse on the Island of Pátmos (1999); Old Town of Corfu (2007)

Guatemala: Antigua Guatemala (1979); Tikal National Park (1979); Archaeological Park and Ruins of Quirigua (1981)

Guinea: Mount Nimba Strict Nature Reserve (1981, 1982)

Haiti: National History Park – Citadel, Sans Souci, Ramiers (1982)

Honduras: Maya Site of Copan (1980); Río Plátano Biosphere Reserve (1982)

Hungary: Budapest, including the Banks of the Danube, the Buda Castle Quarter and Andrássy Avenue (1987, 2002); Old Village of Hollókö and its Surroundings (1987); Caves of Aggtelek Karst and Slovak Karst (1995, 2000); Millenary Benedictine Abbey of Pannonhalma and its Natural Environment (1996); Hortobágy National Park – the *Puszta* (1999); Early Christian Necropolis of Pécs (Sopianae) (2000); Fertö / Neusiedlersee Cultural Landscape (2001); Tokaj Wine Region Historic Cultural Landscape (2002)

Iceland: Þingvellir National Park (2004)

India: Agra Fort (1983); Ajanta Caves (1983); Ellora Caves (1983); Taj Mahal (1983); Group of Monuments at Mahabalipuram (1984); Sun Temple, Konârak (1984); Kaziranga National Park (1985); Keoladeo National Park (1985); Manas Wildlife Sanctuary (1985); Churches and Convents of Goa (1986); Fatehpur Sikri (1986); Group of Monuments at Hampi (1986); Khajuraho Group of Monuments (1986); Elephanta Caves (1987); Great Living Chola Temples (1987, 2004); Group of Monuments at Pattadakal (1987); Sundarbans National Park (1987); Nanda Devi and Valley of Flowers National Parks (1988, 2005); Buddhist Monuments at Sanchi (1989); Humayun's Tomb, Delhi (1993); Qutb Minar and its Monuments, Delhi (1993); Mountain Railways of India (1999, 2005); Mahabodhi Temple Complex at Bodh Gaya (2002); Rock Shelters of Bhimbetka (2003); Champaner-Pavagadh Archaeological Park (2004); Chhatrapati Shivaji Terminus (formerly Victoria Terminus) (2004); Red Fort Complex (2007)

Indonesia: Borobudur Temple Compounds (1991); Komodo National Park (1991); Prambanan Temple Compounds (1991); Ujung Kulon National Park (1991); Sangiran Early Man Site (1996); Lorentz National Park (1999); Tropical Rainforest Heritage of Sumatra (2004)

Iran (Islamic Republic of Iran): Meidan Emam, Esfahan (1979); Persepolis (1979); Tchogha Zanbil (1979); Takht-e Soleyman (2003); Bam and its Cultural Landscape (2004); Pasargadae (2004); Soltaniyeh (2005); Bisotun (2006)

Iraq: Hatra (1985); Ashur (Qal'at Sherqat) (2003); Samarra Archaeological City (2007)

Ireland: Archaeological Ensemble of the Bend of the Boyne (1993); Skellig Michael (1996)

Israel: Masada (2001); Old City of Acre (2001); White City of Tel-Aviv – the Modern Movement (2003); Biblical Tels – Megiddo, Hazor, Beer Sheba (2005); Incense Route – Desert Cities in the Negev (2005)

Italy: Rock Drawings in Valcamonica (1979); Church and Dominican Convent of Santa Maria delle Grazie with "The Last Supper" by Leonardo da Vinci (1980); Historic Centre of Rome, the Properties of the Holy See in that City Enjoying Extraterritorial Rights and San Paolo Fuori le Mura (1980, 1990); Historic Centre of Florence (1982); Piazza del Duomo, Pisa (1987); Venice and its Lagoon (1987); Historic Centre of San Gimignano (1990); The Sassi and the Park of the Rupestrian Churches of Matera (1993); City of Vicenza and the Palladian Villas of the Veneto (1994, 1996); Crespi d'Adda (1995); Ferrara, City of the Renaissance, and its Po Delta (1995, 1999); Historic Centre of Naples (1995); Historic Centre of Siena (1995); Castel del Monte (1996); Early Christian Monuments of Ravenna (1996); Historic Centre of the City of Pienza (1996); The *Trulli* of Alberobello (1996); 18th-Century Royal Palace at Caserta with the Park, the Aqueduct of Vanvitelli, and the San Leucio Complex (1997); Archaeological Area of Agrigento (1997); Archaeological Areas of Pompei, Herculaneum and Torre Annunziata (1997); Botanical Garden (Orto Botanico), Padua (1997); Cathedral, Torre Civica and Piazza Grande, Modena (1997); Costiera Amalfitana (1997); Portovenere, Cinque Terre, and the Islands (Palmaria, Tino and Tinetto) (1997); Residences of the Royal House of Savoy (1997); Su Nuraxi di Barumini (1997); Villa Romana del Casale (1997); Archaeological Area and the Patriarchal Basilica of Aquileia (1998); Cilento and Vallo di Diano National Park with the Archaeological sites of Paestum and Velia, and the Certosa di Padula (1998); Historic Centre of Urbino (1998); Villa Adriana (Tivoli) (1999); Assisi, the Basilica of San Francesco and Other Franciscan Sites (2000); City of Verona (2000); Isole Eolie (Aeolian Islands) (2000); Villa d'Este, Tivoli (2001); Late Baroque Towns of the Val di Noto (South-Eastern Sicily) (2002); *Sacri Monti* of Piedmont and Lombardy (2003); Etruscan Necropolises of Cerveteri and Tarquinia (2004); Val d'Orcia (2004); Syracuse and the Rocky Necropolis of Pantalica (2005); Genoa: *Le Strade Nuove* and the system of the *Palazzi dei Rolli* (2006)

Japan: Buddhist Monuments in the Horyu-ji Area (1993); Himeji-jo (1993); Shirakami-Sanchi (1993); Yakushima (1993); Historic Monuments of Ancient Kyoto (Kyoto, Uji and Otsu Cities) (1994); Historic Villages of Shirakawa-go and Gokayama (1995); Hiroshima Peace Memorial (Genbaku Dome) (1996); Itsukushima Shinto Shrine (1996); Historic Monuments of Ancient Nara (1998); Shrines and Temples of Nikko (1999); Gusuku Sites and Related Properties of the Kingdom of Ryukyu (2000); Sacred Sites and Pilgrimage Routes in the Kii Mountain Range (2004); Shiretoko (2005); Iwami Ginzan Silver Mine and its Cultural Landscape (2007)

Jerusalem (Site proposed by Jordan): Old City of Jerusalem and its Walls (1981)

Jordan: Petra (1985); Quseir Amra (1985); Um er-Rasas (Kastrom Mefa'a) (2004)

Kazakhstan: Mausoleum of Khoja Ahmed Yasawi (2003); Petroglyphs within the Archaeological Landscape of Tamgaly (2004)

Kenya: Lake Turkana National Parks (1997, 2001); Mount Kenya National Park/Natural Forest (1997); Lamu Old Town (2001)

Laos (Lao People's Democratic Republic): Town of Luang Prabang (1995); Vat Phou and Associated Ancient Settlements within the Champasak Cultural Landscape (2001)

Latvia: Historic Centre of Riga (1997); Struve Geodetic Arc (2005)

Lebanon: Anjar (1984); Baalbek (1984); Byblos (1984); Tyre (1984); Ouadi Qadisha (the Holy Valley) and the Forest of the Cedars of God (Horsh Arz el-Rab) (1998)

Libya (Libyan Arab Jamahiriya): Archaeological Site of Cyrene (1982); Archaeological Site of Leptis Magna (1982); Archaeological Site of Sabratha (1982); Rock-Art Sites of Tadrart Acacus (1985); Old Town of Ghadamès (1986)

Lithuania: Vilnius Historic Centre (1994); Curonian Spit (2000); Kernavė Archaeological Site (Cultural Reserve of Kernavė) (2004); Struve Geodetic Arc (2005)

Luxembourg: City of Luxembourg: its Old Quarters and Fortifications (1994)

Macedonia (the Former Yugoslav Republic of Macedonia): Natural and Cultural Heritage of the Ohrid region (1979, 1980)

Madagascar: Tsingy de Bemaraha Strict Nature Reserve (1990); Royal Hill of Ambohimanga (2001); Rainforests of the Atsinanana (2007)

Malawi: Lake Malawi National Park (1984); Chongoni Rock-Art Area (2006)

Malaysia: Gunung Mulu National Park (2000); Kinabalu Park (2000)

Mali: Old Towns of Djenné (1988); Timbuktu (1988); Cliff of Bandiagara (Land of the Dogons) (1989); Tomb of Askia (2004)

Malta: City of Valletta (1980); Hal Saflieni Hypogeum (1980); Megalithic Temples of Malta (1980, 1992)

Mauritania: Banc d'Arguin National Park (1989); Ancient *Ksour* of Ouadane, Chinguetti, Tichitt and Oualata (1996)

Mauritius: Aapravasi Ghat (2006)

Mexico: Historic Centre of Mexico City and Xochimilco (1987); Historic Centre of Oaxaca and Archaeological Site of Monte Albán (1987); Historic Centre of Puebla (1987); Pre-Hispanic City and National Park of Palenque (1987); Pre-Hispanic City of Teotihuacan (1987); Sian Ka'an (1987); Historic Town of Guanajuato and Adjacent Mines (1988); Pre-Hispanic City of Chichen-Itza (1988); Historic Centre of Morelia (1991); El Tajin, Pre-Hispanic City (1992); Historic Centre of Zacatecas (1993); Rock Paintings of the Sierra de San Francisco (1993); Whale Sanctuary of El Vizcaino (1993); Earliest 16th-Century Monasteries on the Slopes of Popocatepetl (1994); Historic Monuments Zone of Querétaro (1996); Pre-Hispanic Town of Uxmal (1996); Hospicio Cabañas, Guadalajara (1997); Archaeological Zone of Paquimé, Casas Grandes (1998); Historic Monuments Zone of Tlacotalpan (1998); Archaeological Monuments Zone of Xochicalco (1999); Historic Fortified Town of Campeche (1999); Ancient Maya City of Calakmul, Campeche (2002); Franciscan Missions in the Sierra Gorda of Querétaro (2003); Luis Barragán House and Studio (2004); Islands and Protected Areas of the Gulf of California (2005); Agave Landscape and Ancient Industrial Facilities of Tequila (2006); Central University City Campus of the *Universidad Nacional Autónoma de México* (UNAM) (2007)

Moldova (Republic of Moldova): Struve Geodetic Arc (2005)

Mongolia: Uvs Nuur Basin (2003); Orkhon Valley Cultural Landscape (2004)

Montenegro: Natural and Culturo-Historical Region of Kotor (1979); Durmitor National Park (1980, 2005)

Morocco: Medina of Fez (1981); Medina of Marrakesh (1985); Ksar of Ait-Ben-Haddou (1987); Historic City of Meknes (1996); Archaeological Site of Volubilis (1997); Medina of Tétouan (formerly known as Titawin) (1997); Medina of Essaouira (formerly Mogador) (2001); Portuguese City of Mazagan (El Jadida) (2004)

Mozambique: Island of Mozambique (1991)

Namibia: Twyfelfontein or /Ui-//aes (2007)

Nepal: Kathmandu Valley (1979, 2006); Sagarmatha National Park (1979); Royal Chitwan National Park (1984); Lumbini, the Birthplace of the Lord Buddha (1997)

Netherlands: Schokland and Surroundings (1995); Defence Line of Amsterdam (1996); Historic Area of Willemstad, Inner City and Harbour, Netherlands Antilles (1997); Mill Network at Kinderdijk-Elshout (1997); Ir.D.F. Woudagemaal (D.F. Wouda Steam Pumping Station) (1998); Droogmakerij de Beemster (Beemster Polder) (1999); Rietveld Schröderhuis (Rietveld Schröder House) (2000)

New Zealand: Te Wahipounamu – South West New Zealand (1990); Tongariro National Park (1990, 1993); New Zealand Sub-Antarctic Islands (1998)

Nicaragua: Ruins of León Viejo (2000)

Niger: Air and Ténéré Natural Reserves (1991); "W" National Park of Niger (1996)

Nigeria: Sukur Cultural Landscape (1999); Osun-Osogbo Sacred Grove (2005)

North Korea (Democratic People's Republic of Korea): Complex of Koguryo Tombs (2004)

Norway: Bryggen (1979); Urnes Stave Church (1979); Røros Mining Town (1980); Rock Art of Alta (1985); Vegaøyan – The Vega Archipelago (2004); Struve Geodetic Arc (2005); West

Norwegian Fjords – Geirangerfjord and Nærøyfjord (2005)

Oman: Bahla Fort (1987); Archaeological Sites of Bat, Al-Khutm and Al-Ayn (1988); Land of Frankincense (2000); *Aflaj* Irrigation Systems of Oman (2006)

Pakistan: Archaeological Ruins at Moenjodaro (1980); Buddhist Ruins of Takht-i-Bahi and Neighbouring City Remains at Sahr-i-Bahlol (1980); Taxila (1980); Fort and Shalamar Gardens in Lahore (1981); Historical Monuments of Thatta (1981); Rohtas Fort (1997)

Panama: Fortifications on the Caribbean Side of Panama: Portobelo-San Lorenzo (1980); Darien National Park (1981); Talamanca Range-La Amistad Reserves / La Amistad National Park (1983, 1990); Archaeological Site of Panamá Viejo and Historic District of Panamá (1997, 2003); Coiba National Park and its Special Zone of Marine Protection (2005)

Paraguay: Jesuit Missions of La Santísima Trinidad de Paraná and Jesús de Tavarangue (1993)

Peru: City of Cuzco (1983); Historic Sanctuary of Machu Picchu (1983); Chavin (Archaeological Site) (1985); Huascarán National Park (1985); Chan Chan Archaeological Zone (1986); Manú National Park (1987); Historic Centre of Lima (1988, 1991); Río Abiseo National Park (1990, 1992); Lines and Geoglyphs of Nasca and Pampas de Jumana (1994); Historical Centre of the City of Arequipa (2000)

Philippines: Baroque Churches of the Philippines (1993); Tubbataha Reef Marine Park (1993); Rice Terraces of the Philippine Cordilleras (1995); Historic Town of Vigan (1999); Puerto-Princesa Subterranean River National Park (1999)

Poland: Cracow's Historic Centre (1978); Wieliczka Salt Mine (1978); Auschwitz Birkenau (1979); Belovezhskaya Pushcha / Białowieża Forest (1979, 1992); Historic Centre of Warsaw (1980); Old City of Zamość (1992); Castle of the Teutonic Order in Malbork (1997); Medieval Town of Toruń (1997); Kalwaria Zebrzydowska: the Mannerist Architectural and Park Landscape Complex and Pilgrimage Park (1999); Churches of Peace in Jawor and Swidnica (2001); Wooden Churches of Southern Little Poland (2003); Muskauer Park / Park Muzakowski (2004); Centennial Hall in Wroclaw (2006)

Portugal: Central Zone of the Town of Angra do Heroismo in the Azores (1983); Convent of Christ in Tomar (1983); Monastery of Batalha (1983); Monastery of the Hieronymites and Tower of Belém in Lisbon (1983); Historic Centre of Évora (1986); Monastery of Alcobaça (1989); Cultural Landscape of Sintra (1995); Historic Centre of Oporto (1996); Prehistoric Rock-Art Sites in the Côa Valley (1998); Laurisilva of Madeira (1999); Alto Douro Wine Region (2001); Historic Centre of Guimarães (2001); Landscape of the Pico Island Vineyard Culture (2004)

Romania: Danube Delta (1991); Churches of Moldavia (1993); Monastery of Horezu (1993); Villages with Fortified Churches in Transylvania (1993, 1999); Dacian Fortresses of the Orastie Mountains (1999); Historic Centre of Sighişoara (1999); Wooden Churches of Maramureş (1999)

Russian Federation: Historic Centre of Saint Petersburg and Related Groups of Monuments (1990); Kizhi Pogost (1990); Kremlin and Red Square, Moscow (1990); Cultural and Historic Ensemble of the Solovetsky Islands (1992); Historic Monuments of Novgorod and Surroundings (1992); White Monuments of Vladimir and Suzdal (1992); Architectural Ensemble of the Trinity Sergius Lavra in Sergiev Posad (1993); Church of the Ascension, Kolomenskoye (1994); Virgin Komi Forests (1995); Lake Baikal (1996); Volcanoes of Kamchatka (1996, 2001); Golden Mountains of Altai (1998); Western Caucasus (1999); Curonian Spit (2000); Ensemble of the Ferrapontov Monastery (2000); Historic and Architectural Complex of the Kazan Kremlin (2000); Central Sikhote-Alin (2001); Citadel, Ancient City and Fortress Buildings of Derbent (2003); Uvs Nuur Basin (2003); Ensemble of the Novodevichy Convent (2004); Natural System of Wrangel Island Reserve (2004); Historical Centre of the City of Yaroslavl (2005); Struve Geodetic Arc (2005)

Saint Kitts and Nevis: Brimstone Hill Fortress National Park (1999)

Saint Lucia: Pitons Management Area (2004)

Senegal: Island of Gorée (1978); Djoudj National Bird Sanctuary (1981); Niokolo-Koba National Park (1981); Island of Saint-Louis (2000); Stone Circles of Senegambia (2006)

Serbia: Stari Ras and Sopoćani (1979); Studenica Monastery (1986); Medieval Monuments in Kosovo (2004, 2006); Gamzigrad-Romuliana, Palace of Galerius (2007)

Seychelles: Aldabra Atoll (1982); Vallée de Mai Nature Reserve (1983)

Slovakia: Historic Town of Banská Štiavnica and the Technical Monuments in its Vicinity (1993); Spišský Hrad and its Associated Cultural Monuments (1993); Vlkolínec (1993); Caves of Aggtelek Karst and Slovak Karst (1995, 2000); Bardejov Town Conservation Reserve (2000); Primeval Beech Forests of the Carpathians (2007)

Slovenia: Škocjan Caves (1986)

Solomon Islands: East Rennell (1998)

South Africa: Fossil Hominid Sites of Sterkfontein, Swartkrans, Kromdraai, and Environs (1999, 2005); Greater St Lucia Wetland Park (1999); Robben Island (1999); uKhahlamba / Drakensberg Park (2000); Mapungubwe Cultural Landscape (2003); Cape Floral Region Protected Areas (2004); Vredefort Dome (2005); Richtersveld Cultural and Botanical Landscape (2007)

South Korea (Republic of Korea): Haeinsa Temple Janggyeong Panjeon, the Depositories for the *Tripitaka Koreana* Woodblocks (1995); Jongmyo Shrine (1995); Seokguram Grotto and Bulguksa Temple (1995); Changdeokgung Palace Complex (1997); Hwaseong Fortress (1997); Gochang, Hwasun and Ganghwa Dolmen Sites (2000); Gyeongju Historic Areas (2000); Jeju Volcanic Island and Lava Tubes (2007)

Spain: Alhambra, Generalife and Albayzín, Granada (1984, 1994); Burgos Cathedral (1984); Doñana National Park (1984, 2005); Historic Centre of Cordoba (1984, 1994); Monastery and Site of the Escurial, Madrid (1984); Works of Antoni Gaudí (1984, 2005); Altamira Cave (1985); Monuments of Oviedo and the Kingdom of the Asturias (1985, 1998); Old Town of Ávila with its Extra-Muros Churches (1985); Old Town of Segovia and its Aqueduct (1985); Santiago de Compostela (Old Town) (1985); Garajonay National Park (1986); Historic City of Toledo (1986); Mudejar Architecture of Aragon (1986, 2001); Old Town of Cáceres (1986); Cathedral, Alcázar and Archivo de Indias in Seville (1987); Old City of Salamanca (1988); Poblet Monastery (1991); Archaeological Ensemble of Mérida (1993); Route of Santiago de Compostela (1993); Royal Monastery of Santa María de Guadalupe (1993); Historic Walled Town of Cuenca (1996); La Lonja de la Seda de Valencia (1996); Las Médulas (1997); Palau de la Música Catalana and Hospital de Sant Pau, Barcelona (1997); Pyrénées – Mont Perdu (1997, 1999); San Millán Yuso and Suso Monasteries (1997); Rock Art of the Mediterranean Basin on the Iberian Peninsula (1998); University and Historic Precinct of Alcalá de Henares (1998); Ibiza, Biodiversity and Culture (1999); San Cristóbal de La Laguna (1999); Archaeological Ensemble of Tárraco (2000); Archaeological Site of Atapuerca (2000); Catalan Romanesque Churches of the Vall de Boí (2000); Palmeral of Elche (2000); Roman Walls of Lugo (2000); Aranjuez Cultural Landscape (2001); Renaissance Monumental Ensembles of Úbeda and Baeza (2003); Vizcaya Bridge (2006); Teide National Park (2007)

Sri Lanka: Ancient City of Polonnaruwa (1982); Ancient City of Sigiriya (1982); Sacred City of Anuradhapura (1982); Old Town of Galle and its Fortifications (1988); Sacred City of Kandy (1988); Sinharaja Forest Reserve (1988); Golden Temple of Dambulla (1991)

Sudan: Gebel Barkal and the Sites of the Napatan Region (2003)

Suriname: Central Suriname Nature Reserve (2000); Historic Inner City of Paramaribo (2002)

Sweden: Royal Domain of Drottningholm (1991); Birka and Hovgården (1993); Engelsberg Ironworks (1993); Rock Carvings in Tanum (1994); Skogskyrkogården (1994); Hanseatic Town of Visby (1995); Church Village of Gammelstad, Luleå (1996); Laponian Area (1996); Naval Port of Karlskrona (1998); Agricultural Landscape of Southern Öland (2000); Kvarken Archipelago / High Coast (2000, 2006); Mining Area of the Great Copper Mountain in Falun (2001); Varberg Radio Station (2004); Struve Geodetic Arc (2005)

Switzerland: Benedictine Convent of St John at Müstair (1983); Convent of St Gall (1983); Old City of Berne (1983); Three Castles, Defensive Wall and Ramparts of the Market-Town of Bellinzone (2000); Jungfrau–Aletsch–Bietschhorn (2001, 2007); Monte San Giorgio (2003); Lavaux, Vineyard Terraces (2007)

Syria (Syrian Arab Republic): Ancient City of Damascus (1979); Ancient City of Bosra (1980); Site of Palmyra (1980); Ancient City of Aleppo (1986); Crac des Chevaliers and Qal'at Salah El-Din (2006)

Tanzania (United Republic of Tanzania): Ngorongoro Conservation Area (1979); Ruins of Kilwa Kisiwani and Ruins of Songo Mnara (1981); Serengeti National Park (1981); Selous Game Reserve (1982); Kilimanjaro National Park (1987); Stone Town of Zanzibar (2000); Kondoa Rock-Art Sites (2006)

Thailand: Historic City of Ayutthaya (1991); Historic Town of Sukhothai and Associated Historic Towns (1991); Thungyai-Huai Kha Khaeng Wildlife Sanctuaries (1991); Ban Chiang Archaeological Site (1992); Dong Phayayen-Khao Yai Forest Complex (2005)

Togo: Koutammakou, the Land of the Batammariba (2004)

Tunisia: Amphitheatre of El Jem (1979); Medina of Tunis (1979); Site of Carthage (1979); Ichkeul National Park (1980); Punic Town of Kerkuane and its Necropolis (1985, 1986); Kairouan (1988); Medina of Sousse (1988); Dougga / Thugga (1997)

Turkey: Göreme National Park and the Rock Sites of Cappadocia (1985); Great Mosque and Hospital of Divriği (1985); Historic Areas of Istanbul (1985); Hattusha: the Hittite Capital (1986); Nemrut Dağ (1987); Hierapolis-Pamukkale (1988); Xanthos-Letoon (1988); City of Safranbolu (1994); Archaeological Site of Troy (1998)

Turkmenistan: State Historical and Cultural Park "Ancient Merv" (1999); Kunya-Urgench (2005); Parthian Fortresses of Nisa (2007)

Uganda: Bwindi Impenetrable National Park (1994); Rwenzori Mountains National Park (1994); Tombs of Buganda Kings at Kasubi (2001)

Ukraine: Kiev: Saint-Sophia Cathedral and Related Monastic Buildings, Kiev-Pechersk Lavra (1990, 2005); L'viv – the Ensemble of the Historic Centre (1998); Struve Geodetic Arc (2005); Primeval Beech Forests of the Carpathians (2007)

United Kingdom of Great Britain and Northern Ireland: Castles and Town Walls of King Edward in Gwynedd (1986); Durham Castle and Cathedral (1986); Giant's Causeway and Causeway Coast (1986); Ironbridge Gorge (1986); St Kilda (1986, 2004, 2005); Stonehenge, Avebury and Associated Sites (1986); Studley Royal Park including the Ruins of Fountains Abbey (1986); Blenheim Palace (1987); City of Bath (1987); Frontiers of the Roman Empire (1987, 2005); Westminster Palace, Westminster Abbey and Saint Margaret's Church (1987); Canterbury Cathedral, St Augustine's Abbey, and St Martin's Church (1988); Henderson Island (1988); Tower of London (1988); Gough and Inaccessible Islands (1995, 2004); Old and New Towns of Edinburgh (1995); Maritime Greenwich (1997); Heart of Neolithic Orkney (1999); Blaenavon Industrial Landscape (2000); Historic Town of St George and Related Fortifications, Bermuda (2000); Derwent Valley Mills (2001); Dorset and East Devon Coast (2001); New Lanark (2001); Saltaire (2001); Royal Botanic Gardens, Kew (2003); Liverpool – Maritime Mercantile City (2004); Cornwall and West Devon Mining Landscape (2006)

United States of America: Mesa Verde National Park (1978); Yellowstone National Park (1978); Everglades National Park (1979); Grand Canyon National Park (1979); Independence Hall (1979); Kluane / Wrangell-St Elias / Glacier Bay / Tatshenshini-Alsek (1979, 1992, 1994); Redwood National and State Parks (1980); Mammoth Cave National Park (1981); Olympic National Park (1981); Cahokia Mounds State Historic Site (1982); La Fortaleza and San Juan National Historic Site in Puerto Rico (1983); Great Smoky Mountains National Park (1983); Statue of Liberty (1984); Yosemite National Park (1984); Chaco Culture (1987); Hawaii Volcanoes National Park (1987); Monticello and the University of Virginia in Charlottesville (1987); Pueblo de Taos (1992); Carlsbad Caverns National Park (1995); Waterton Glacier International Peace Park (1995)

Uruguay: Historic Quarter of the City of Colonia del Sacramento (1995)

Uzbekistan: Itchan Kala (1990); Historic Centre of Bukhara (1993); Historic Centre of Shakhrisyabz (2000); Samarkand – Crossroads of Cultures (2001)

Vatican City (Holy See): Historic Centre of Rome, the Properties of the Holy See in that City Enjoying Extraterritorial Rights and San Paolo Fuori le Mura (1980, 1990); Vatican City (1984)

Venezuela (Bolivarian Republic of Venezuela): Coro and its Port (1993); Canaima National Park (1994); Ciudad Universitaria de Caracas (2000)

Viet Nam: Complex of Hué Monuments (1993); Ha Long Bay (1994, 2000); Hoi An Ancient Town (1999); My Son Sanctuary (1999); Phong Nha-Ke Bang National Park (2003)

Yemen: Old Walled City of Shibam (1982); Old City of Sana'a (1986); Historic Town of Zabid (1993)

Zambia: Mosi-oa-Tunya / Victoria Falls (1989)

Zimbabwe: Mana Pools National Park, Sapi and Chewore Safari Areas (1984); Great Zimbabwe National Monument (1986); Khami Ruins National Monument (1986); Mosi-oa-Tunya / Victoria Falls (1989); Matobo Hills (2003)

Index

Acknowledgments

Concept, design and maps by Collins Geo, HarperCollins Reference, Glasgow

Editorial by Collins Geo and Essential Works Ltd

Origination by Essential Works Ltd, 168a Camden Street, London NW1 9PT
www.essentialworks.co.uk
Editors for Essential Works: Nina Sharman, Cathy Lowne
Designer for Essential Works: Kate Ward

The World Heritage List, images, brief descriptions, nomination files, and background material: thanks to the United Nations Educational, Scientific and Cultural Organization (UNESCO) and its World Heritage Centre.

The UNESCO World Heritage Centre and its staff including: Francesco Bandarin, Kishore Rao, Guy Debonnet, Yvette Kaboza, Cedric Hance, Yacoub Raheem, Christian Manhart, Eric Esquivel, Barbara Blanchard, Fabien Ferry, Marta Severo, Art Pederson, Lynne Patchett, Joanna Sullivan, Florian Monnerie, Vesna Vujicic-Lagasy, Mechtild Rössler, Anna Sidorenko-Dulom, Junko Okakhashi, Giovanni Boccardi, Salamat Tabbasum, Junhi Han, Veronique Dauge, Mounira Baccar, Karim Hendili, Franca Miglioli, Nuria Sanz, Marc Patry, Claire Servoz, Ann Lemaistre, Alessandro Balsamo, Luba Janikova.

Thanks to: Mario Santana Quintero, Tito Dupret, Ian Kean, Paul Morrison, Doug Hebenthal, Maurizio Forte, Claudia Liuzza, Daniël Pletinckx, Scot Refsland, Josh Litwin, Mark Altaweel, Peter Miglus, Soroor Ghanimati, Laurence Beasley, Melody Di Piazza, Bruce Beasley, James Graff, Predrag Matejic, Pasha Johnson, Bob Allison, Brian Donovan, Michael Milojevic, Ileana Vásquez, Carmen Daly Schelbert, Deborah Klimburg-Salter, Gianni Maragno, Arthur Chen, Rand Eppich, Naymuzzaman Prince, José Tello, José Kalpers, Juan Pablo Moreiras, Thalia Liokatis, Kes and Fraser Smith, Sue Stolton, Carolina Castellanos, Africa Parks Foundation, Flora and Fauna International, the International Committee to Save Lascaux, the Foundation of the Hilandar Holy Monastery, the World Monuments Fund, Wikipedia, Wikimedia and the Creative Commons community, NASA, USGS, US Library of Congress, UNEP, IUCN, ICOMOS, and the WCMC.

With additional thanks to Elaine, Eleanor, and Henry Addison, for their support and patience.

Image credits

12 Tito Dupret/WHTour.org
13 UNESCO 1963
14 left & right Tito Dupret/WHTour.org
15 left UNESCO/A. Lézine
15 right UNESCO WHC News
16 Getty Images
17 Nico Tondini/Robert Harding World Imagery/Getty Images
18 José Tello
19 UNESCO/APF-José Kalpers – Africa Parks Foundation
20 Dave Bartruff/Corbis
21 John Reader/Science Photo Library
22 UNESCO/APF-José Kalpers – Africa Parks Foundation
23 Juan Pablo Moreiras/FFI
23 left Finbarr O'Reilly/Reuters/Corbis
24 right Patrick Robert/Sygma/Corbis
25 Martin Harvey/Corbis
26 UNESCO/Horst Gödicke
27 Danny Lehman/Corbis
28 UNESCO/Franca Miglioli
29 Maynard Owen Williams/National Geographic/Getty Images
30, 31 Mario Santana Quintero
34 De Agostini/Getty Images
35 Kes and Fraser Smith
36 Reto Kuster
37 Wendy Stone/Corbis
38 UNESCO-Evergreen
39 Mary Ann McDonald/Corbis
40 Dieter Biskamp

41 Shawn Baldwin/epa/Corbis
42, 43 left & right D. Sims/Environmental Investigation Agency/CIP
44 Flip Nicklin/FLPA-images.co.uk
45 UNESCO/Michael Calderwood
46 UNESCO/Giovanni Boccardi
47 Royal Geographical Society
48 UNESCO/Giovanni Boccardi
49 top left UNESCO/M.Baccar, C. Sintes, F. Souq
49 top left, bottom left & bottom right UNESCO/Giovanni Boccardi
50 UNESCO/Mark Patry
51 Sue Stolton
52 left UNESCO/Mark Patry
52 right Sue Stolton
53 UNESCO/Mark Patry
56 Prof. Dr. Mark-Oliver Rödel
57 top Nicolas Granier
57 bottom Herb Caudill
58, 59 (CC by-sa 2.5) Ali Imran
60 Library of Congress, USA
61 (CC by-sa 2.5) Wikimedia user: Kolossos
62 Michael Dunning/Getty Images
63 Taxi/Getty Images
64 left UNESCO/Francesco Bandarin
64 right Nicole Duplaix/National Geographic/Getty Images
65 Courtesy of Power
66 Claudia Liuzza
67, 68 left UNESCO/Veronique Dauge
68 right, 69 Claudia Liuzza

70 UNESCO/Junko Okahashi
71 Mark Edwards/Still Pictures
72 Pete Oxford/Minden Pictures/Getty Images
73 Mike Kemp/Corbis
74 Tito Dupret/WHTour.org
75 Courtesy Digital Globe
76 UNESCO/Francesco Bandarin
77 top Brian A. Vikander/Corbis
77 bottom Faramarz Mirahmadi/AP/ PA Photos
80 Alonzo Addison
81 Martin St-Amant/Wikimedia Commons
82 left Alonzo Addison
82 right UNESCO/Nuria Sanz
83 Alonzo Addison
84 UNESCO-Evergreen
85 Donald Nausbaum/Stone/Getty Images
86, 87 Images reproduced by kind permission of UNEP
88, 89 left & right, 90, 91 Mario Santana Quintero
92 Ted Mead/Stone/Getty Images
93 IKONOS image courtesy of GeoEye
94, 95, 96 left Alonzo Addison
96 right UNESCO/Francesco Bandarin
97 NASA
98 Tito Dupret/WHTour.org
99 Keren Su/China Span/Getty Images
100 UNESCO/Kishore Rao
101 Remi Benali/Corbis
102, 103 UNESCO/Giovanni Boccardi
104 Anders Blomqvist/Lonely Planet Images/Getty Images
105 Guy Edwards/Taxi/Getty Images
108, 109, 110 left & right, 111 Courtesy South Florida Water Management District
112 UNESCO/Paul Morrison (www.portfolios.com/paulmorrison)
113 Simeone Huber/Stone/Getty Images
114 left UNESCO/Doug Hebenthal
114 right Steve Kaufman/Corbis
115, 116, 117 UNESCO/Paul Morrison (www.portfolios.com/paulmorrison)
118 UNESCO/Veronique Dauge
119 Jake Rajs/Photonica/Getty Images
120 www.halongbay-vietnam.com
121 Steven Vidler/Eurasia Press/Corbis
122 UNESCO/Giovanni Boccardi
123 top & bottom Image State/Alamy
124 Hideo Kurihara/Stone/Getty Images
125 Bettmann/Corbis
126, 127 Mario Santana Quintero
128 UNESCO-Evergreen
129 Jaques Descloitres, MODIS Land Rapid Response Team, NASA/GSFC
130 (CC by 2.0) Paata Vardanashvili
131 UNESCO/Mark Simons
134 2001 UNESCO/Alain Brunet
136 Richard Powers/Corbis
137 Hasan Sarbakhshian/AP/EMPICS
138 UNESCO/Mark Patry
139 IKONOS image © CRISP 2004
140 left & right Perry van Duijnhoven 2007
141 Ian Singleton
142, 143 Heinz Wohner/LOOK/Getty Images
144 left & right, 145 Jens-Ulrich Koch/AFP/ Getty Images
146 Kevin Schafer/Corbis
147 Stephen L Alvarez/National Geographic/Getty Images
148 left Reuters/Corbis
148 right Charles & Josette Lenars/ Corbis

149 James Sparshatt/Corbis
151 top & bottom Brian Donovan
152 UNESCO/Barbara Blanchard
153 Frank Chmura/Nordic Photos/ Getty Images
154 left Hiroshi Higuchi/Photographer's Choice/Getty Images
154 right UNESCO/Barbara Blanchard
155 AFP/Getty Images
156 Tito Dupret/WHTour.org
157 Apichart Weerawong/AP/PA Photos
158 Vincenzo Lombardo/Taxi/Getty Images
159 Mimmo Jodice/Corbis
160, 161 UNESCO/Giovanni Boccardi
164, 165 Jayanth Sharma
166, 167 UNESCO/Claudio Margottini
168 left & right Mario Santana Quintero
169 UNESCO/Claudio Margottini
170 Heinz Rüther, University of Cape Town
171 Carmen Daly Schelbert
172 UNESCO/Giovanni Boccardi
173 Mark Altaweel
174, 175 Carolina Castellanos
176 left J. M. Fdez. Díaz-Formentí/ San Marcos
176 right National Institute of Culture, Peru
177 J. M. Fdez. Díaz-Formentí/San Marcos
178, 179 T. Vives/San Marcos
180 J. C. Muñoz/San Marcos
181 Martyn Colbeck/Oxford Scientific
182 Waqas Muhammad/Wikipedia
183 Rand Eppich/Mario Santana Quintero
184 UNESCO/Jim Williams
185 UNESCO/Francesco Bandarin
188 UNESCO/M. Rio
189 (CC by 2.0) Wikimedia user: Niro5
190 Reuters/Corbis
191 Steve McCurry/Magnum Photos
192 UNESCO/Veronique Dauge
193 Tito Dupret/WHTour.org
194, 195 UNESCO/Alessandra Balsamo
196, 197 UNESCO/Veronique Dauge
198, 199 Justin Clements/flickr-Guistino
200 Jake Rajs/Getty Images
201 Hugh Sitton/Stone/Getty Images
202 left Darrell Gulin/Photographer's Choice/Getty Images
202 right UNESCO/Dominique Roger
203 Upperhall/Robert Harding World Imagery/Getty Images
204, 205 UNESCO/Francesco Bandarin
206 Stacy D. Gold/National Geographic/Getty Images
207 Paul Chesley/Stone/Getty Images
208 Michael Poliza/Gallo Images/ Getty Images
209 UNESCO/Mark Patry
210, 211 Antonella Infantino
214, 215 UNESCO/Mark Patry
216 UNESCO/Claire Servoz
217 UNESCO/Daniel Fitter
218 UNESCO-Evergreen
219 Harvey Lloyd/Taxi/Getty Images
220 Tito Dupret/WHTour.org
221 2007 Shunya
222, 223 Fleur Gayet
224 Rowan Trebilco
225 Jenny Scott
226, 227 Amaury Oliver Laporte (www.alaporte.net)
228 UNESCO-Evergreen
229 Theo Allofs/Corbis
231 UNESCO/Francesco Bandarin
232 Nikolas Konstantinou/Stone/

Getty Images
233 NASA/Science Photo Library
236 Harvey Lloyd/Taxi/Getty Images
237 Dave Pattison/Alamy
238 NASA/Goddard Spaceflight Center, Scientific Visualization Studio
239 Nina Schwendemann/Reuters/Corbis
240, 241 Guillaud Jean Michel/Corbis Sygma
242 Paul Morrison (www.portfolios.com/paulmorrison)
243 top NSIDC/William O. Field
243 bottom NSIDC/Bruce F. Molina
244 left UNESCO/S. Stewart, Parks Canada
244 right, 245 Paul Morrison (www.portfolios.com/paulmorrison)
246 Scot Refsland
247 IKONOS image courtesy of GeoEye
248 left Spencer Platt/Reportage/ Getty Images
248 right Scot Refsland
249 Louie Psihoyos/Science Faction/ Getty Images
250 2002 Jacob Lautrup, Geological Survey of Denmark and Greenland (GEUS)
251 MODIS/NASA
252, 253 2002 Jacob Lautrup, Geological Survey of Denmark and Greenland (GEUS)
254 Nikhil Devasar
255 Jesse Allen, NASA Earth Observatory, using data from University of Maryland's Global Land Cover Facility
256 left & right Naymuzzaman Prince (www.ebonyivory.net)
257 2007 Shunya
258, 259, 260 left & right, 261 Alonzo Addison
262 Courtesy of the Great Barrier Reef Marine Park Authority for and on behalf of the Commonwealth of Australia 1996–2007
263 MODIS/NASA
264 left Theo Allofs/Photonica/Getty Images
264 right NASA
265 Ove Hoegh-Guldberg, Centre for Marine Studies, University of Queensland

Tito Dupret/WHTour.org (www.world-heritage-tour.org) is a non-profit organization documenting World Heritage sites in panography – 360 degree imaging – thanks to the support of the J. M. Kaplan Fund from New York, USA.

CC by 2.0 These works are licensed under the Creative Commons 2.0 Attribution License. To view a copy of this license, visit http://creativecommons.org/licenses/by/2.0/

CC by 2.5 These works are licensed under the Creative Commons 2.5 Attribution License. To view a copy of this license, visit http://creativecommons.org/licenses/by/2.5/

CC by-sa 2.5 These works are licensed under the Creative Commons Attribution ShareAlike 2.5 License. To view a copy of this license, visit http://creativecommons.org/licenses/by-sa/2.5/